Implementing and Sustaining Total Quality Management in Health Care

Hugh C.H. Koch

BSc, PhD, Dip Clin Psych
Managing Director, Koch Consulting Services
Cheltenham, UK

Associate, Health Services Management Centre
University of Birmingham

LONGMAN

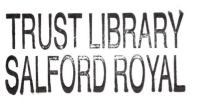

IMPLEMENTING AND SUSTAINING TOTAL QUALITY MANAGEMENT IN
HEALTH CARE

Longman Group UK Limited, Longman Industry and Public Service
Management Publishing Division, Westgate House, The High, Harlow, Essex
CM20 1YR
Tel: Harlow (0279) 442601
Fax: Harlow (0279) 444501

First published 1992

A catalogue record for this book is available from the British Library

ISBN 0-582-20903-X

Typesetting by Next Step Training, London
Printed and bound in Great Britain by
Dotesios Ltd, Trowbridge, Wiltshire.

For Sue

Contents

Chapter 1   Quality Health Care and Total Quality Management (TQM)

Defining Quality Care

The NHS was a visionary initiative started by Bevan (Webster, 1992) in 1948. He described this new service as composed of highly skilled men and women who were devoted to providing high quality care to their many patients. At this early stage in the life of the NHS quality was at the top of the health agenda.

Now, 44 years later, NHS managers and clinicians all see the need for an increasing emphasis to be placed on quality in health care provision. Guidance from the Department of Health's Management Executive (NHSME) repeatedly refers to the need for systematic approaches to quality of service.

But what is *quality*? What does it mean? Who defines it? In general parlance it suggests expensive and desirable products. Can we transfer this to health care? Are there any problems in using the *Search for Excellence Approach?* (Peters, 1982)?. One difficulty is that no simple relationship between patient satisfaction and 'successful', high quality care exists as is usually found in the commercial world. (Pfeffer, 1992). Nevertheless, there are some relatively universal ways to define quality which are appropriate to health care:

- What is quality?
  - — Quality is continually satisfying **customer** (purchaser/patient) requirements;
  - — Total quality is to achieve quality at lowest cost;
  - — Total quality management (TQM) is achieving total quality care and service by **harnessing everyone's commitment**.

Relating this to the public services, there are six main components of quality (Maxwell, 1984).

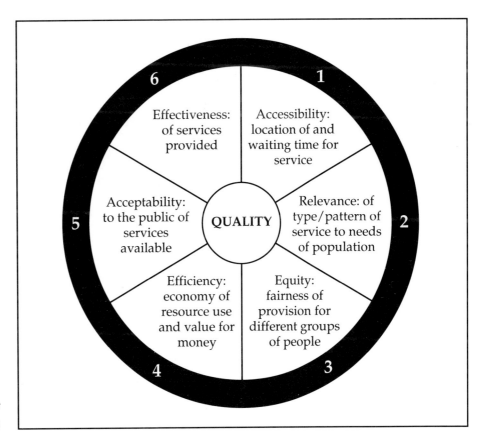

Figure 1.1. Six components of quality in public services

All six areas easily relate to the components of relevance and equity are more the province of purchasers than clinicians — efficiency is of importance to all. Without efficiency, accessibility, and to a certain extent effectiveness, cannot be achieved.

As part of the NHS reforms in general and the contracting process, in particular, guidance was given by the DoH suggesting that contracting for quality should involve:

- Appropriate treatment and care;
- Achievement of optimal clinical outcome;
- All clinically recognised procedures to minimise complications and other preventable events;
- Attitudes which treat patients with dignity as individuals;
- An environment conducive to patient safety, reassurance and contentment;
- Speed of response and minimal inconvenience;
- Involvement of patients in their own care.

This was the precursor of many later quality definitions such as that from the Western Health and Social Services Board (WHSSB, 1990).

- Maximising positive outcomes (clinical and consumer);
- Ensuring high quality care in both acute and continuing care services;
- Minimising the provision of poor quality care;
- Ensuing cost effective use of resources;
- Provision of consumer orientated modes of care; and
- Ensuring appropriate targeting of resources.

Of all these several types of definition, the one which affords the greatest opportunity for improving quality of care is the understanding of our patients' expectations. Our identification of who our several *customers* are and their views of the technical care and non-clinical service received is crucial. One of the expectations which we hold when needing health care is easy access via short waiting times. This has been perhaps the thorniest issues for successive governments to deal with, and one of the greatest tests of their commitment to quality delivery of care. This complex issue has recently been tackled via the *Patient's Charter* (1991). A service's ability to meet the expectations of short waits for outpatient and admission to hospital is a hard but important test of quality.

Prior to the General Election of April 1992, each of the three main parties debated their vision for post-election health policy with regard to quality. They all reinforced the need for standards against which performance could be compared and monitored, partly externally, leading to innovation and quality improvement with greater consumer involvement. They implied the need for organisational development to integrate quality initiatives with the overall business planning and management of health care delivery (*HSJ*, 1992).

Much of the election hype frustrated the health care professionals: many felt that the NHS reforms were already providing improvements in the quality of patient care; greater efficiency; and greater access. It was felt, and still is, that the reforms 'affirmed the principles on which the NHS was founded' (McColl) with delegation of decision making responsibility to local level ie unit/trust being very important.

The NHS objectives and targets set out the strategic direction and centre on:

- Improving the health of the population;
- Raising standards, improving quality and making services more responsive to the needs of individuals;
- Targeting provision on those with greatest need;
- Ensuring value for money in the use of resources;
- Creating the management framework to achieve these objectives.

Political Context

It is clear that the quality dimension of public sector services has gained momentum over the past two to three years. The government shows greater and greater interest in how services provide high quality to their *customers* through well managed systems and workforce, and how this quality is best monitored and improved.

Public *not-for-profit* services have several characteristics which differentiate themselves from other manufacturing and service sector companies. These include:

- Public accountability;
- Cash limits;
- Pronounced national and local *image*;
- Routine and emergency services;
- Former/current monopoly now *under threat*;
- Performance not always *easily* measurable;
- Undergoing major changes; and
- Essentially *people* profession.

It has been suggested that some of these characteristics make the implication of quality management systems more difficult than in the private sector. Without fully exploring and debating the validity of these 'differentiating factors' suffice it to say that they do have definite impact on the process of introducing quality systems and need to be fully taken into account.

The term *quality* applied to any public sector service has at least six main components:

- Accessibility: location of service to population it services and waiting time for service;
- Relevance: of type/pattern of service to needs of population;
- Equity: fairness of provision for different groups of people (age, ethnic origin, etc);
- Efficiency: economy of resource use and value for money;
- Acceptability: to the public of services available;
- Effectiveness: of services provided.

The many and varied public services are progressing at very different rates in terms of quality improvement systems and culture. Most have in-built quality assurance processes. However, the extent to which these are comprehensive and *total* is variable. In addition, the evidence of other aspects of a total quality organisation is gradually developing including:

- Culture and management commitment;
- Teamwork, staff recognition and empowerment;
- Process improvement (standards; costing) flow charting;
- Consumerism;
- Training for quality improvement.

The tide is now turning away from the concept that the public service, often monopolistic in nature, knows what is best for the public and towards the concept that service must find out what the customer wants and provide it, or even exceed his/her expectations.

The National Health Service and some local authorities are implementing total quality strategies, although the level of awareness and understanding of total quality approaches is currently developing from a fairly low base.

The high visibility of the NHS, plus the professionalism and training of their many and varied staff groups, predicts perhaps a rapid rate of quality management implementation. It is motivated by a growing awareness of the need to 'delight' the customer who is quite rightly becoming better-informed and more assertive in communicating his/her rights, as a citizen and taxpayer, to high quality public service.

Since general management was introduced in 1983, professional managers have been getting to grips with how to *manage* health care delivery, in general, and to *assure* its quality. From the start of general management it was important that quality assurance should be understood as covering both professional processes: clinical audit and consumer/patient concerns.

In the first review of general management and quality (Pollitt et al, 1990) the recognition of bureaucracy and the move towards more flexible, friendly managerial style was acknowledged. However there was a dichotomy between clinical and non-clinical services in quality assurance (QA) with more QA action in the non-clinical services. It was clear that resource issues watered down efforts in QA.

Clinically there was little systematic quality assessment and a general managerial reluctance to become involved due to other priorities; ambivalence about the legitimacy of management input; and anticipated resistance from doctors.

Pollitt et al concluded that this situation would only change if:

- Greater priority is given to quality improvement;
- Better data on quality is available;
- General cultural change occurs;
- Relations between doctors and managers improve.

In particular, with the development of the *Patient's Charter* John Major has moved away from the *right* way, both literally and metaphorically to manage health care as the Government *knew best* to a more consumerist way emphasising ten patient/charter rights:

- To receive health care on the basis of clinical need, regardless of ability to pay;
- To be registered with a GP;
- To receive emergency medical care at any time, through your GP or the emergency ambulance service and hospital accident and emergency departments;
- To be referred to a consultant, acceptable to you, when your GP thinks it necessary, and to be referred for a second opinion if you and your GP agree this is desirable;
- To be given a clear explanation of any treatment proposed, including any risks and any alternatives, before you decide whether you will agree to the treatment;
- To have access to your health records, and to know that those working for the NHS are under a legal duty to keep their contents confidential;
- To choose whether or not you wish to take part in medical research or medical student training;
- To be given detailed information on local health services, including quality standards and maximum waiting times;
- To be guaranteed admission for treatment by a specific date no later than two years from the day when your consultant places you on a waiting list; and
- To have any complaint about NHS services — whoever provides them — investigated and to receive full and prompt written reply from the chief executive or general manager.

It was designed to lead any patient to experience high quality clinical and customer care as displayed in the DoH video *Ivor Wright goes to hospital* about the *Patient's Charter*:

- Clear sign-posting creates a positive first impression.
- A personal welcome to the hospital from people who work there helps the patient feel reassured.
- An immediate clinical assessment on arrival at the accident and emergency department is undertaken by a trained nurse (triage).
- Information on how long the patient can be expected to wait, with clear names of staff on duty, should be provided in waiting areas.
- The patient should be able to identify all staff from their clear name badges.
- A named nurse will greet the patient when admitted to a ward.

- Relatives and friends will be informed, subject to the patients wishes, about the progress of treatment.
- Upon discharge, patients will have the reassurance of knowing what arrangements are being made for any continuing health or social care needs they may have.
- Patients in the outpatients department will be seen within 30 minutes of their appointment time.
- Local charter standards will be publicly displayed.
- Information to patients is provided at a desk, where patients are encouraged to 'help us to help you'.
- Access to the hospital is available for people with special needs.

Background to TQM

When TQM is mentioned key names emerge tagged with the grandiose title *guru*. They are names such as: Deming, Juran, Crosby, Ishikawa and all offer managers in industry the values as in Figure 1.2 alongside top management commitment and quality policy development. If you are particularly interested in the differences between these people, a lighthearted way of doing this is offered by the quality guru questionnaire Figure 1.4 (Timmers & Van Der Wiele). The author also reviews and compares these people for their own contributions.

The conclusion is that they all contribute to a general quality management framework as shown in Figure 1.3.

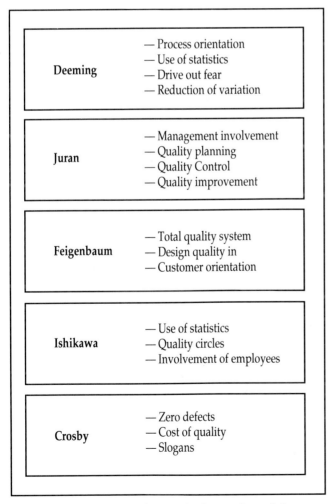

Figure 1.2. Comparison of the gurus

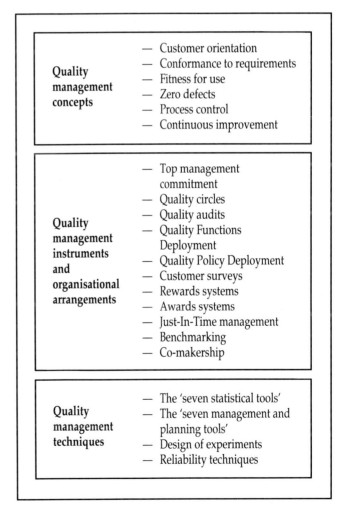

Figure 1.3. Quality management framework

Quality guru quiz

	Deming	Juran	Feigenbaum	Ishikawa	Crosby
1. Zero defects as a slogan means that the term is adopted as a kind of banner to fly during a company's 'drive' to improve quality.	☐	☐	☐	☐	☐
2. There must be an awakening to the crisis, followed by action– management's job.	☐	☐		☐	☐
3. Quality must be designed and built into a product; it can not be exhorted or inspected into it.	☐	☐	☐	☐	☐
4. You can get rich by preventing defects.	☐	☐		☐	☐
5. When ideas are implemented, standardise the process and establish controls so that the process will not deteriorate.	☐	☐	☐	☐	☐
6. Customers' needs do not remain static. There is no such thing as a final list of customers' needs.	☐	☐	☐	☐	☐
7. Cash or financial awards are not personal enough to provide effective recognition.	☐	☐	☐	☐	☐
8. The next process is the customer.	☐	☐	☐	☐	☐
9. Costs and errors can be reduced by standardisation and by establishing units of measure.	☐	☐	☐	☐	☐
10. Barriers against realisation of pride of workmanship may in fact be one of the most important obstacles to the reduction of cost and improvement of quality.	☐	☐	☐	☐	☐
11. A process that is in statistical control (stable) furnishes a rational basis for predicting the results of tomorrow's run.	☐	☐	☐	☐	☐
12. Quality is free. It is not a gift, it is free.	☐	☐	☐	☐	☐
13. Total quality programmes are perhaps the single most powerful change agent for companies today.	☐	☐	☐	☐	☐
14. Morale is one of the most critical control items in the workshop.	☐	☐	☐	☐	☐
15. In broad terms, quality planning consists of developing the products and processes required to meet customer's needs.	☐	☐	☐	☐	☐
16. Good things only happen when planned; bad things happen on their own.	☐	☐	☐	☐	☐
17. The best way to make products and offer services quicker and cheaper is to make them better.	☐	☐	☐	☐	☐
18. When you see data, doubt it! When you see the measuring instrument, doubt it!	☐	☐	☐	☐	☐
19. The workforce should be regarded as internal customers who can tell us a great deal about quality needs.	☐	☐	☐	☐	☐
20. Quality systems engineering is the foundation for true Total Quality Management.	☐	☐	☐	☐	☐
21. The greatest waste in America is failure to use the abilities of people.	☐	☐	☐	☐	☐
22. In the 1980s the number one quality role for the senior manager was to be a speechmaker.	☐	☐	☐	☐	☐
23. Many companies are facing serious losses and waste as a result of deficiencies in the quality planning process.	☐	☐	☐	☐	☐
24. Costs of warranty are plainly visible, but do not tell the story about quality. Anybody can reduce the cost of warranty by refusal or delayed action on complaints.	☐	☐	☐	☐	☐
25. Quality has much in common with sex.	☐	☐	☐	☐	☐
26. There is no substitute for knowledge. But the prospect of the use of knowledge brings fear.	☐	☐	☐	☐	☐
27. Creativity is nothing but the result of everyone's effort to identify problems and to think and use inherent wisdom.	☐	☐	☐	☐	☐
28. It takes four or five years to get people to understand the need for, and learn to have confidence in an improvement programme.	☐	☐	☐	☐	☐
29. Quality is what the customer says it is — not what an engineer, marketeer or merchant says it is — and it is a continually upward moving demand.	☐	☐	☐	☐	☐
30. The method of studying techniques must be related with how those techniques are to be applied in the workshop.	☐	☐	☐	☐	☐
31. Attributes:	☐	☐	☐	☐	☐

A   B   C   D   E (R.I.P.)

Information: Timmers & Van Der Wiele (1991)

Figure 1.4. Quality guru quiz

Developing TQM in the NHS

Many now point to the need for concepts and practices of *total quality* to be part of the corporate culture of a successful organisation (Cylenburg). It is built on an awareness of many varied processes which contribute to make any *business* work — three major ones being:

- Zero defect — very difficult to attain;
- Meeting customer requirements — an ever increasing task; and
- All employee involvement.

These all lead to continuous quality improvement.

The power of the process improvement approach is that it provides the systematic, measurable 'side of the coin' balanced by the human resource cultural value. The first side emphasises the processes of:

define/measure/analyse/improve.

Cylenburg from his considerable industrial experience with Mercury Communications cites improvement in employee motivation and company performance in two to three years with greater willingness to meet customer requirements, which in the 1990s are becoming more vocal.

However, some have found a serious dearth of industrial understanding by UK's leading plcs of TQM and its benefits (Howard, 1991) with only a minority aware, interested, or endorsing TQM. Half the companies he examined were service companies. He used a questionnaire probing *continuous business improvement* characteristics.

Characteristics for Continuous Business Improvement

1. Are you familiar with the techniques of
    Total Quality Management (TQM)?   Yes   Unsure   No

2. Do you believe that process thinking as
    opposed to output thinking will better
    sustain business improvement?   Yes   Unsure   No

3. Would you like to see companies report
    on year by year reductions in the total
    costs which they incur solely to ensure
    that their customers do not receive
    defective products and/or services?   Yes   No

4. Do you believe that certain key non-financial
    indicators of company performance (such
    as service level; product defect rates;
    quality cost; employee accident rates) should
    be reported alongside the traditional numbers?   Yes   No

5. Would you please order-rank the aspects of business managment
    from the following list which contribute to continuous business
    improvement, deleting those which you consider to have a negative
    effect?
    >   Top-down leadership
    >   Auditable process systems
    >   Company mission statement
    >   Evidence of process/product innovation
    >   Evidence of supplier/customer bonds
    >   Status-quo management
    >   Management by measurement
    >   Command and control management
    >   Evidence of hourly paid employee development
    >   Constancy of purpose
    >   Search for never ending performance

Figure 1.5. Continuous business improvement

His findings indicated a serious lack of understanding of TQM, although they do not necessarily indicate agreement or disagreement with it. The vital message concerning the superior performance of business-type process management rather than pure financial management is still being disregarded or misunderstood by many manufacturing and service companies.

In a similar study of UK and Netherlands based companies in manufacturing, commerce, and service sectors, Dale (1991) found clear understanding of many aspects of TQM especially of the five main components:

- Satisfying external customers;
- Reducing costs;
- Partnership with customers;
- Employee involvement and development; and
- Satisfying internal customers.

Most companies in this study indicated commitment to TQM but cited many common difficulties in getting commitment and sustaining TQM.

Inhibitors	Number of respondents (N=117)
Lack of top management commitment and vision	41
Company culture and management style	41
'Flavour of the month' type attitude	40
Department-based thinking and actions	31
Poor appreciation of concepts and principles of TQM	30
Lack of structure for TQM activities	27
Deciding how to start	21
Gaining the involvement of non-manufacturing departments	16
Ineffective leadership	16

Figure 1.6. Main difficulties experienced in introducing TQM

Inhibitors	Number of respondents (N=88)
Time pressure, workload and resources	51
Lack of top management commitment	30
Company culture	25
Departmental boundaries	24
Organisational restructuring	22
Managing the process of improvement	16
Complacent with the progress being made	14
Coping with the rate of change	13
Union resistance	6
Promotion of individuals	4

Figure 1.7. Main difficulties experienced in sustaining TQM

Within the health care setting evidence is beginning to emerge of quality being 'managed' and hospitals' organisation becoming more sensitive to the practices of quality management.

In Boston, USA, at an annual TQM conference, the New England Memosiar Hospital (NEMH) presented its TQM program (Ferguson, 1991). It encompassed all areas looking at medical, nursing, productivity, data process planning and materials management, and a greater sensitivity to patient expectations and needs. A goal of 'half life' improvement was adopted, ie attempting to achieve 50 per cent improvement in an area deemed achievable in a relatively short time — the remaining 50 per cent taking much longer. A second US symposium TQO, held years earlier by KPMG Peat Marwick Main & Company (1988) elicited 148 responses from purchasers and providers of health care in the USA and found a high level of agreement on the relationship between cost and quality in health care, and which elements of quality are important.

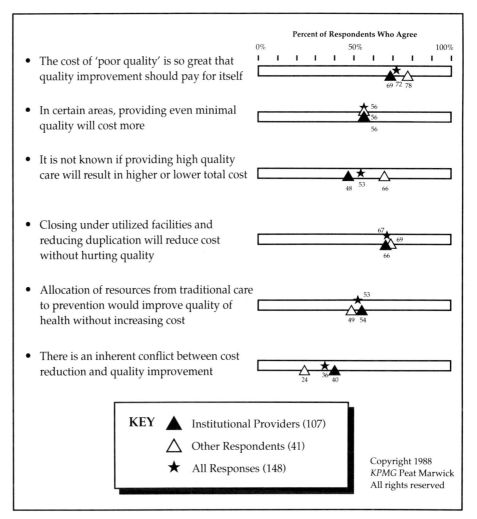

Figure 1.8. What is the relationship between cost and quality?

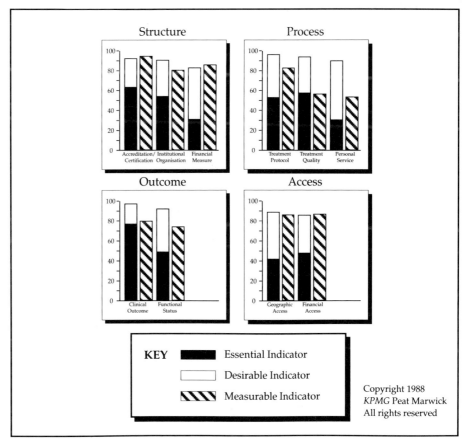

Figure 1.9. What elements of quality are important? Can these elements be measured?

In the UK the priority for quality to be taken more seriously has spread with the NHS over recent years (Koch, 1991). One of the early surveys of NHS attitudes to quality was undertaken by a York University team (Carr-Hill & Dalley, 1990) from the Centre for Health Economics and showed how the responsibilities for quality varied in the 122 districts who responded.

It is clear from this study in 1988 that a wide range of quality activities were taking place at all levels of the service. But they were frequently uncoordinated and needed some formula or approach to consolidate the management of these various initiatives. In July 1990 ODI Mosaic Management Consultancy Group (ODI, 1990) undertook a survey to examine the implementation of quality in the NHS. The findings from 100 respondents of 376 managers surveyed showed that most had established some type of QA system and were happy with it, but had not established TQM although it was planned.

More recently the Department of Health has embarked on a programme to encourage health units in the UK to introduce TQM-type initiatives in the NHS. With funding available to *pump prime* initiatives, 17 in the first year (1989), and 23 sites in the second year (1990) took the opportunity to harness their aspirations and skills, as demonstration sites to develop TQM. As Brooks (Brooks, 1992) describes: 'a clearly defined concept with a well documented history'. She cites several reasons why the NHS is ready for TQM:

- Caring culture;
- Untapped talent;
- Growing *management* culture;
- Committed staff;
- Public support, involvement, and expectation;
- Purchaser/provider culture;
- Developing corporate goals; and
- High quality failure costs.

In 1990 at one of the first UK NHS conferences on TQM (Chase, 1991) some of the progress was *hung on the line* and despite problems of cynicism at all levels its benefits were beginning to be predicted. More importantly, early on in the life of TQM the commitment, dedication, and professionalism of staff involved were again emerging: one delegate commented: ' We have the best health care providers in the world. What we need is an integrated customer-focused management system to transform the existing NHS into best health system anywhere'…by TQM.

So far so good. From a background of lack of managerial insight, the NHS is emerging as an organisation which, unlike many of its UK counterparts, can develop TQM…or can it? To answer this, one has to be aware of some of the initial or basic obstacles to the total application of TQM. Like any new initiative, accounts can be glossy and optimistic (Wilkinson & Witcher, 1991). These authors indicate that TQM might be expected to be 'just the cure the company doctor ordered'. However, consistent obstacles have been reported:

- Short termism;
- Organisational fragmentation;
- Ambivalent managers; and
- Sceptical workforce.

However, forewarned is forearmed, and the emerging TQM proponents in the NHS will do well to anticipate these difficulties and build solutions into their programmes.

Contracting for quality

Before outlining the emerging models of TQM within UK health care, it is appropriate to cover what the DoH in 1989 perceived as the main driver of quality — the concept of contracting, and the management of the purchaser/provider split. In manufacturing industry, TQM is associated with improving relationships with suppliers. In the NHS interest in TQM is associated with increasing emphasis on controlled competition: the NHS being asked to provide that competitive edge. To achieve this real or imagined advantage and to implement TQM requires a good cooperative relationship between purchasers and providers based on:

• Clear, unambiguous specification of quality;
• Positive adult relationships between purchasers and providers;
• Clear and effective monitoring;
• New funding opportunities;
• Better public information (to/from) about quality.

The reforms *Working for Patients* had quality and customer responsiveness as their base. Purchasers, providers, and patients all have different expectations about how to define, measure, and control quality. The most practical way to balance expectations is to build into a TQM approach better information about what constitutes quality care. With workable criteria of quality and accompanying standards, it will be possible to assist the purchaser and public to obtain maximum value for their health care expenditure and greater customer satisfaction.

The system for developing these explicit criteria for quality should come from the same system that the provider uses to develop his total approach to quality. Main purchasers and providers should both access the same information but at different levels.

Setting the scene for TQM in the NHS

These introductory sections have added to the overall picture of the NHS' readiness for TQM initiatives, already cited in Koch (1991). Throughout the UK in demonstration sites and other units, who have utilised regional, district, or their own funds to *pump prime* their TQM phase 1 programme, a considerable amount of TQM-type activity is taking place.

In the work the author has undertaken in both advising and training staff at all levels of provider units, some initial frameworks for visualising TQM in health care have emerged. None are necessarily correct or comprehensive, however, they may be helpful to readers developing their own approach.

TQM is about:

• **Total patient orientation;**
• **Quality management; and**
• **Measuring performance.**

Patient orientation involves attempting to *delight* them. In many instances NHS staff achieve this based on their staff's professionalism: not in its strictest sense, but on their ability to *do the job* well.

Figure 1.10. Goals of TQM

TQM in the NHS must strive to achieve several benefits:

- Good and better service;
- Delighted customers;
- Satisfied staff;
- Staff working well across agencies; and
- Reduced operating costs.

TQM therefore involves the interweaving of culture teamwork tools and techniques. Each of the five models in Figures 1.11 to 1.15 achieve this integration in different ways.

Figure 1.11. Interweaving of culture teamwork

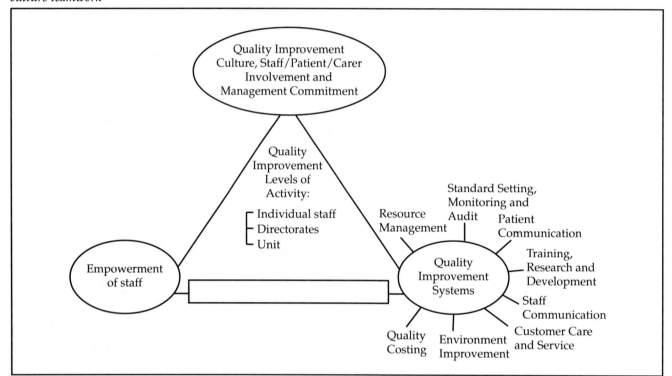

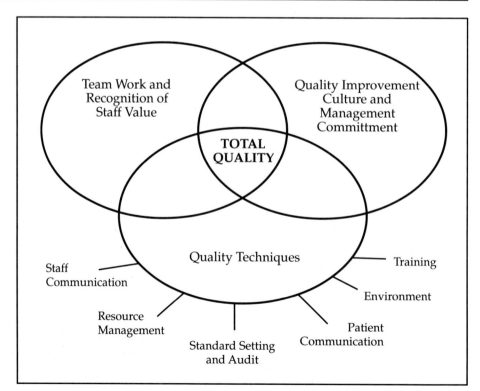

Figure 1.12. Requirements for achievement of total quality

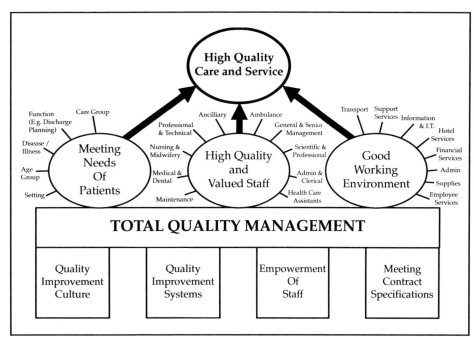

Figure 1.13. Teamwork tools and techniques

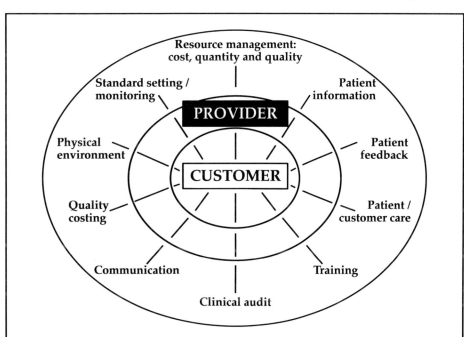

Figure 1.14. Total Quality Management culture

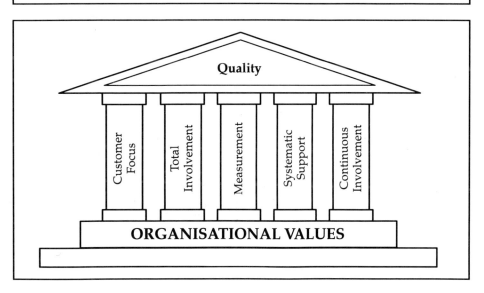

Figure 1.15. Do you measure up?

In attempting to account for the inevitable complexity and diversity of quality issues, the model which *works* best ie, can accommodate whatever issue is thrown its way, is in fact the simplest one. The working model which informs the author's work, makes sense of his experience as clinician, manager, and management consultant to date. It informs many aspects of the structure of this book as shown in Fig 1.16.

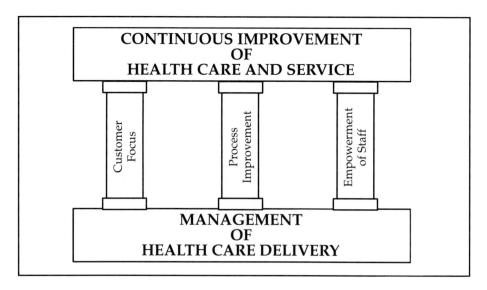

Figure 1.16

In summary, as a colleague very simply put to me, 'the aim of TQM is to do the job well' so producing health care of high quality which is continuously improving. To do this, attention must be paid to:

• Customer focus (communication to/from patients. GPs and purchasers);
• Process improvement (standard setting/monitoring, quality costing, corrective action, flow charting); and
• Empowerment (recognition, appraisal, training, QA teams, staff amenities and conditions).

Not only attention and intervention, but a clear explicit and organised management of all three of these *building blocks*.

This book will address ten of the major thrusts of TQM within health care in an ordered and practical way. The text will vary from the simple example (car parking!; your desk; telephone behaviour) to the complex, or diverse example (comprehensive standard setting). The simpler the example, perhaps the better the message. The book addresses the following issues in its subsequent chapters:

• Staff commitment and developing a strategy
• Management and organisation of TQM;
• Measuring quality;
• Designing health care;
• Controlling health care processes;
• Empowering staff and problem solving;
• Customer responsiveness;
• Training for quality improvement;
• Sustaining commitment and momentum.

I sincerely hope that you enjoy these chapters and find your own experiences mirrored here with some useful pointers to help you in your own endeavours to implement TQM.

Chapter 2   Gaining and sustaining staff commitment: developing a strategy

**Leadership and
*firing on all
cylinders***

Introducing TQM into an unsettled industry like health care, requires strong leadership and direction *from the top*; a coherent strategy; and practical implementation. To help a provider health care unit *fire on all cylinders* during TQM, the path followed needs to incorporate a *cascade* method to roll down TQM into the whole organisation.

Four key steps in this roll out plan are shown in Figure 2.1 below:

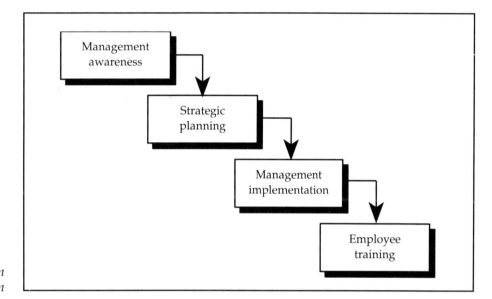

*Figure 2.1. The implementation
roll out plan*

The four steps are:

* Management awareness, vision and personal commitment;
* Strategic planning and staff involvement;
* Management implementaion, with analytical and behavioural aspects being integrated; and
* Staff training.

Leadership should, of course, come from the Chief Executive/UGM and his/her board. In some units, it may be the Director of Quality who shows leadership if the style of the CE is aligned with financial management rather than TQM. TQM can thrive in either of these environments, but the former is likely to be more rapid and ultimately more successful.

**Gaining staff
commitment Part 1:
*Aren't we
committed Already?***

With any new management/organisational initiative, it is unlikely that it is totally *new*. In this case, which certainly applies to TQM, some, if not all, staff will wonder if it offers them anything new. Or is it just a repackaging of management objectives? In relation to TQM staff will often think, and indeed say, that they are already committed to providing quality care and service. This is undoubtedly true — however, commitment and increasing commitment requires:

* Increasing knowledge about quality;
* Developing new skills; and
* Fitting personal contribution into an organisational picture of quality management.

To *say* staff are committed to quality improvement and quality core values is not enough. Senior clinicians and managers must show their commitment to quality in everything they *do*. Role modelling within quality can be displayed in many ways by senior staff, eg working alongside *front line* staff (nurses, porters) to experience patient care at first hand; personally investigating complaints.

More in keeping with the typical management role, the following behaviours should be displayed:

1.   Setting a clear vision (short, medium, long);
2.   Ensuring clarity and integration of unit objectives. It is important that everyone has a clear understanding of these;
3.   Running effective meetings and time keeping;
4.   Communicating well — don't lose the message in the technique; and
5.   Investing in training — train for prevention.

Recently, the psychology of TQM was articulated by Ullah (199?) in emphasising the need to focus on and change people rather than technology — easy to understand but difficult to achieve. To shape attitudes that result in quality conscious behaviour, it is important to focus attitudes towards specific job related behaviour, rather than general attitudes about the need for quality and the importance of customer satisfaction. We need to know how values relate to behaviour via our **expectations** and **beliefs** about our own abilities.

Consider for one moment these non-corporate, non-quality comments and consider your own reaction to them:

Receptionist:	I haven't got any change . . . . . that's this Authority for you.
Fracture Clinic Sister:	Go to the X-ray department and complain — I've tried, I can't get them to do anything right.
Anyone:	It's not my job to do that.
Porter:	I don't know why they make us do this job like this.
Manager:	My job is to sort out crises in this hospital.
Nurse:	The main problem in this hospital is our lack of funds — but no one listens to us.
Doctor:	I need my own car space because I get emergency calls.

Vision of quality

Reading the literature across industries about implementation underlying principles and core values are relatively consistent. Figure 2.2 illustrates the main values of an individual in an organisation successfully implementing TQM.

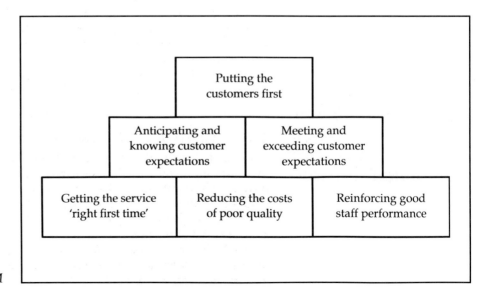

Figure 2.2. Core values of TQM

1. Putting the patient first (and other customers first)

Health care should reinforce the individuality of its customers via the care planning process. However, both staff and the public recognise that the ability to realise the *individuality* embodied in this core value — putting the patient first — can vary both clinically and non-clinically.

Does the patient: Have priority over staff in car parking in front of the hospital?

Have a choice of appointment?

Get offered a cup of coffee?

Have access to a telephone?

Get asked his/her views on treatment?

2. Meeting and exceeding patient expectations

Once a clinician is trained and experienced at his/her work, there is an inevitable tendency to generalise people's problems and behaviours into *types* which make the world of the clinician a little tidier. However, people are different and there is a skill in being sensitive to finding out what people expect in order that these expectations can be met, if not exceeded. In fact, the goal in many industries now is *to delight the customer*. Do you think that staff in your service *delight their patients*? I'm sure they do.

3. Getting the service *right first time*

Given the way that the NHS developed since 1948, mainly at the hands of doctors and nurses and their professionalism, the service has a very high quality without a thorough service specification. In many cases we do not know what the right service is, or if we do, we have two or more versions of what is right. We need to aim for a single specification which once agreed, is put into practice first time — by everyone involved.

At this stage of TQM development in the NHS an intriguing and vital point is: what should happen if and when the service is not provided *right first time*? The correct service must be provided *right second time*, immediately. A unit whose staff are keen to find out at the earliest opportunity when they have failed first time in order to immediately *put it right* are well on the way to TQM.

4. Reducing the costs of poor quality

The words *quality* and *cost* are felt by some to be in opposition in their everyday implications: for example, the nurse who only sees quality improving if more funds are made available. If one asks those in the manufacturing industry about how they consider quality and cost, their initial response would be to discuss how to measure the success of their organisation in terms of the level of quality costs, ie how much resource is wasted by not getting it right first time? A key value should be to make every effort continually to identify and reduce the failure costs of a health care unit.

5. Reinforcing good staff performance

A successful unit is able to make its staff feel from the moment of their induction that they are valued as individuals, as members of their team, and have an important role to play in the unit.

Organisations like Marks and Spencers have partly built their success on their human relation stategies which put their staff second on their list of priorities, with the public first.

TQM effectiveness is, according to Seddon and Jackson, often reduced by failure to consider the relationship between core values, cultural behaviour, and productivity. Cultural change does not happen overnight. It is based on senior staff's commitment to TQM and is created through a shift in value systems, based on belief: a passion for change and improvement.

The impact of TQM on a hospital or community service is brought about by ensuring that senior staff adopt a *prevention mentality* with mind set to promote the *right first time* approach to clinical and non-clinical situations (Oakland 1989). To understand what mind set is adopted, the following questions need to be asked:

- Do you assess the costs of treatment or service errors, complaints — are these costs small or large as a percentage of revenue budget?
- Is quality management and standard setting given a high priority?
- Does the service hold quality systems, documentation, policies and procedures in an organised manner?
- Are staff well versed in how to prevent problems?
- Are staff well trained to get it *right first time*?

TQM is concerned with changing attitudes and skills so that the health care culture is one of preventing failure and getting it right first time.

Outlining the strategy

TQM strategy for any health care unit should be tailormade or *doctored* to the specific characteristics and culture of that unit. However, there are, from experience gained, several key components which should be addressed in developing the strategy that will inform quality management action and behaviour for 1-3 years, before revision and review. Key components include:

1. Introduction to quality and quality improvement — setting the scene;

2. Outline of TQM:
   - Quality culture and vision;
   - Management and clinician commitment;
   - Teamwork and empowerment;
   - QI systems, tools, and techniques; and
   - Patient/consumer orientation.

3. Relevance of TQM to other key management processes:
   - RMI;
   - Medical audit;
   - Business planning;
   - Contracting; and
   - Patient charter;

4. Detailed description of key components:
   - Communication of strategy;
   - Patient and staff communication;
   - Standard setting, monitoring and audit;
   - Quality costing;
   - Use of information;
   - Enhancing teamwork and empowering QIT's; and
   - Training for quality.

5. Responsibilities for implementation:
   - All staff;
   - Key people;
   - Role of steering group;
   - Role of medical and nursing staff; and

6. Implementation programme:
   - First 6-12 months; and
   - Objectives/responsibilities/timescale.

AYLESBURY VALE PRIORITY CARE SERVICES

'TOWARDS TOTAL QUALITY' — A STRATEGY FOR ACTION

1. Introduction

The Unit provides Mental Health, Mental Handicap, Physical Rehabilitation, Palliative Care and general Community services of high quality. As outlined in the Trust Application (April 1991) the Unit is and will continue to be responsive to local demands, informative, and rewarding to its staff and to improve the quality of service by implementing a strategy 'Towards Total Quality'.

2. Total Quality

The two guiding principles of Total Quality are our wish to give our 'customers' the best possible service at all times and to do this by supporting and reinforcing the professionalism of our staff.

This commitment to high quality services in Aylesbury Vale requires that all aspects of service are managed and provided to the best possible level. They should meet the needs of the people being served. Efforts should be continously made by all staff in both clinical and non-clinical services to improve this service. It is characterized by:-

■ A Quality Improvement 'culture', with staff (and patient/carer) involvement and management commitment and leadership.

■ Establishing Quality Improvement Systems (eg standard-setting, audit, Quality Costing) to monitor and review key aspects of care and service of all departments/teams.

■ Facilitating effective team work, inter-agency co-operation, staff recognition and providing appropriate training and support.

■ Ensuring quality of services provided, meets, if not exceeds, that expected by our 'purchasers' via the contracting process.

3. Components of strategy

The Unit's overall quality strategy includes the following components:-

■ **Management Strategy** — the Unit Executive Board Sub-Group (Quality) will take action to ensure rapid and effective development and co-ordination of Quality Initiatives. There will be regular communication throughout the Unit outlining progress. The establishment of Quality Improvement Teams and training of facilitators will be an integral part of this. (An experienced external adviser will facilitate the management of the strategy in the early stages).

■ **Patient and Staff Communication Strategy**. The Unit will develop an explicit plan to communicate with the people it serves — patients, carers and General Practitioners. It will determine their needs for and satisfaction with health care services provided, in line with the Patients Charter. The needs of the Units's internal customers — the network of clinical and non-clinical adminstrative staff — will be identified and met.

■ **Quality Standards Setting, Monitoring and Audit** — Maintaining Quality improvement systems, will include:-
— Setting agreed and measurable standards of quality.
— Monitoring performance to conform with these standards.
— Medical, Nursing, PAM and Management Audit of care and service including positive and negative outcome monitoring.
— Implementing identified quality improvements.

■ **Quality Costing and Releasing Wasted Resources** — identifying the hidden costs continuing 'poor quality' where it exists. Raising staff awareness of these costs and motivation to reduce these costs by better appraisal and prevention methods. Planning investment in quality in proportion to possible savings. Ensuring savings in time or financial resources are appropriately re-invested and staff initiative duly recognised and rewarded.

■ **Information Strategy and Measurement** — ensuring the appropriate data is collected, analysed and produced as management information to enable staff to be fully aware of trends and progress in quality indicators.

■ **Enhancing Individual and Team Working** — staff, working individually as carers, therapists and clinicians, as members of multi-disciplinary teams must be valued and be supported by their managers and colleagues. The reinforcement of positive appraisal and personal development, backed up by a sound, well resourced Training, Research and Development Programme is essential.

■ **Marketing Service and Increasing Resources** — with increasingly well-managed, high quality services, the Unit will become able to recognise its marketing capabilities with the potential to attract additional revenue from nearby purchasers. Realising this 'potential' will facilitate highly desirable developments in clinical services. These are summarized in Figure 2.3.

4. Responsibilities for implementation of quality service

The Unit General Manager, the Management Board and particularly the Unit Nurse Manager lead the implementation of the Quality Strategy. They support all managers and clinicians in executing quality activities in their services. As illustrated in Figure 2.4, success of moving towards Total Quality is dependent upon the enthusiasm and involvement of all staff throughout the Unit.

5. Short-term programme to implement quality strategy

1. Finalise TQM Strategy   6/91

2. Develop Communication Strategy   8/91

3. Discussion with all staff, via service management groups, followed by training seminars on a quarterly basis to reinforce key principles and further develop expertise.
                                                                          10/91

4. Development of Quality Improvement Teams in all service areas and nominate facilitators.
    a) Mental Handicap   8/91
    b) E.M.I.   9/91
    c) Physical Rehabilitation   9/91
    d) Community   10/91
    e) Adult Mental Health   10/91
    f) Palliative Care   11/91

5. Provide initial training for facilitators   10/91

6. Develop comprehensive standards setting and monitoring strategy   10/91

7. Develop Quality Costing Strategy   10/91

8. Prepare bid for Quality funds from Unit Budget   11/91

9. Explore the formation of Quality circles in all care groups
                                                                          11/91

10. Review Existing Quality initiatives   1/92

11. Develop three year Total Quality Improvement Programme in all care groups and Unit functions   3/92

12. Review year one of Total Quality Strategy   5/92

John Sabugueiro & Hugh Koch
July, 1991
Manor House, Bierton Road
Aylesbury

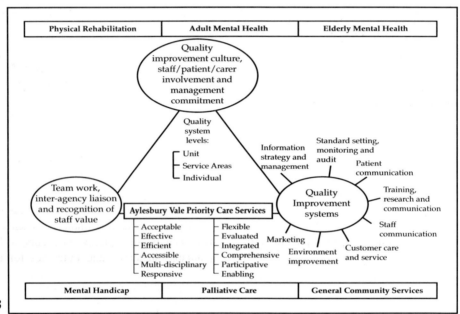

Figure 2.3

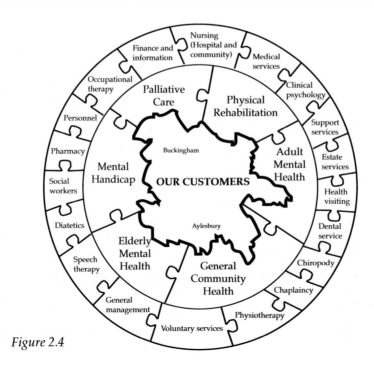

Figure 2.4

West Glamorgan Health Authority District Services Unit

Total Quality Management Strategy for Action (1992/93)

1) Introduction

This Unit is committed to providing the highest possible standards of care and service within the resources available. The key to achieving this 'vision' is the Unit's 'Total Quality Management' strategy. This is in line with previous Unit papers and District and Principality Directives. The TQM strategy will complement and harness the quality of service which is typically offered to all patients, through the professionalism of our staff. Quality of care is in no way 'new' to the Unit, but the coordination and maximum recognition, reinforcement and increasing consistency of quality improvement via this strategy perhaps is.

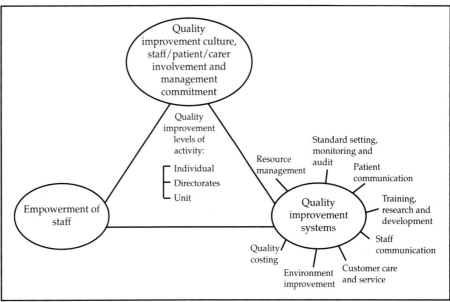

Figure 2.5. Total Quality Management Approach

2) Towards Total Quality Care and Service in West Glamorgan

The Unit will achieve the following objectives of

a) meeting agreed needs and expectations of patients in West Glamorgan;

b) providing and maintaining staff, with high quality skills, attitudes and morale;

c) maintaining a working environment for effective and efficient clinical services to be provided;

through a Total Quality Management approach (see Figure 2.5).

This is characterised by:

* a Quality Improvement 'Culture' with all staff (and where appropriate patient) involvement and both management and clinical commitment at all levels;
* establishment of Quality Improvement systems (eg standard setting, audit, quality costing) to monitor and review aspects of care and service which are 'key', 'variable' or 'problematic'; these include principles of the 'Patients Charter';
* empowerment of staff to facilitate effective teamwork, inter-department liaison, staff reinforcement, recognition and training;
* ensuring the quality of services provided meets, if not exceeds, that specified by the Unit and our 'purchasers' via the contracting process.

3) Components of Strategy

The Unit's overall quality strategy includes the following components:-

Management Strategy — The Unit Management Team will continue to develop and coordinate Quality Initiatives in clinical and non-clinical areas via the Quality Steering Group. Through a straightforward 'Quality Planning' approach, it will ensure that the Unit as a whole, and each service, develops its own plan of key quality indicators with measurable and attainable standards and outcomes for each indicator, as appropriate. This process will ensure the reinforcement of the following key quality values within each and every part of the Unit:

Putting the customers/patient first		
Anticipating and knowing customer/ patient expectations		**Meeting and exceeding customer/ patient expectations**
Getting the service 'right first time'	**Reducing the costs of poor quality**	**Reinforcing good staff performance**

Fig 2.6 Core values of TQM

This information will serve as a basis for contract management between Purchaser/Unit Team/services with documentation already found to be effective and 'user friendly' in other Units.

Establishing and Maintaining High Standards for Each Service — Considerable work has already been put into departmental/professional standard-setting and audit. Maintaining continuous quality improvement of our service requires:-

- establishment of comprehensive agreed and measurable standards covering aspects of care which are 'key', 'variable' and/or 'problematic' across all groups/services;
- monitoring performance to ensure maximum conformance to these standards;
- auditing of positive and negative outcomes of care through efficient, clear and 'owned' audit processes.

Improving Quality and Releasing Resources — Identifying and reducing the hidden costs of continuing 'poor quality' (eg failures, wasted consumables, wasted time) where it exists, and increasing time spent on prevention of operational problems is essential. Through increasing awareness of these costs, staff initiative to improve the 'patient trail' and reduce its costs can be encouraged and duly rewarded by reinvestment of savings made.

Communicating with Patients and Staff — The Unit intends to reinforce and further develop ways of communicating with the people it serves — patients, carers and General Practitioners. It will determine their satisfaction with the health care services provided by the Unit, in line with the concept of a patient's charter recently outlined, in Parliament (HMSO, July, 1991). The needs of the Unit's internal customers — its staff — will also be identified and, wherever possible, met.

Empowerment of Staff — Following on from keeping staff well informed (above) it is essential that staff feel empowered to take maximum responsibility for creative problem-solving and practical action on service improvements. Key features of empowerment which will be reinforced and developed for this are:-

- staff-centredness, relying on staff's own experiences and ideas;
- top-management support;
- multi-disciplinary team-led quality improvements (Quality Improvement Teams);
- well resourced Training, Research and Development programmes (including customer care);

leading to benefits for staff in terms of increased confidence and morale.

With the principle components in place (see Figure 2.6), the Unit will be increasingly able to recognise, monitor and support the high quality services provided and also be aware of its potential for attracting additional revenue from its purchasers. Realising this 'potential' will facilitate highly desirable developments in clinical services.

4) Responsibilities for Implementing Quality Strategy

Success in moving towards Total Quality services is dependent upon the involvement and support of all staff in this strategy. The Unit General Management and the Management Team lead the implementation of the strategy. They will support all clinicians and managers in identifying current and future quality activities in their own services.

5) Short Term Programme to Implement Quality Strategy 1992-93

A broad strategic outline for the implementation of Total Quality Management has been identified as follows:

February 1992	Establishment of Unit TQM Steering Group comprising Senior Managers and Clinicians both to oversee the TQM process and to monitor the outcomes.
April 1992	By this stage 101 Managers will have undertaken training on the concept and principles of TQM.
September 1992	Each Manager will have identified individual departmental Quality Improvement Teams who will have undertaken a course on 'team building'.
December 1992	Each Quality Improvement Team to have submitted its first set of targets to the TQM Steering Group for approval and inclusion, as appropriate, into the Business Planning process.
April-September 1993	TQM Steering Group to monitor progress of Quality Improvement Teams and provide guidance, as appropriate, to enable targets to be met.
September 1993	The first phase of the TQM process to be reviewed. Second round of target setting to commence.

6) Achieving Benefits from TQM

It is worth noting that to fully realise the benefits of this approach, the Unit and its staff, both clinical and non-clinical, must clearly relate the various components discussed above with their *own* working activities. There is considerable interest, enthusiasm and commitment throughout the Unit to continue providing high quality services and improve these further. This strategy and implementation plan, once it is communicated to *all* the Unit staff, will serve as a basis for the next year's activity.

Mr H P J Butcher (Unit General Manager)
Unit Management Team
Dr H Koch, Management Consultant in Quality Management

May, 1992

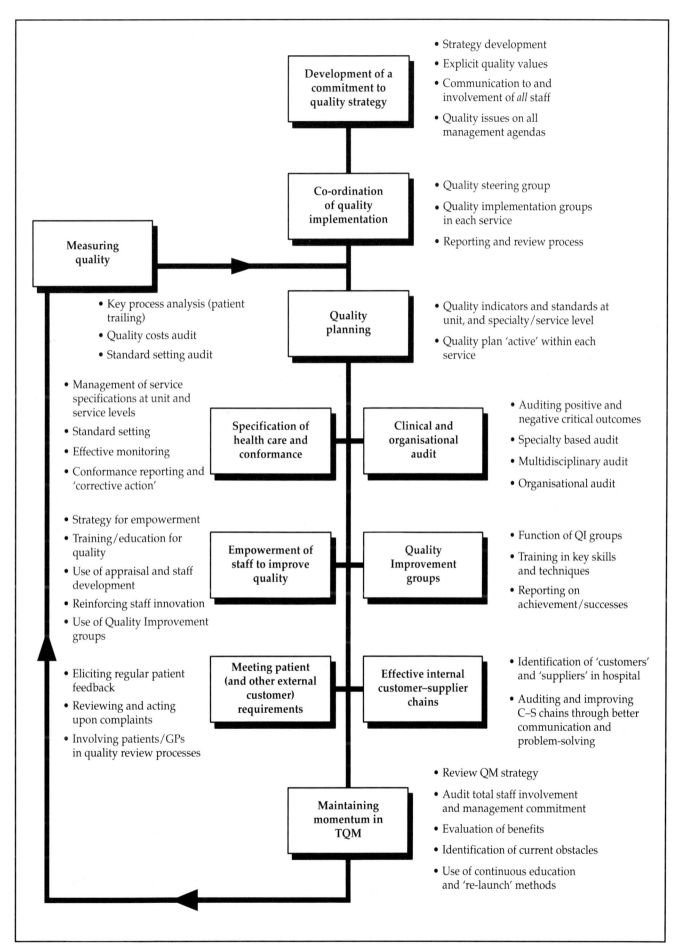

Figure 2.7. Implementing total quality

Who's involved in developing the strategy?

If a provider unit is to commit itself to the quality process, the senior management board must commit itself to it as rigorously as the staff. According to Deming, 'quality is made in the board room'. Trust or unit senior executives must explain to the unit, via its strategy, what its quality process means to the organisation and all its staff. It is the management responsibility to be accountable for the success or failure of the strategy. Management has the responsibility to communicate; to lead by example; and to put the quality process, via the strategy, in place. And be accountable for the end result. As in other public and private sector industries, the board in a provider health care unit must show the way in the *drive for excellence*. See Figure 2.8.

A mechanism for involving both trust/unit management and next-in-line senior staff in developing the strategy, is 1-2 day workshop which has been well tried in many units with considerable success. The aims of the workshop are to:

1.   Develop the unit specific model of quality management;
2.   Integrate quality management with other key initiatives;
3.   Link the strategy with current quality problems in the unit;
4.   Engender in the staff present a feeling of involvement with the emerging strategy;
5.   Produce a draft strategy for further discussion and consultation in two weeks.

Usually, the workshop is facilitated by an external agent with experience of quality management, health care management and clinical work.

Dependent on how much time is to be committed to developing the first draft strategy, a cascade approach can be used to ensure *total staff involvement*.

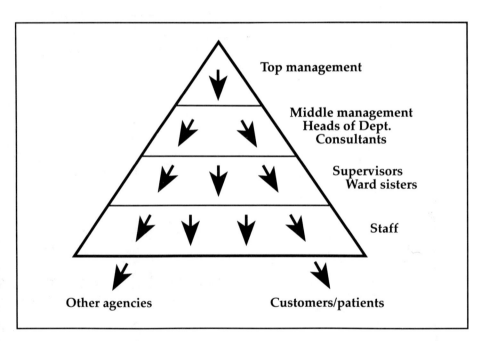

Figure 2.8. Total Quality Management starts at the top

All groups within a provider unit are essential to realising any aspect of total quality. However, one group of staff, the medical staff need special mention because of their atypical position within public sector health care. Unlike many industries where the expert technical staff are clearly managed within the hierarchy of management in public health care, the medical consultant has ambiguous management relationships with the unit management board/CEO and despite the development of general management ethos within the NHS, consultants because of their contractual relationships, still retain a model of accountability based on their professional code of conduct rather than corporate accountability. Therefore in the development of a quality management strategy, there input must perhaps be treated in an atypical way which takes into account their:

1. Important clinical leadership role;
2. Training and subsequent expertise in health care delivery;
3. Particular interest and expertise in audit; and
4. Importance as key opinion formers in the service.

This *treatment* usually takes the form of medical meeting where the background to TQM and its local application is presented and discussed. The tenor and content of the discussion follows a pattern illustrated by eight hospital consultants (clinical co-ordinators) who attended a seminar with a TQM consultant employed to develop the quality management strategy. Key issues raised by consultants were:

- Quality must be *new resource* linked;
- We never get involved in management;
- We have not time to be involved in audit let alone quality management;
- Health care shouldn't be organised by non-clinicians;
- We hold the quality values and show them everyday; and
- Management *don't* learn by their mistakes.

The role of the main purchasing agency for most provider units — namely the *old* district authority — in contributing to the development of a unit's TQM strategy can take the form of:

1. Clear contractural expectations via quality specifications;
2. Expectations of provider units to develop a sound quality management system;
3. Making *up-front* funding available to *pump prime* a unit's development of TQM.

Overcoming potential obstacles

Experience from several TQM demonstration sites around the UK and in most hospital and community services implementing major quality assurance projects, indicates several difficulties in introducing TQM, all of which can be overcome by skill and perseverance.

Lack of top management commitment and vision

The difficulty here is to ensure that there is a clear understanding of what quality of care and service already exists and how quality management can be implemented in the future. If there is a clear strategy, the next issue is to ensure that senior managers are committed, really committed, to the basic concepts of TQM.

'Flavour of the month/year' attitudes

At a recent TQM seminar, I was asked by a surgeon, 'Is this Initiative No. 991?' An understandable attitude, which belies a desire not to be disappointed by good, well-intentioned initiatives which are not sustained. The 'believer's' enthusiasm and the 'traditionalist's' cynicism must be joined to produce sound and sustained implementation.

Hospital/community service culture and management style

Each service has developed its own culture and style. TQM fits well with a corporate style based on effective, efficient communication and a high performance ethic, linked to staff motivation. However, many provider units do not display this culture and style and will either adopt TQM concepts at an intellectual level only or implement it half-heartedly.

Poor appreciation of TQM concepts, principles and practices

The introduction of TQM into the NHS in the UK has invited managers and clinicians to learn rapidly TQM ideas and practices. In the past two years, perhaps related to the obstacle of culture and management style, as described above, some provider units have rapidly learnt the required information and skills, whereas others are still implementing very worthwhile QA projects which do not get near the prerequisites of TQM and do not predict, therefore, the achieving of optimal benefits in quality improvement.

Lack of structure for TQM activities

Such is the huge potential offered by implementing TQM that there is a need to have a sound organisational framework for its planning and implementation. The senior steering group, the work-line related TQM Groups (eg theatres, outpatients, health centres) and quality improvement/quality-circle type groups all require an organisational framework which links the potential outcomes from each. Unfortunately, this framework or structure is difficult to establish in many units, especially if the next obstacle exists.

Medical uninvolvement

According to Dash (Dash, 1992), before attempting to devise a means of bringing doctors into the quality arena, it is important to consider why they have excluded themselves from the management of health care for so long. Perhaps one of the reasons is that they feel themselves poorly treated by the NHS: eg excessive junior doctor hours, personnel support, inadequate management training.

Managers or administrators?

With the rapid development of general management ethos since 1983, and with the advent of general managers from primarily nursing and administrative backgrounds the fact that only a small number of the current general managers have been able to benefit from the NHS GMTS scheme or external MBA qualification has resulted in the retention in some of:

1. An administrative approach to management overemphasising financial management; and

2. Crisis management rather than prevention of problems.

   For quality management to be effective, the senior managers must, in showing leadership abilities, develop general management skills incorporating a vision for corporate quality improvement and a *bias for action*.
   Rather than seeing obstacles as an unfortunate consequence of perhaps *getting it wrong* at some stage, a view which makes sense of obstacles as the psychotherapist helps the client to learn from his *defences*, and repeatedly shows the unit organisation that it can learn from its own obstacles and mature in the direction of total quality.

Where is your culture now?

Developing and running a total quality programme is a complex task. It is essential to keep track of where a unit's culture currently is and to map its progress towards a total quality culture. Most management textbooks attempt to provide frameworks or questionnaires to help the reader measure culture. In attempting wide coverage, these inevitably are non denominational or non industry specific. This results in their utility and application to the NHS being reduced as staff feel very ambivalent to using a management tool which does not take into account the special caring, individual, patient centred aspects of

NHS work. However the reader is referred to key texts in Handy (1988).

In developing an NHS specific *culture barometer*, an article by Atkinson (Atkinson, 1990) provided two useful non-NHS lists of indicators of corporate culture and categories of strong culture:

Indicators of corporate culture

A group of managers brainstormed the factors they thought important in indicating the predominant culture within a company. The results are below.

- Ethos — the way things were laid out.
- Spirit or teamwork.
- Warmth and friendship.
- Ideals — company messages and how they were displayed.
- Management style — what people did, not what they said.
- How they talk to you, the tone and manner of communication.
- Listening to us — is there evidence.
- Attitudes to employees portrayed through noticeboards.
- Involvement — did people incorporate the ideas of others.
- Ambiance — was it a nice place to be.
- Telephone response.
- Promises not kept — especially between departments.
- Events — was there evidence of a corporate get together.
- Criteria for selection/appraisal — was it a pleasant experience.
- Type of communication.
- Negative rumours and the failure to address them.
- Reception — staff entrances and goods inwards and outwards.
- Stereotypes of departments — what is projected by opinion leaders.
- Answering the telephone — was there concern for helping.
- Tidiness in all areas.
- Clutter in non-manufacturing areas.
- Participation — did people participate.
- Belonging — did they feel at home.
- Motivation — the process — was it carrot and stick.
- Shared corporate values — were they known by all and displayed.

Organisational performance and strong cultures

In studying the performance of 80 companies, Deal and Kennedy found that the most successful companies were those which had strong cultures. The strong culture was categorised as:

- Had a widely shared philosophy of management.
- Emphasised the importance of people to the success of the organisation.
- Encouraged ritual and ceremonies to celebrate company events.
- Had identified successful people and sung their praises.
- Maintained a network to communicate the culture.
- Had informal rules of behaviour.
- Had strong values.
- Set high standards for performance.
- Possessed a definite corporate character.

The majority are relevant and helpful to the NHS. These have been taken into account alongside a very useful matrix developed by Shell Netherlands (De Kievit and Finlow-Bates, 1992) which categorised 11 main areas for cultural diagnosis. These have been *translated* to apply to the NHS:

1. Commitment by CEO and unit officers (clinical and management)
2. Quality organisation and structure;
3. Quality training;
4. Indicators of quality improvement;

5. Existence and functioning of quality improvement groups/circles;
6. Quality specifications and standardisation;
7. Realistic customer expectations (patient);
8. Realistic customer expectations (purchaser);
9. Process control; and
10. Costs of poor quality.

The matrix in Figure 2.9 is constructed so that these ten categories (A to J) are shown horizontally, and the various steps to total quality are shown vertically (1 to 10). Thus a simple visual aid is available for determining where a unit stands in its TQM implementation process in Figure 2.9.

Figure 2.9 Shell Netherlands Quality Matrix

↕ QUALITY LEVEL ↔ QUALITY ELEMENTS					
	A	B	C	D	E	F
	COMMITMENT BY HIGHEST RESPONSIBLE LINE MANAGER	QUALITY ORGANISATION AND STRUCTURE	QUALITY TRAINING	INDICATIONS OF OPPORTUNITIES FOR IMPROVEMENT	FUNCTIONING OF PROJECT IMPROVEMENT TEAMS	QUALITY CERTIFICATION ISO 9000, BS 5750 OR OTHERS
10	Quality improvement is normal part of organisations culture, hold reviews and audits also in other 'units'.	Quality improvement is part of day-to-day activities and culture organisation.	Everybody trained, quality a natural component of training programmes.	Mentality for acceptance of continuous improvement philosophy achieved.	Project approach normal part of daily work practice.	Continuous improvements of systems achieved. Regular reviews and audits.
9	Communicates quality improvement information to customers and to own organisation.	Quality improvement element of new activities. System improvements permanent. Cost savings measurable.	All staff have mastery of quality techniques.	Customer/supplier relationship focused on improvement.	Systematic identification of new projects.	Certificate awarded.
8	Quality improvement is integral part of tack 'target' setting and also staff appraisals.	Quality audits held. Project groups functioning well. Proposals systematic implemented.	Supplementary quality training available.	Quality costs known and measured. All processes and system descriptions prepared.	Experience with project approach very positive.	Quality documentation complete. Staff trained.
7	Quality improvement is agenda item in meetings, manager gives lectures an publishes on quality.	QITs functioning well. Regular communication concerning improvements.	Middle management trained and these managers give training.	Performance indicators introduced for continuous measurement and control.	Half of all personnel have been actively involved in quality projects.	First internal quality audits and reviews in line with norm. First work instructions completed.
6	Stimulates quality improvements in the organisation, gives lectures and is involved in training.	First phase project groups completed. Implementation plan actively supported.	Training in quality techniques. SPC system description etc. Supplementary facilitator training.	Quality reviews and audits started.	Positive results of projects become recognised.	Procedures written. First work instructions written.
5	Has taken part in an improvement project.	Regular adjustments made to plans, progress monitored.	Whole organisation acquainted with the planned quality programme.	Performance indicators identified.	Implementation of first projects with system to hold the gains.	First procedures written following norm and first staff trained.
4	Involved in progress of project groups and makes necessary resources available.	Quality plan established. Quality information system set up. Fully active QIT programme. Facilitators appointed.	Facilitators and project leaders trained. Part of organisation has received quality awareness lectures.	Project selection criteria identified and first projects selected.	A number of project groups functioning.	Quality handbook written, programme plan established, and staff awareness program begun.
3	Quality goals defined and published.	Steering Committee meets regularly. A few QIT's functioning. First system description written QIT plan created.	QIT workshops commenced. Training available for facilitators and project leaders.	QIT has charted the most important work processes.	First project progress reports to QIT.	Work procedures and systems sketched in following norm guidelines.
2	Is chairman of the Steering Committee or QIT.	Steering Committee convened, first QIT initiated and quality adviser appointed.	Quality advisor trained. Managers have followed Quality Managers Workshop Training programme developed further.	QIT has identified the most important systems and has ranked them.	QIT monitors progressing projects.	Choice of norm made and decision taken to write work procedures.
1	Quality principles know, verbal support given but no personal involvement.	Quality focal point appointed but not yet an advisor.	Quality training programme selected.	Systems identified for which QIT responsible criteria defined for selecting those of most importance.	First project team initiated.	Aware of quality guidelines.
0	Obviously has no interest.	Structure completely lacking.	Quality training not started.	No progress.	No quality improvement projects.	No programme.

Gaining staff commitment Part II

Having developed the draft strategy and assessed the current status of the quality culture, it is essential to communicate the TQ message to all staff. Often, managers underestimate the power of effective communication in developing and accelerating change (Chase, 1991). At the outset, a provider unit needs an exciting unit-specific communication programme for spreading the quality management messages using a mixture of the most effective communications tools:

1. Unit wide open forum meetings;
2. Departmental meetings; and
3. Staff newsletter.

Figure 2.9. contd.

↕ QUALITY LEVEL ↔ QUALITY ELEMENTS				
G REALISTIC CUSTOMER SPECIFICATIONS	**H** TRAINING 'WORK INSTRUCTIONS'	**I** STATISTICAL PROCESS CONTROL	**J** SUPPLIER QUALITY	**K** COST OF POOR QUALITY AND PERFORMANCE INDICATORS
10 Realistic specifications periodically reviewed and agreed with internal and external customers.	Training in writing work instructions.	All processes fully controlled using SPC techniques.	Quality contracts drawn up with all important suppliers. Suppliers control their processes.	Quality costs & performance indicators as standard management tool.
9 100% review and agreement with customers.	Everyone trained. New staff trained as part normal company training programme.	All important processes controlled using SPC techniques.	Suppliers of critical products demonstrate their quality using statistical control methods.	Monthly overviews of quality tools and performance indicators.
8 Programme for continuous appraisal of specifications and procedures established and implemented.	Everyone trained.	90% of processes in control.	90% of goods from most important suppliers meet specs.	Monthly measurement of quality costs. Regular measurement of performance indicators.
7 Responsibilities for all important procedures agreed in principle with customers.	50% of staff trained.	75% of processes in control.	80% of goods from most important suppliers meet specs.	Regular measurement of quality costs.
6 Specifications for all procedures agreed in principle with customers.	Training programmes developed further.	50% of processes in control, capability studies commenced for remainder.	Specifications agreed with most important suppliers.	Structure for measurement of quality costs developed. Overview of performance indicators complete.
5 A number of new procedures agreed with customers.	First training sessions completed.	25% of processes in control, all important processes identified.	Key materials and components identified and specifications established.	Overview of quality costs available.
4 Improvement procedures outlined and first discussions on these procedures held with customers.	Training programme established and approved.	First process declared as 'in control'.	Problem-causing materials and components identified for spec's review.	First regular measurement of some quality costs. First performance indicators established.
3 Most important problems with non conformance identified with customers.	Training explained to staff.	Programme extended in a number of critical processes.	Desired quality levels discussed with all important suppliers.	Some quality costs established.
2 Most important areas identified for the establishment of customer specifications.	Training discussed with management.	First data collated and preliminary control limits established for one process.	Monthly report on supplier quality.	Search for performance indicators (own 'norms').
1 Responsibility established for determining customers specifications.	Programme for, and description of how to write and implement work instructions.	First subject for process capability study identified.	Quality programme with supplier started.	First discussions concerning quality costs.
0 No progress.	No programme.	Not started.	No programme.	No activity.

Roy (1991) analysed various communication methods utilised in the top US companies. He found the above three methods most widely used and effective in companies at TQM stage 1-3 years and outlines a 10 point checklist which has been adapted here for the NHS:

Ten point checklist for quality communication
Are you following this checklist?

1. *Do you regularly refine your views of quality from hearing your staff views?*
2. *Are messages about TQM regularly appearing from the top?*
3. *Is there a unitwide quality statement?*
4. *Have you developed a written quality communication plan?*
5. *How do you ensure individual audiences, eg medical, porters, are targeted?*
6. *How do you communicate good practice and QI success?*
7. *How do you reinforce QI more than product improvement?*
8. *Do you use all the main communication tools?*
9. *Do you track, analyse and publicise QI progress?*
10. *Do you regularly refine your views of quality as a result of hearing patients' views?*

Planning implementation

A flavour of short term objectives and implementation plans for TQM have been given in the sample strategies and in Koch (1991). A more comprehensive implementation programme is shown in Figure 2.7. The components are dealt with in detail in later chapters.

These components can be translated into *milestone* timetables, two examples of which are shown in Figures 2.10 and 2.11.

Months	1	2	3	4	5	6	7	8	9
Preliminary Workshop	X								
Diagnostic Investigation	——		——						
Appoint TQM Co-ordinator			X						
Commitment Workshop				X					
Set up Steering Group				X	-	-	-	-	-
Management Workshops				——		——			
Appoint Facilitators				X					
Train Facilitators				——					
Modular Training Cascade					——		——	-	-
Improvement Projects				——			——	-	-

Figure 2.10. Milestones in the TQM process 1

Months	Oct	Nov	Dec	Jan	Feb	March	Apr	May	June
Set up Steering Group	X								
Preliminary TQM Workshops			▬▬	▬▬					
Current Initiative Review		▬▬	▬▬	▬▬					
Establish Senior level Co-ordinating Groups			▬▬						
Construct Strategy				▬▬					
Consult on Strategy					▬▬	▬▬			
Commitment to Strategy Workshops					▬▬	▬▬			
Operationalise Purchaser Quality Specification (a) general			▬▬						
(b) specific monitoring				▬▬					
Establish Quality Improvement Groups			▬▬	▬▬	▬▬	▬▬			
Nominate Facilitators				▬▬					
Customer Relations/Service Workshops				▬▬	▬▬	▬▬			
Improvement Projects			▬▬	▬▬	▬▬	▬▬	▬▬	▬▬	▬▬
Benefits Review							X No1		

Source: M. Trafford (1989)

Figure 2.11. Milestones in the TQM process 2

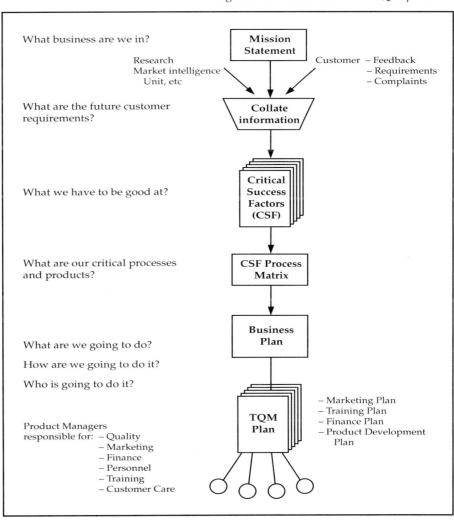

Figure 2.12. Avon TEC's strategy to TQM planning process

Integration of TQM with business planning

One main cause of poor commitment to TQM is the uncertainty about how TQM will achieve the provider units' strategic goals. Without the integration of TQM with other planning and implementation initiatives, it becomes *yet another initiative*. TQM must be part of the ongoing strategic planning process to maintain its momentum.

A helpful diagrammatic representation of this is given in Marsh (1991) from work with TEC (Training and Enterprise Council) which is easily translated into health care. See Figure 2.12.

The NHS has completed two years of business planning and is approaching its third. In previous years, the way to identify a unit's commitment to quality might often have been to turn to a particular section (often No. 5!) labelled *quality* or *quality assurance*, rather than see quality or QI as an integral part of the current and future direction of the unit. Units, whether they be trusts, potential trusts, or DMU's, now have the opportunity, through a greater awareness of what constitutes TQM, to ensure a coalescing of business planning and TQM strategy, as illustrated by the business plan index (1993/1994) in Figure 2.13.

Business plan 1993/94

Section I   Introduction and overview

Section II   (a) Review of current services
Assessment of services needs;
(b) Management of estate;
(c) Human resource strategy;
(d) Current market analysis
(Feedback from patients, purchasers and GPs)
(e) Future service strategy
Summary of each director's future plan,
Risks analysis and financial strategy;

Section III   Directorate business plans structure
(a) Current service description and review
(Activity, quality);
(b) Management of service
Structure,
Leadership,
Management of space, buildings, equipment,
Communication and teamwork,
Use of information (+RMI),
Staff/HR strategy including training,
Budgeting control and reducing *failure*, costs;
(c) Quality improvement
Key quality indicators,
Development and monitoring of standards and
protocols,
Responding to feedback (patient, GP, purchaser),
Audit approaches and outcomes,
Quality improvement problem solving;
(d) Summary of future service strategy.

Section IV   Conclusions

Figure 2.13

Would you get the *European Quality Award* yet?

In 1990 the European Foundation for Quality Management (EFQM) started to define criteria and weightings for a quality award to quality conscious companies. The conclusion of Chapter 10 (EFQM, 1991) illustrates eight criteria with definitions and weightings. Translating the *company* into the trust unit, it is useful and interesting to consider — the development of strategy and gaining staff commitment ..... whether your unit is on line for achieving quality improvement in these eight areas!

Chapter 3   Management and organisation of continuous quality improvement

Optimal use of management structure

1. How is the service currently managed?

All provider units have an organisational structure which defines accountability of staff and services to individual managers or clinicians. No two units' structures will be identical: a typical structure is shown in Figure 3.1.

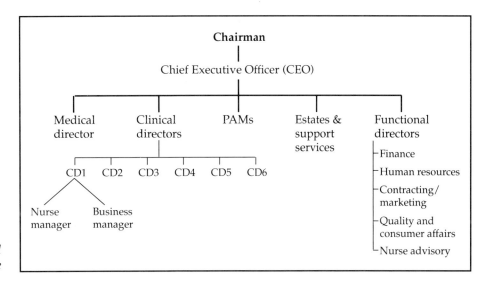

Figure 3.1. A typical organisational structure

The description of a unit should affect the way people behave if:

1.   Structure is agreed and widely understood;
2.   Managers and staff relate behaviourally to the accountabilities illustrated; and
3.   Management objectives and initiatives reflect the structure.

Functional directors do not have line responsibilities, over and above their own, usually small group. However, their *influence* is no less real and in some cases can be greater than their peer line managers.

Structure must imply and reflect the fact that quality is *part of everyone's job*, not an add-on. However, the role of the quality director (to be described later) will involve developing a shadow organisation as shown in Figure 3.2:

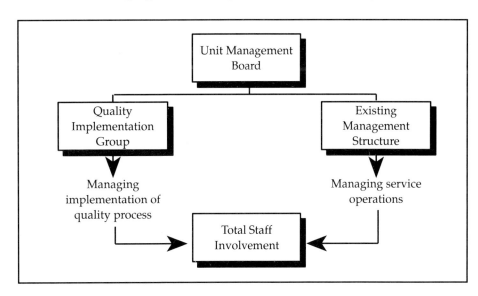

Figure 3.2.

This is not meant in any way to compete with the main organisational structure into which it will be absorbed in due time. To begin with their different functions and activities need to be distinguished.

As most units have implemented some form of directorate structure as the most effective way of delivering high quality health care, there are five key areas which must be addressed to ensure successful implementation and ability to drive quality upwards (REA, 1992):

1. **Structuring directorates**
    Key to this is the ability to manage a discrete patient service: grouping clinical services so that patients can have an integrated, seamless service. In many units this is a move away from traditional organisational nurses and doctors. Secondly, the directorate must be of optimal size and appropriate span of control;

2. **Awareness of staff within directorate**
    A big inhibitor of mobilising staff's quality initiative is a lack of understanding of why directorates have been established;

3. **Involvement of doctors in management**
    Many doctors have the management skills and awareness in addition to their considerable clinical experience to offer within the role of clinical director and coordinator;

4. **Inter-directorate relationships**
    There is a need to reinforce healthy internal competition for resources alongside appropriate collaboration and cooperation in the benefit of patients' need for integrated care and service. Two good examples of this are; surgical and anaesthetic services, and acute and priority services;

5. **One directorate and the rest of the service**
    It is important that one directorate is fully aware of the services and problems of the service around it, in order to reduce *tribal boundary* disputes! This is particularly relevant between clinical directorates and services of personnel human resources, porters, administrative and clerical, and estates and support services.

Thus, the successful implementation of a clinically led management structure is both innovative and challenging to all concerned and the most likely way of organising service delivery effectively.

2. Levels of work and defining responsibilities

Some provider units successfully developed their management structure based on, or informed by, Brunel University's extensive research on levels of work illustrated below:

LEVELS OF WORK

Level 7 —   **Total Field ('Metafield') Coverage**
defining the basic nature of needs and services and creating agencies and directives to them to provide what is required.
eg. Ministerial responsibility for health and health care.

Level 6 —   **Conglomerate Management**
shaping services by ensuring providing agencies implement L–7 directives and by ensuring coordination amongst the providing agencies

eg. Regional responsibility for Districts

Level 5 — Local Field Coverage (Operational Coverage)
shaping and providing the totality of services in relation to provision by other agencies within a territory
eg. reponsibility for health services in a District with maximal responsiveness to the community and its agencies.

Level 4 — Comprehensive Provision
dealing with a given range of services for a social territory with concern for unmet needs.
eg. developing over years a community nursing service, or a large general hospital; providing a comprehensive district personnel service.

Level 3 — Systematic Provision
dealing with a flow of complex situations (or cases)
eg. developing and introducing a new admissions procedure, or a new system for staff development; running a medical practice.

Level 2 — Situational Response
dealing with one-off, open-ended, complex situations
eg. making a diagnosis, handling a busy ward, dealing with a complex personnel problem.

Level 1 — Prescribed Output
carrying out tasks whose objectives are completely specifiable beforehand so far as is significant
eg. carrying out some routine nursing, or cleaning or clerical, procedure or task.

Although merely an abstraction of how *work* in a unit can be conceptualised, a commonsense interpretation is:

Level 4	Comprehensive provision	CEO/unit board/clinical directors on board
Level 3	Systematic provision	Directorates (clinical, functional) Heads of departments
Level 2	Situational response	Ward Sisters, therapists CMH teams Supervisors
Level 1	Prescribed output	Routine nursing Activities

To establish clear direction of quality improvement initiatives and management, there must be a clear allocation of responsibilities between each level:

Level 4	Director responsible for quality improvement;
Level 3	Each director responsible for the general management of the quality of all functions within that directorate;
Level 2	Ward managers responsible for ensuring clinical services run smoothly, performance of staff is satisfactory, and that the quality of service is improving.

At each level, there needs to be a feeling of responsibility for quality in all staff. For those interested in the application of *BS5750*, it must be recognised that the clarity of definition of management structure, levels of work, and definition of responsibilities is essential to meet the requirements of section 1 of the standard.

3. Involvement of clinicians in management

Berwick and Bunker (1992) argue that each unit should encourage clinicians to play a central part in the development of the unit's capability to improve its processes. In one sense, clinicians should learn how to *heal the organisation* or *improve its health*.

The role of clinicians, both doctors and other therapeutic staff, eg nurses, PAMs, is crucial to the development of a TQM approach to delivering health care. In particular, the experience and maturity of medical staff, both clinically and, in many cases, managerial, complements the other available management skills and practices.

In general, medical involvement in QI can and should occur in several ways and at levels, via:

- Medical director (on board);
- QI steering group;
- Medical professional machinery;
- Clinical director coordinator;
- Clinical audit committee;
- Clinical teams;
- GP liaison;
- Service specifications; and
- Business planning.

4. Role of chief executive/UGM

The crucial *top led* nature of TQM requires active and visible leadership which first and foremost is provided by this person. This demanding role requires a person with considerable stamina, expertise, and stability, who can display:

- Organisational skills;
- Effective communication skills;
- Ability to operate with short and long term objectives;
- Tolerate stress and ambiguity;
- Commitment to quality; and
- Awareness and understanding of TQM techniques.

5. Role of the clinical director/coordinator

With the adoption of the directorate model in most acute units and some district-wide trusts, the role of the clinical director is crucial in managing and improving quality. The clinical director is the manager of staff in the directorate and holds the budget. Most clinical directors are practising clinicians for whom management is a part-time activity. Supported by a business manager and or a nurse manager, the clinical director is responsible and accountable for:

- Planning of services;
- Allocation of resources;
- Activity and workload management;
- Maintaining good relationships with other directorates; and
- Maintaining good working relationships within directorate.

The challenge for the clinical director is to draw clinicians meaningfully into management and decision making and involving them in:

- Contract management;
- Quality cost reduction; and
- Defining quality care and its monitoring.

Key obstacles which need to be overcome are the problems of work overload and the apparent or real lack of management skills.

6. Role of senior manager

All line managers, whether next in line to the CEQ, or departmental head, or clinical director, should understand both what quality of care is, what it means to the patient, and also contribute to the delivery of this quality.

Performance and response of the manager should be assessed in terms of the impact on patient care and/or patient satisfaction. Management activity which does not add value from a patient's point of view should be challenged.

Managers need to be involved in, relate to, and understand patients and staff — not be preoccupied with demands of servicing the internal unit machine and bureaucracy. The manager is a facilitator or coach helping staff to access and harness resources relevant to the performance of their role and satisfying patient requirements.

A common problem in units embarking on TQM is the ambivalent commitment of senior and middle managers because of apparently conflicting/competing priorities and lack of quality management development. As some managers either lose, or never find, their way, they may behave in ways which hinder change either deliberately, due to self protection and anxiety containment, or inadvertently because of lack of skills or alternative ideas (Seddon, 1991).

Middle managers are the custodians of the CEO's vision of quality health care delivery. According to Seddon, when this is successfully achieved, managers feel they:

- Know what the units purpose and mission are;
- Feel empowered;
- Relate well to other managers; and
- Feel their manager is open to suggestion.

This requires a shift in many unit managers beliefs. Seddon's research indicates that in service organisations, managers need to acquire more knowledge, better decision making skills, control of workload and conflict resolution.

Managers from a non-clinical background also need to understand clinical operational issues and become less preoccupied with administration (Iles, 1992). They require:

- Clinical vocabulary and understanding;
- Awareness of the educational and regulatory framework of professions;
- Ability to translate managerial issues into language clinicians use; and
- Skills for interacting with clinicians.

7. Quality management competences

This has been addressed partly elsewhere (Koch, 1991). However some of the main competences required by a NHS manager (general manager or clinical director) are:

Leadership and influence	• Vision and strategic planning ability, • Individual leadership, • Conflict resolution, • Effective communication, • Ability to develop staff;
Decision making skills	• Problem solving, • Information retrieval and organisation, • Calculated risk taking, • Bias for action;
Management skills	• Control of time and workload, • Focusing ability, • Delegation and support, • Evaluation of progress, • Ability to change direction;

Personal

- Commitment to quality in own work,
- Tolerance of stress,
- Positive impact on others,
- Adaptability,
- Customer orientation.

Quality function and director

1. Role of director

With the present type of unit/trust management board, there is usually one board director designated as having responsibility for quality — this is often combined with one other key responsibility such as:

- Consumer affairs;
- Marketing;
- Professional nursing advice; or
- Contracting.

The key responsibilities of this role are as follows:

JOB DESCRIPTION

JOB TITLE: DIRECTOR OF NURSING/CONSUMER SERVICES

ACCOUNTABLE TO: CHIEF EXECUTIVE

SUMMARY OF ROLE

As an Executive Director the postholder will have corporate responsibility as a member of the Board for the overall formulation of policy and strategic direction of the Trust. The Director will provide leadership to nurses and health visitors through the development, implementation and evaluation of policies for the Trust consistent with its statement of aims and values.

The Director will also have overall responsibility for implementation of the Trust Total Quality strategy, including ensuring that quality standards defined in contracts with purchasers are implemented and monitored.

To participate in the development of the Trust as a customer-focused organisation through the development of all staff working in the Trust.

PRIME FUNCTIONS

1. *RESPONSIBLE FOR THE IMPLEMENTATION AND MONITORING OF THE TOTAL QUALITY STRATEGY.*

- To ensure that quality systems become an integral part of operation activities throughout the organisation.

- To develop in conjunction with clinical general managers, methods to measure, evaluate and update service standards.

- To facilitate, support and coordinate service quality initiatives.

- To plan and facilitate staff awareness of quality issues and the methods of high quality services.

- To act as a catalyst and champion to develop 'quality in everybody's business' culture in the organisation.

- To monitor all complaints and accolades, particularly reviewing trends and areas of poor performance, in particular to be alert for claims of negligence.
- To promote and facilitate customer surveys.
- To coordinate the implementation into contracts the guide-lines for service delivery by the Department of Health.
- To ensure that standards of service delivery contained in contracts are implemented and monitored.
- To promote and develop a process of clinical audit, involving all professions, recognising that initially each profession will develop unidisciplinary audit, developing into multi-disciplinary.

2. *RESPONSIBLE FOR THE PROFESSIONAL STANDARDS OF NURSING PRACTICE AND PERFORMANCE*

- To exercise professional leadership and ensure the provision of safe, efficient, cost effective nursing services.
- To provide advice to the Chief Executive, Board and other managers on all aspects of nursing strategy, practice, education and training.
- Establish and implement standards of nursing practice consistent with the UKCC and ENB.
- To provide advice to the Chief Executive, Board and other managers on appropriate methods to determine the requirements for skilled nursing staff, the deployment and utilisation of nursing resources.
- To promote the development of nursing practice and foster awareness of research activities.

3. *CORPORATE RESPONSIBILITY AS A MEMBER OF THE BOARD*

- To participate in the development of Trust strategy, and policies.
- To participate in the overall monitoring of the Trust's performance, ensuring financial viability and service quality.
- To contribute to the overall leadership of the Trust, actively promoting devolution of responsibility to ensure fast, responsive decision making.

It is often suggested that such a post detracts from the aspect of quality as *part of everyone's job*. This could also be said, presumably about any one of the functional directors, eg finance, personnel, all functions of which are part of line management. However, the role of these directors is to provide and develop the expertise in these functions, not to manage these within the unit — a subtle difference. In other words, the director of quality is there to facilitate and assist line managers in managing the quality of service, not to manage it *per se* him/herself.

The typical background of this postholder is nursing, for historical and pragmatic reasons: historical in the sense that the majority of QA has been carried out in the nursing services; and pragmatically due to the need to represent the largest part of the workforce.

2. Quality improvement (QI) steering group

Inherent in the third initial of TQM — *M for management* — is the need for quality improvement to be coordinated and managed with the unit. Actual service improvement is managed in the line management system. But the overall TQM process, led by the CEO, needs coordinating by the director of quality (DOQ) and his/her steering group with purpose and responsibilities:

Purpose
- Develop strategy and implementation planning;
- Provide leadership and resources;
- Instigate and monitor action for the implementation and communication of a continuous quality improvement process.

Responsibilities
- Accept the implementation of the quality plan;
- Develop key issues, strategy and objectives;
- Set and review priorities;
- Manage the overall implementation schedule and timetable;
- Assign responsibilities for action throughout the unit;
- Provide initial leadership and guidance to the improvement process;
- Develop and promote awareness raising and training;
- Facilitate and support the implementation of the necessary systems for process improvement, consumer responsiveness, and staff empowerment; and
- Review the TQM process and agree criteria for regular reporting, evaluation and feedback.

Membership of the QI steering group does not need to be representative of the various groups, clinical and non-clinical, within the organisation, in the strictest sense. It requires members who have skills and expertise and vision in the continuous QI process. However, it is useful and practical to have members who can bridge any real or apparent gaps between line managers and clinicians eg medical audit chairman, senior nurse.

Chairmanship of the group can vary with the most likely contenders being:

- CEO — DOQ — Medical audit chairman.

Each have advantages and disadvantages — the main criterion for the post is an ability to promote a vision of TQM and turn it into effective action.

3. Quality task project subgroups

The steering group will soon find itself requiring time and effort spent on particular projects, developing specific strategies or techniques systems. This necessitates the formation of time limited subgroups examining areas such as:

- Training and education;
- Standard setting/monitoring/corrective action;
- Measurement/charting;
- Empowerment and QI teams;
- Quality costing;
- Customer care; and
- First impressions.

Each project group reports back to the main steering group with the outcome of its work.

Business planning, quality strategy and directorate service plans

1. Recent experience of business planning in the NHS

Over the past two to three years, NHS senior management have been learning about developing a business planning approach, on an annual basis, with an approximate nine month preparation time. This has usually meant a tight round of meetings at directorate or specialty level to look at an agenda clarifying issues of activity, quality and cost of service.

This plan provides the vision for where the unit wishes to be in the next one, two or three years. The strategy aims to unify and motivate all staff towards a common goal. In many business plans quality has not shown through as the main driving force. It has frequently been financially led, with *quality* being found as an individual section without high priority.

Secondly, partly as a result of this low priority being given to quality, clinicians have not necessarily adopted their business plan to drive the organisation and delivery of health care in their speciality forward for the next year. Therefore it has lost much of its power and influence and some have seen it as a paper exercise.

2. Integration of quality strategy with business planning

Units/trusts are now developing the vision to combine these two planning processes. In a recent initiative, an acute unit developed a framework for their business planning round:

Business Plan — 1993/94

INTRODUCTION AND OVERVIEW

a) Future Service Strategies (Based on each Directorate Business Plan and Risk Analysis).
b) Review of current services.
c) Management of Estate.
d) Management Strategy.
e) Quality Strategy.
f) Finance Strategy.
g) Human Resources Strategy.
h) Market Analysis.

DIRECTORATE BUSINESS PLANS

a) Future Service Strategies (the development of Strategies based on clinical priorities and requirements, market opportunities, quality and the empowerment of staff).
b) Current service description and review (including trend analysis).
c) Management of Services.
   — Structure
   — Leadership
   — Management of space, buildings and equipment
   — Use of information (including RMI)
   — Human resources strategy
   — Financial management and reducing 'failure' costs.
d) Quality Improvement.
   — Key indicators
   — Development and monitoring of Standards and Protocols
   — Audit approaches and outcome
   — Responding to feedback (Patients, GPs and Purchasers)
   — Quality Improvement 'Problem Solving'.

This allowed the developing quality strategy to be seen to complement the business plan and provide a more corporate business policy for the next 12 months. It also achieved a greater involvement and commitment from the clinicians, and reduced the split between financial, activity and quality issues — a split which is unreal in clinical practice.

3. Outline directorate plan

As outlined in section 3.3.2 an essential feature of managing quality improvement is to involve the major *factory lines* — the clinical and non-clinical directorates — in planning for the future. Part of this process is to organise directorate-specific quality business plans.

Part of this is the development of quality plans — one format of which is shown below:

BRIEF FOR SEMINAR OF SENIOR STAFF
QUALITY PLANNING WITHIN DIRECTORATES

Introduction

There has been considerable effort put into providing quality care and service within the Acute Unit. Recently a draft quality plan for the Unit was developed, coincident with the appointment of a Quality Facilitator, plus external consultancy help.

A central part of the Quality Plan is the development of Directorate specific quality plans within each of the twelve clinical directorates, six functional directorates and other clinical and non-clinical support services. The Directorate planning ensures that the authority for developing plans to improve quality rests near to the patient(s) receiving care, and crucially involves the medical and nursing staff. It will also link with existing work on Collaborative Care Planning.

A framework has been prepared (which can be altered!) for each Directorate which helps to assess current progress on several key aspects of Quality Management.

Structure and Quality Management Framework

In Figure 3.3 is the overall Unit structure with each Directorate or Service numbered for this Quality Planning exercise.

Figure 3.3

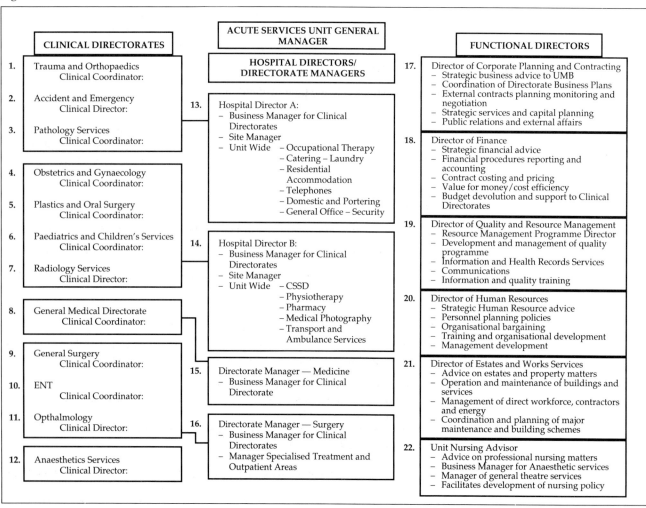

In Figure 3.4 below a Quality Management (QM) framework depicts the various components of QM which each Directorate will be asked to look at.

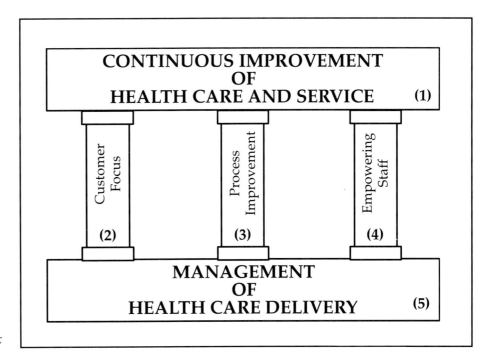

Figure 3.4. QM framework

Quality Planning Process and Timetable
The collation of these plans will produce a document covering:

(a)   Unit-wide Quality Planning Issues: Patient Charter
                                                Purchaser Requirements
                                                Unit Issues

(b)   Clinical Directorate Quality Plans (12)

(c)   Functional Directorate Quality Plans (6)

(d)   Clinical and Non-clinical Support Service Plans (12 approx)

As part of the next round of Business Planning (1993/94) meeting, there is an approximate timetable for raising awareness and drafting these quality plans, as follows:

Preparation of Framework

Meeting with Senior Directorate Coordinators, Managers/Clinicians   July 1992

Work with each Directorate   July/October 1992

1 hour Completion 1st Draft Meetings with Senior Staff   October/November 1992

What will the Benefits be?

1.   Feeling of involvement with management quality improvement and its integration with overall Business Planning in the Unit.

2.   Well organised activity in each Directorate to:
    (a)   Improve the consistency of the main processes of care and service
    (b)   Meet patient expectations
    (c)   Keep staff satisfied with working in the Dudley Group of Hospitals
    (d)   Reduce wasted resources.

More information can be obtained from Lynette Holliday, Paul Brennan or Hugh Koch.

QUALITY PLANNING WITHIN DIRECTORATE

Introduction

Quality Planning is a structured and organised approach to reinforcing and improving the current health care delivery in the Acute Unit and is part of the overall Business Planning approach. It progresses the Unit Quality Plan (1992/93) recently discussed within the Unit.

Please complete this as best you can. We will be happy to help in anyway we can. The purpose of this is two fold. Firstly, it helps develop your own directorate plan for your own internal purposes and secondly contributes to the Unit's Business Plan.

Directorate Structure

Please draw below (or attach separately) a structure showing wards, departments (as appropriate) within the Directorate.

Communication

Please show below what meetings occur within the directorate within a 1-8 week period. If meetings occur irregularly, please show:

Meeting Name	Wk 1	2	3	4	Irregular but is monthly	5	6	7	8	Irregular but bi-monthly

Identification of Quality Indicators

Using the sheet attached, please identity the many key quality issues in your Directorate which will require standards being set and/or corrective action being taken. These may be:

(a) Key Issues and Processes eg   Patient Charter
                                           Admission, Discharges etc.
                                           Purchaser and/or Unit issues
                                           Directorate — specific issues

(b) Problem issues eg   Medical bed availability
                                           Complaints

(d) Variable Issues eg   Care Planning
                                           Discharge Planning

The general framework for this is the Patient Trail shown below. Work is currently underway to integrate this approach with Collaborative Care Planning.

⇒	Accept Patient	→	Patient Entry	→	Assessment & Diagnosis	→	Treatment	→	Discharge	

Standard Setting and Monitoring

The Unit is developing a comprehensive approach to standard setting and monitoring. Please develop an action plan to take each of the above Quality Indicators and describe explicit standards (1 or more) for each, plus appropriate monitoring mechanisms (see example layout below and sheets attached). Please also set regular review dates to review performance and also the standards themselves.

Quality Indicator	Standard Statement	Monitoring	Performance Record

Issues to be aware of:

1. Timescale and how much of above can be achieved by when?

2. Directorate-wide standards, then departmental standards.

Patient Feedback/Staff Feedback

The Unit will be developing two simple questionnaires for your consideration, one to give to Patients (and relatives), the second to staff using your service (if appropriate). Please consider and describe how you might plan to elicit patient feedback and staff feedback on a regular (quarterly) basis. The outcome of this will be (a) information on which to base improvement and (b) numerical score to observe change over time.

Audit (Medical/Clinical/Management)
If not already mentioned under standard setting, please describe how outcomes (positive and negative) are recorded, monitored and lead to improvements in the service are delivered.

Positive Outcomes	Negative Outcomes	Method & Frequency of Recording

Regular Information
What information do you collect and monitor on a regular basis which either informs you about important quality variables (eg waiting times) or problem areas?

Staff Awareness Raising and Training
Describe plans currently being implemented to ensure all groups of staff in Directorate are kept updated as appropriate.

Staff Recognition and Empowerment
How do your staff regularly receive reinforcement, feedback and encouragement?
Have you in existence: (a) Appraisal (inc IPR)
                             (b) QI Group(s)?

Budgetary Control and Quality Costing

1. Do you feel you have sound control of your Directorates budget(s)?

2. Are you regularly overspent (Monthly)?
   If so, why is this!

	Yes / No	Comments

	Problem	Approx. Annual Wastage
1.		
2.		
3.		
4.		
5.		
6.		

3. What are the main problems which 'waste' resources (time, effort, revenue) in your Directorate

Once you have completed a draft of this plan, please let me have a copy for further discussion.

Many thanks.

Staff involvement in managing quality

1. Structure for organising quality

In the first section of this chapter, a *shadow* organisation was outlined showing how the implementation group linked to line management. The objective of the managing and organising of continuous quality in its initial stage is to *set the scene* for ongoing total staff involvement. There are many important *drivers* of quality improvement — total staff involvement is one such driver. Every attempt should be made by staff in both the formal line management and the quality improvement steering group to inform all staff — not just most of them or those that happen to attend team briefing etc. It sounds a tall order and *hard work*. But it is harder work in the long run not to, because of the resistance that will be caused consciously or unconsciously by uninformed or partially informed staff.

2. *'Part of everyones job'* — implications

Quality management is *top-led and bottom-fed* — an awful phrase but of some significance. The management and organisation so far described relies on senior managers and clinicians to develop strategic action plans for the unit and directorates to consider. Once informed by them about what is intended, the bulk of the staff at operational level, must believe that it is their responsibility to interpret these plans and intentions into maintaining and raising the performance and standards of their own particular work. This motivation should ideally be encouraged via their:

- Own personal commitment;
- Team allegiances; and
- Wish to meet their managers' expectations, in return for their managers' recognition and positive reinforcement.

3. Quality improvement teams (QITs)

Staff involvement in many aspects of TQM in general and problem solving in particular is achieved via the exciting development of QITs/quality circles — an initiative described in full in chapter 9.

This *'subversive'* approach to raising quality is an inevitable and necessary complement to any type of management structure even the most effective and positively styled. Like any family, staff need to feel able to counteract, ignore, or even oppose their management in a constructive and approved way. QITs provide this opportunity and complement the other more mainstream ways of involving staff — watch this space for more details!

Chapter 4   Measuring quality and quality improvement (QI)

Introduction

A key component of managing health care is the facility to *measure* — measure where we are now; where we should like to be; measure key aspects of service delivery. In Chapter 6 more details will be given concerning standard setting and the monitoring of standards, which many in the NHS may associate with the concept of measurement.

However, this chapter will address four key aspects of measurement which relate to the early stages of implementing TQM in health care:

1. Preparedness for TQM and current QI activity;
2. General measurement frameworks for key areas of health care, eg environment, outpatients;
3. Measurement of quality costs; and
4. Use of visual information and charting.

Preparedness for TQM and current QI activity

In many TQM programmes, the first phase will need to be some form of *diagnosis* of the current climate and situation in which TQM will eventually sit. The background to a diagnostic review was briefly described in Koch (1991). Outlines of different methods for assessing this climate are:

General attitudes

Simple checklists questionnaires are useful to start the ball rolling and aid discussions as in Figure 4.1. They can be developed into a more detailed staff questionnaire, similar to that used by a PA consulting group with Trafford General Hospital (Manchester), one of the leading NHS demonstration sites.

	1 (low)	2	3	4	5 (high)
Please show your rating for each question by ticking one of the boxes. Tick one box only for each question.					
1 How serious is management about quality?					
2 How serious are staff about quality?					
3 How serious are you about quality?					
4 How good is staff morale?					
5 How do you rate the Trust on management development/education?					
6 How do you rate the Trust on staff communication?					

Figure 4.1. Assessment 3 (attitudes)

TRAFFORD HEALTH AUTHORITY

Total Quality Initiative — Staff Questionnaire — March 1990

No of responses	THA 124	Hos 62	Com 35	Mgt 41	Non-Mgt 62	Sth 8	Nth 20	Admin 38	Medic 15	Nurse 31	Para/M 22
	Net percentage + ve or -ve perceptions										
1. I understand what THA is trying to achieve	73	71	71	85	60	88	40	55	87	77	77
2. All THA staff share the same overall goals	-28	-24	-34	-56	-16	-63	-20	-34	-40	-23	-41
3. THA promotes good health in the district	66	68	71	54	69	38	70	55	53	68	77
4. THA provides the highest possible standards of health care within its resources	31	45	20	10	39	13	50	37	20	45	0
5. I continuously try to satisfy the requirements of my customers (internal and external)	94	90	97	95	94	75	90	95	93	90	100
6. My department continuously tries to satisfy the requirements of all its customers	90	87	97	88	94	100	85	87	87	90	100
7. THA continuously tries to satisfy the requirements of all its customers	57	60	57	71	50	38	50	53	53	61	68
8. Management positively encourages suggestions for improved quality of service	16	29	26	32	11	13	15	11	13	13	45
9. My service/speciality has a business plan	-22	-26	-6	-32	-10	-50	-15	-29	-40	-13	5
10. I understand the business plan of my service/ speciality	-3	0	-11	2	-5	-25	-10	-5	-7	-6	9
11. THA actively promotes staff welfare	-19	-31	0	-44	-10	25	5	-8	-33	-42	-18
12. There is little interdepartmental conflict	19	15	37	24	21	13	25	18	40	19	14
13. My immediate manager/supervisor is a good motivator	52	55	54	41	61	63	55	50	27	61	64
14. I am always treated with respect	43	39	51	37	47	0	70	53	0	48	36
15. THA gives me appropriate skills and knowledge	10	11	20	-5	16	-13	-10	11	-27	23	9
16. I am encouraged to identify real and potential problems	48	48	63	34	50	75	70	34	13	68	45
17. Management is fair	32	37	34	44	37	38	25	39	33	29	50
18. Management is firm	62	63	66	63	60	38	55	58	67	71	50
19. I know the standards of performance I am expected to achieve	67	69	71	71	65	75	55	58	100	65	59
20. I have performance measures to enable me to monitor my own performance	20	24	9	46	8	-13	25	42	27	-10	23
21. The "way we do things" is regularly reviewed and improved	45	48	54	54	42	63	25	11	73	71	64
22. I am always clear what my customers expect from me	52	56	40	41	63	25	65	55	47	61	45
23. My suppliers are always clear what I expect from them	16	13	20	22	10	0	20	29	-7	19	5

Figure 4.2. Trafford Health Authority Staff Questionnaire

Characteristics and awareness of TQM

Prior to implementing TQM, an assessment of how much knowledge and awareness there already is within the unit of TQM-related processes will help. The checklist in Figure 4.3 was used in one unit at the start of their programme and covered five areas of:

- Awareness;
- Involvement;
- Customer feedback;
- Information to patients; and
- Standard setting.

Figure 4.3. TQM audit commitment

DEPARTMENT:

TQM Characteristic	Current	Future Plans

1. Awareness and Commitment
   Quality Assurance and Total Quality
   Management:-

   a) Have all your staff seen TQM strategy?
   b) Do staff agree in principle with contents?
   c) Do staff *in principle* want quality to improve?
   d) Do staff *in principle* feel able to implement *some* Quality Improvements themselves?

2. Involvement of *all* staff in department in Quality issues

   a) Do you have regular discussions with all staff about Quality Issues or Quality Improvements?
   b) Do you encourage *junior* staff and *new* staff to raise new ideas on Quality Improvement?
   c) Do you have specific group/meeting for generating Quality Improvements eg 'Quality Circle'?

3. Getting Feedback from our patients and relatives

   a) Do you regularly survey patients, (quarterly, annually)?
   b) Do you *review* complaints received, (quarterly) to learn any lessons?
   c) Do you have any form of 'user' group meeting (eg quarterly) where patients can 'air' their views with you?

4. Giving patients well-produced and relevant information

   a) Do you give patients written information?
   b) Are you happy with the quality of this?
   c) Have you plans for developing further information giving?

5. Has set standards which are

   a) Understood by *all* staff
   b) Reviewed regularly (6-monthly or yearly)

Current activity and initiatives

A substantial approach to assessing the readiness of a provider unit for comprehensive TQM approach is to carry out a QI audit. This invites staff via an open ended yet structured questionnaire to let the quality manager know what current initiatives and ongoing activity are in place to improve quality. It does not *per se* measure current quality. It measures or audits QI processes.

A small number of variables are chosen and given to all operational heads (clinical directors, HODs, ward sisters) for completion and return in four to eight weeks. An example framework sent to staff is shown in Figure 4.4.

QUALITY IMPROVEMENT INITIATIVES	
	Activity
Clinical practice	
Standard setting and monitoring	
Patient information	
Clinical and management audit	
Physical environment	
Staff recognition and value	
Patient feedback	
Communication	
Training	

Figure 4.4. QI audit form

It covers areas of:

- Clinical practice;
- Standard setting and monitoring;
- Patient information;
- Clinical and management audit;
- Physical environment;
- Staff recognition and value;
- Patient feedback;
- Communication; and
- Training

This approach immediately attests to the notion that TQM is not new — that QI activity is alive and well in all units to a certain extent. The collection and collation of this information reinforces the staff's feeling that their current QI activity, although they may not call it this, is valuable and recognised. Once collected and collated, the communication of the information back to the staff is essential:

1. Backed by the UGM CEO — a *front intro* from a UGM which speaks for itself:

    7th February 1992

   Dear Colleague,

   In May last year I approached Managers and clinical staff across the Unit, asking for information about quality improvement initiatives underway in wards and departments. I asked for this information to help me get a picture of the many and varied initiatives that had been developed by individual wards and departments. This information could then form a baseline before we implemented the Towards Total Quality strategy. My colleagues and I thought it was very important to understand and recognise the considerable effort put in to improving quality before we started the Towards Total Quality initiative as we wanted to build upon all the work already underway.

   This is a summary of the responses received. The list is impressive and indicates the tremendous enthusiasm and commitment staff in the Unit have always had to delivering a high quality service. We ought to be proud of this.

   Our TOWARDS TOTAL QUALITY strategy was launched at the end of July last year. This will enhance, support and promote the commitment already existing. A considerable amount of work has already been developed and many others are being considered by the Quality Improvement Teams.

   I am sure this summary gives us all one message — that out Towards Total Quality strategy has a very firm base to build upon.

   Unit General Manager
   Priority Care Services Unit

2. Present the information in a readable form. When the information comes back it is a daunting task to collate it. However, for staff to either feel valued or to learn from the review, it must be readable and interesting. Figure 4.5 illustrates a format for collating this information.

Figure 4.5. Collation of QI activity cont'd

Aylesbury Vale Priority Care Services

Physical environment
People visiting our many units will immediately form impressions from us from the appearance of our facilities. The appearance and fabric of the buildings in which care is offered is crucial to satisfied patients, clients and relatives. Initiatives currently underway are:

Control of hazardous substances (COSSH)
Security systems (Health and Safety)
Near-miss reporting (Health and Safety) and appropriate training
Evaluation of incident rates
Maintenance and renovation of residences: *Eliminating Hazards * Involving clients
Replacement/servicing of equipment/furniture
Availability of department funds for low cost environment improvements
Staff involvement in equipment need determination
Improved decorating schedule
Waiting times: *Individual appointment system * Review of waiting times
Checking supplies of psychological test forms/materials for ordering
Multi-sensory learning disability project
'Personalising/normalising' residences
Updating of planned maintenance programme
Geographical clinic access

Communication with staff
Increasingly, effective communication of information and understanding between departments, hospitals and services is very important to ensure appropriate services are offered and received. Current initiatives to reduce the quote 'They never tell us anything' are:

Safety Management monthly journal (Health and Safety)
In-house Unit Newsletter
Departmental communication strategy
Team briefing
Informal staff groups
Awareness meetings on Unit Plan
Distributor of monthly performance figures
(Health and Safety)
Staff involvement in service planning (speciality)
Quality action group (Cromwell Ward)
Single maintenance contact point
New services requisitioning system estates
Management accounting service reply slips
Staff feedback meetings (Finance)

Chiropody staff hand book
Chiropody 'open door' policy
Staff feedback on service
Credentialing (Occupational Therapy)
IPR
Staff support groups
'Smokestop' support

Team building services
M/D team development
Quality issues in job descriptions
Team Chiropody System
'Open door' policy by HOD

Staff Training
A key component to quality improvement is the continual education, awareness raising and training of us all in the latest methods of delivering and organising our work. Ways of identifying training needs, types of training offered and ways of evaluating training are given:

Methods/sources for identifying training needs
Health and Safety committee
Staff Health & Safety representatives
Review of accident/incident records
IPR

Departmental meetings
Journal Club discussions
Staff survey

Types of training
Induction
In-service training
COSSH
Handling loads at work
Basic Health & Safety
Food hygiene training

Bereavement training
Counselling training
IPP (Continuous Care) training
Cognitive rehabilitation
Facilitating staff support services
Lifting training

cont'd Figure 4.5

Cook-chill training
Paediatric clinic observation (Speech Therapy)
Use of video camera training (Speech Therapy)
Behavioural family therapy
C.M.H.T. training
Front-line management training

Financial management training

Basic CPR (Dental)
Recovery training (Dental)
Radiation protection
Fire Drill

Evaluation of Training
Health & Safety evaluation questionnaire
Explicit Health & Safety training strategy (Health & Safety)
Informal review with staff
Feedback on courses attended

Getting it right first time
*Standard setting and monitoring
*Clinical and management audit

One key element in Quality Management is ensuring staff have clear and measurable 'standards' written, documented and used in a way which they and/or others can regularly monitor. This helps staff to have their high level of skill regularly acknowledged and valued and to ensure 'below standard' performance is picked up and improved upon.

Issues addressed in standard setting
Training records
Training evaluation
Staff awareness
Accident incident rates
Existing legislation
Use of information services
Sickness rates
External award achievement
HSE Inspectorate report
Occupational disease/allergy rates
Health screening: pre-appointment/during work
Regular vaccination
Priority staff treatment
Use of Occupational Health

Recruitment and retention
Budget maintenance
Professional standards
Ordering/purchasing food
Hygiene auditing
Waiting times monitoring (Speech Therapy)
Screening —
(pre-appointment) (Speech Therapy)
Client-specific standards (Speech Therapy)
General QA standards —
(OT/Clinical Psychology)
Nursing standards
Management accountancy standards
Systems manual —
(Administration/Mental Health)
Physiotherapy standards

Standards monitoring group/committee
Health & Safety Committees: fire, policy review, violence, COSSH, handling loads at work, 1992 requirements
Catering monitoring group and multi-disciplinary monitoring teams
Occupational Therapy QA group
Nursing (LD)

Other monitoring methods
IPR. systems manual (Administration/Mental Health)*

Explicit modification of 'nonconformity' to standards
Dietetics

Information to compile this edition was received from:
Catering
Dietetics
Health & Safety
Support Services
Financial and Information Services
Community Dental
Nursing (Acute Mental Health, Community, Learning Disabilities, Physical Rehabilitation)

Planning and Contracting Services
Speech and Language Therapy Services
Chiropody
Clinical Psychology
Occupational Therapy

* Major documentation of all areas

General measurement of quality

In trying to organise the overall approach to quality care and service, experienced practitioners, be they clinicians or nonclinicians, move between a *professional–experienced eye* model. In this process maturity, experience, and previous training lend themselves to gaining impressions of whether quality is high or low. Also the systematic checklist approach leads to the search for definitive checklists of quality in particular areas. Experience with both these approaches teaches one that they complement each other and are insufficient on their own. Checklists are endless in any organisation — but below are examples of different checklists available in the NHS. They are not an exhaustive list! Different formats will help inform quality managers how to approach their measurement task.

Social acceptability of care

As part of ones region's (SWRHA) pursuit of social acceptability factors in health care delivery, they devised a list of 27 items which were relevant to explore:

South Western Regional Health Authority

Social Acceptability of Care

Checklist for quality

The checklist for quality encompasses elements of environment, personal service, care and support for staff.

1. Environment
   (a) External first impression/signposting;
   (b) Car parking;
   (c) Accessible entrances;
   (d) Internal first impression/signposting;
   (e) Reception areas (patient information);
   (f) Waiting areas;
   (g) Art in public/patient areas;
   (h) Corridors; and
   (i) Local environments (wards, clinics etc).

2. Personal service
   (a) Mission statement/organisational values — for consumers;
   (b) Providing patients and relatives with information;
   (c) Staff empowerment/action to create a personalised service;
   (d) Management support/facilitation;
   (e) Staff attitudes/behavioural issues;
   (f) Standards in personal/nonclinical care;
   (g) Consumer involvement; and
   (h) Staff appearance (uniforms etc).

3. Care and support for staff
   (a) Mission statement/organisational values — for staff;
   (b) Recruitment and selection processes;
   (c) Induction;
   (d) Education and training;
   (e) Monitoring and appraisal processes;
   (f) Facilities for staff;
   (g) Services for staff;
   (h) Counselling/crisis and change management;
   (i) Preparation for demographic changes; and
   (j) Informing staff.

Figure 4.6 was developed into a useful checklist *creating a quality environment* which concentrated on one aspect of quality — the physical environment — as seen through the eyes of a patient or a visitor entering a hospital. Its objective was to identify problems needing to be addressed.

Figure 4.6. Creating a quality environment cont'd

QUALITY: EVERYONES BUSINESS

CREATING
A
QUALITY ENVIRONMENT

CHECKLIST
OF
QUALITY ISSUES
AND
THE PHYSICAL ENVIRONMENT

South West Regional Health Authority
October 1990

SWRHA

INTRODUCTION

E(90)MB17 reiterates the emphasis given in the White Paper to '...the high importance which Ministers attach to the quality of care and the provision of a service which is sensitive to the needs of its customers across the NHS' and requires health authorities to instigate procedures to assess and improve quality of services and customer relations.

Money has been allocated to Regional Health Authorities by the Department of Health to progress these initiatives, part of which will be used to enhance the quality of the physical environment.

South West Health has already taken positive steps in this direction by producing a framework on quality issues to ensure that '...quality statements are being translated into tangible benefits on the ground'.

The checklist which follows is arranged in the form of a questionnaire and concentrates on one aspect of quality — the physical environment — as seen through the eyes of a patient or a visitor entering a hospital. Its objective is to identify problems which need to be addressed. It is not exhaustive and does not seek to provide solutions.

cont'd Figure 4.6

PATIENT INFORMATION — CHECKLIST OF QUALITY ISSUES AND THE PHYSICAL ENVIRONMENT

1   Appointment Information
   a)   Are the directions and information to attend the appointment clearly defined?
   b)   Is the information concerning the locations of car parks or bus stops clear?
   c)   Does the information regarding car parks include parking charges and directions to the patient/visitor as to what to do if the Hospital car park is full?
   d)   Does the information include a plan or a pictorial perspective view of the Hospital?
   e)   Does the information give details of catering facilities?

2   Planning the Visit

2.1.   Pedestrian.
   a)   Are there sufficient buses/trains to take you to the Hospital?
   b)   Does the bus enter the Hospital site or 'set down' the patient outside the site? (If the latter what would be the problems of extending the bus service nearer to the main entrance?)
   c)   Where buses enter the site have shelters been provided?

2.2.   Car
   a)   Is the Local Authority signposting to the Hospital satisfactory?
   b)   Is the signposted name of the Hospital commonly recognised by most people (locals/outsiders)?

3   Arrival at the Hospital

3.1   Pedestrian
   a)   How close to the Hospital does the bus/train bring you?
   b)   Is the directional signposting from that spot satisfactory?
   c)   Are the pedestrian footpaths/walkways:-
      — In good condition?
      — Clearly marked?
      — Adequately illuminated?
      — The shortest practicable route to the destination?
      (If not, could they be or is there a reason for them not to be?)
   d)   Are there any obstructions to the route? (eg Major Building Contracts). If so, are they clearly marked and any alternative route adequately signposted?
   e)   Are adequate drop kerbs provided at road junctions for perambulators or wheelchairs?
   f)   Are the drop kerbs in safe locations?
   g)   Does the layout of the footpaths take into account the security of the users? Unlit or unsupervisable stretches are possible places for personal assault.

3.2   By Car
   a)   What provisions have been made to restrict the speed of on-site vehicles? Are they signposted and illuminated?
   b)   Is the Main Car-Park clearly signposted? If designated a letter or number is this shown on the information leaflet '1' above?

cont'd Figure 4.6

4   Parking
   a)   How easy is it to park?
   b)   Is the surface of the car-park satisfactory — free of pot-holes, solid and 'secure-feeling' under foot?
   c)   Is the location of the car-park reasonably close to your destination?
   d)   Is the layout of the car-park adequate?
   e)   Is parking space wide enough to allow car door to open fully to allow unobstructed transfer into a wheelchair, either unassisted or assisted?
   f)   Are there parking spaces adjacent to the building(s) for disabled users to minimise the distances to be travelled?
   g)   Is the location of the disabled parking spaces such that the approach route to the building/facility is not obstructed by other parked cars and away from moving traffic?
   h)   Are there covered bays for motor cycles and bicycles?
   i)   Are non parking areas clearly marked?
   j)   Are there adequate signs to identify the reserved parking spaces and the best routes into the premises?
   k)   If the parking is 'Pay and Display' is there a change machine conveniently sited to the ticket machine?
   l)   Is the fact that a car park is 'Pay and Display' shown on the information leaflet '1' above?
   m)   Is there a litter bin adjacent to the ticket machine and at other locations on the site?

THE FIRST IMPRESSION OF THE HOSPITAL IS OFTEN FROM THE CAR-PARK

   n)   Does the car park portray a feeling of safety to both persons and vehicles?
   o)   Is the landscaping and lighting designed/maintained to mitigate risk of theft, vandalism and personal attack?
   p)   Does the landscaping obstruct a clear view of the cars/directional signs?
   q)   Are the sight-lines good on exit?
   r)   Are there low level walls, rails, bollards or signs which could damage the vehicle due to non-visibility whilst reversing or parking?
   s)   Is there sufficient clearance for the overhang of the car?
   t)   If the car-park is full are there signs to point you to 'overflow' parking areas? (See also 1c above).
   u)   Is the directional signposting from the car park to the Hospital satisfactory?

3.3   By Ambulance/Car/Taxi
   a)   Can ambulances discharge patients under cover within close proximity of the entrance?
   b)   Is the surface adequate?
   c)   Is the area under cover from the elements?
   d)   Is it close to the required entrance?
   e)   Is there provision to allow taxis to wait close to the entrance?

4   Signposting
   SIGNPOSTING IS OFTEN A MAJOR CAUSE OF CONFUSION ON THE HOSPITAL SITE. IT MAY BE EXPEDIENT TO APPOINT A SIGNPOSTING COORDINATOR TO REDUCE THE CONFUSION.

cont'd Figure 4.6

a)   Is the information given clear?
b)   Is the location satisfactory?
c)   Is the signposting confusing or over-provided?
     (The main signs are:- MAIN ENTRANCE, *i*, EMERGENCY,
     MATERNITY.
     Any others are only required when the patient/visitor reaches the
     hospital building.)
d)   Are the signs adequately illuminated?
e)   Do they follow HTM 65?
f)   Are the symbols or directional lines used? If so, do they work?

5   **Approach to Building**
     a)   Is the approach route smooth, slip resistant (whether wet or dry),
          free from incidental obstructions or hazards?
     b)   Are all public approach routes at least 1200 wide? (Approved
          Document M) — 2 wheelchairs cannot pass on this width.
     c)   Are road level and roadside kerbs blended at intersections? — if
          slightly raised section unavoidable, this must be clearly defined
          with colour contrast and good illumination, be feathered in detail
          and not exceed 25mm in height.
     d)   Are footpaths, ramps and crossings adequately lit to ensure
          security of footing?
     e)   Is the pavement surface textured at the crossing location to assist
          blind and partially sighted users?
     f)   Are handrails provided on all slopes and resting places provided
          at intervals where a ramp or approach is long?
     g)   Are drop kerbs constructed so that the gradient of the ramps is
          within 1:10 maximum?
     h)   Does ramp have a raised kerb at least 100mm on any open side?

6   **Arrival at the Main Entrance**
     a)   What was the walking time from the car-park/bus stop?
     b)   Are all public entrances to the building/facility accessible?
          (Ramps max 1 in 12, preferred 1 in 20).
     c)   Are access doors wide enough to facilitate wheelchair
          movement?
     d)   Are thresholds eliminated or kept to a minimum?
     e)   Are there handrails to ramps or steps? — if so, does handrail
          design obstruct wheelchair manoeuvring and is handrail high
          enough to facilitate free and safe arm movements?
     f)   Do door characteristics and dimensions of related spaces allow it
          to be opened (and closed) easily by independent wheelchair
          users, moving in either direction?
     g)   What doors can be eliminated?
     h)   Is the Entrance in the right place?
     i)   Would re-location or provision of a secondary entrance improve
          the overall functioning of the department?
     j)   Has the design of the Main Entrance followed HBN 51?

7   **First Impressions Upon Entry**
     a)   Is the Reception desk easy to find?
     b)   Is the *i* apparent?
     c)   Is the design/colour satisfactory?
     d)   Are you aware of any deficiencies in the Decor, lighting,
          temperature or general ambience?

cont'd Figure 4.6

e) How much information is on view in the shape of signs, noticeboards, notices or leaflets? Is it too much or confusing? (The Signposting Coordinator referred to above could also maintain the noticeboards.)

f) Is the Resception Area staffed?

g) If not, is it easy to locate someone?

h) Has the 'corporate image' of the uniform and design been used?

8   The Reception

a) Is the Reception desk in the right place?

b) Is the counter enclosed?

c) How? — Glazed screen/solid/louvres?

d) Is there privacy at the counter?

e) Is the attitude and personality of the staff satisfactory?

f) If queuing is necessary is it ordered?

g) What system is used to control appointment times for patients? Is it satisfactory?

h) Is the Waiting Area visible from the Reception?

i) Can patients in chairs use the reception desk conveniently and privately?

THE RECEPTION AREA SHOULD HAVE A FEELING OF OPENNESS WHILE MAINTAINING AN ASPECT OF SECURITY.

(Sometimes achieved by the provision of a second Reception Area, for security purposes, in the Casualty Department).

9   The Waiting Area

a) Are waiting areas protected from draughts as patients move in and out through the entrance doors?

b) Is the ambience satisfactory? (As 6d above).

c) Are there adequate facilities — drinks dispenser, magazines, litter bins, public telephones, free taxi phones and WCs? Are they all clearly marked?

d) Is there a WC for disabled people?

e) Are the magazines up-to-date?

f) Is the area comfortable?

g) Is there 'musak'?

h) Are there plants around the area?

i) Is the seating varied in size, design, material — and comfort?

j) Is the seating arranged in a way to provide visual interest to the patient?

k) Can patients using wheelchairs (their own or hospital chairs whilst waiting for treatment), sit with other patients without obstructing the corridors or circulation areas?

l) Are the floors carpeted?

m) Is there a 'view' from the Waiting Area? (ie into a landscaped courtyard) if so, has consideration been given to providing features or plants to attract birds or butterflies?

n) Are telephones and other public mechanisms accessible to wheelchair users? Are knobs, dials, switches, handles and other controls operable and within convenient reach?

o) Is there artwork on the walls?

p) Could the area be used to show artwork as an exhibition (local Artists, schools, college) or For Sale, either for the Artist or as a source of revenue for the Hospital?

q) Are the Waiting Areas, or adjacent Courtyards, suitable for sculpture or craft demonstrations?

cont'd Figure 4.6

r)   Are there external areas which, by the introduction of planting or screening to provide wind shelter, will allow patients to sit outside in comfort?

s)   Has consideration been given to turning a courtyard into an outdoor room or atrium by the partially or fully glazing the roof to maximise the use of space?

THE STANDARD OF INTERIOR DESIGN SHOULD BE HIGH IN THIS AREA, INCLUDING THE LIGHTING.

t)   Do the staff provide an updating of information service?

10   Internal Circulation (Corridors)

a)   Are the lobby sizes adequate and safe both for independent and assisted wheelchair use?

b)   Are corridor and approach routes satisfactory? Do they allow passing and turning of wheelchairs and take adequate account of corridor traffic conditions?

c)   Have all obstructions and projections from walls (or ceiling) or similar hazards at floor level — such as changes of level — been avoided? If unavoidable are they clearly discernible?

d)   Are internal doors widths adequate to allow wheelchairs turning through 90° from the corridor or lobby? Should either or both be increased?

e)   Have safety handrails been provided on corridors, ramps, steps or at other points where they are required by persons with impaired mobility? Have they been produced where they can be used as locational aids by visually impaired people?

f)   Are any large areas of glass close to circulation areas marked or framed so as to be clearly discernible to partially sighted people?

g)   Are seats available at intervals to permit an ambulant disabled and elderly person to take a short rest when faced with long corridors to negotiate?

h)   Are there clear, well lit signs posted to ensure easy circulation within the building?

i)   Do they follow HTM 65?

j)   What is the impression of the lighting and decor?

k)   Are there artwork, murals or photographs on the walls?

l)   Would the doors be difficult for the disabled to operate?

m) Is the flooring materials non-slip?

n)   Is there wall protection on one side/both sides of the corridor?

o)   Is it in the right location for the various types of trolley used?

p)   Are refreshment areas accessible to disabled people?

11   Vertical Circulation

a)   Are staircases safe and optimally comfortable for elderly and disabled people? Are handrails and landing characteristics satisfactory?

b)   Are staircases clearly signposted?

c)   Are lifts available, conveniently placed, accessible and clearly signposted?

d)   Are there location plans in the lift lobbies?

e)   Are list controls accessible to the independent wheelchair user? Are the visual and audible signals, alarms and floor designations satisfactory? Are digits embossed and satisfactory for blind or partially sighted persons? Is there a tip-up-seat, or a support rail available?

cont'd Figure 4.6

12   Toilets
a)   Are there correctly designed Unisex toilets (ie where a husband and wife may enter the cubicle together) available in the public areas of the premises?
b)   Are there suitable cubicles for wheelchair users in other male and female toilets in the building?
c)   Do cubicles for wheelchair users provide adequate manoeuvring space within, or is turning space provided outside? Is the level of privacy afforded satisfactory?
d)   Are there cubicles available with appropriate grab rails for the use of ambulant disabled people?
e)   Are the WC and wash basin arrangements accessible to independent wheelchair users? Are the grab rails, mirrors, towels, door closing bars and other aids placed satisfactorily?

13   Treatment Areas
a)   Are all consulting and treatment areas fully accessible to disabled patients?
b)   Are there changing cubicles suitable for wheelchair users, with room for assistance to be given if required?

14   Ward Facilities
a)   What are the impressions of the ambience, decor, lighting and floor material?
b)   Is wallpaper used?
c)   Are the Ward floors noisy or slippery?
d)   Could consideration be given to carpeting selected areas around beds?
e)   Is the 'night lighting' in a position to annoy or prevent a patient from sleeping?
f)   Do sanitary facilities offer maximum independence and privacy to disabled patients, both those who will be using wheelchairs and those who have walking difficulties?
g)   Is the day room easily located and accessible, with a variety of seating heights to help ambulant disabled people? Are all notices clear to see and understand?
h)   Are window controls, radio and television and call bells easily reached by disabled people and do they all function?
i)   Can disabled visitors conduct private conversations with their friends in bed or in the ward?

15   Other Features
a)   Are emergency evacuation routes and emergency exits satisfactory?
b)   Are fire alarms readily accessible to the semi-ambulant and wheelchair disabled? Are emergency call facilities stalled to summon assistance in remote locations?
c)   Are audio/visual alarms signals provided?

5/KE-002/3
16.10.90

Many ideas inherent in this questionnaire can be found in the framework in Figure 4.7 — an environmental quality audit — which relates service areas in a DGH with environmental issues and possible improvement methods.

Figure 4.7. Environmental quality audit

ENVIRONMENTAL QUALITY AUDIT

Issues \ Location	External Entrances & Approach	Reception	Outpatient Areas	Wards	Departments	Theatres	Corridors	Methods
Signposting								'First Impressions' Group or 'Quest' Team
Telephones/Bleeps								
Cleanliness/Bins								External Customer Information (Surveys, Visitors' Complaints)
Toilets								
Pictures								M.B.W.A. and Management Audit
Offices								
Plants/Gardens/Landscaping								Comparison between Hospitals
Availability of Goods/Shops/etc								
Colours								Prioritising of Effort
Lighting								
'Welcome' Impressions								Ownership by D.G.M./U.G.M. & Staff
Noticeboards								
Decorating/Painting								Local 'Monitors'
Photograph Boards								
Reading Material								Involvement of Estates Function
Seating and Furniture								
Information								Quality Improvement Annual Programme
Eating Areas								
Individualised Appearance								Costing of Improvements
Smoking Areas								
Storage/Tidiness								Allocation of Funds
Temperature								
Leisure Areas								Corporate Strategy
Curtaining								
Relatives' Rooms								Relevance of Environment on Clinical Outcome
Reception Desk Appearance								
Car Parking								Need to Attract Patients & 'Marketing'
External Fabric								
Ventilation								Maintenance of Standards
Privacy								Open Meeting with Staff to gain Ideas and Commitment

Physical and social environments are crucial in any health care setting. The DoH have placed considerable emphasis on this variable, by supporting and encouraging quality improvements by a programme of centrally funded initiatives. A booklet *Demonstrably different* (DoH, 1991), illustrates the first six outpatient projects (1989/90); summarises key features; outlines lessons learned; and highlights ideas for good practice.

Shop window

A key component of the environment in hospitals and clinics is the quality of its *shop window* — of the receptionist, front line staff, their attitudes, behaviour and facilities. An early checklist was devised at the Kings Fund Centre (Hinks, 1973) *Spotlight on shop window staff*. It is a hospital manager's checklist and uses a very simple format to identify current performance on many shop window behaviours. An example relating to the shop window team is shown in Figure 4.8.

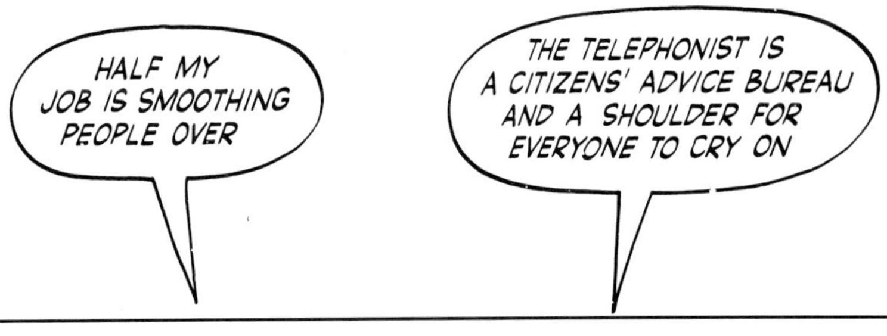

Figure 4.8. Shop window

Outpatient department services (OPD)

OPD services have been subject to considerable scrutiny in terms of the quality of service provided. Work undertaken by the Trent RHA outlined key aspects of the OP process which covered:

1. Informing the GP;
2. Acknowledgement process;
3. Making the first appointment;
4. The visit; and
5. Environment.

The Outpatient Process
PRINCIPLES

Informing the GP

1 GPs should be provided with information on outpatient and inpatient waiting times **for each consultant** and indicating areas or special expertise (which might include, where appropriate, knowledge of further languages).

2 A mechanism should exist to involve GPs in deciding the format of information.

3 GPs should be provided with a protocol, where necessary by specialty or individual consultant and including advice on diagnostic tests required, for making an urgent referral.

Acknowledgement Process

4 All patients should receive a prompt acknowledgement that their GP's referral has been received.
The hospital should ascertain at this early stage any language, gender or cultural issues which may require special consideration throughout the patients period of care.
The hospital should also ascertain the style of address preferred by the patient for all communications.

Making a First Appointment

5 A maximum desired waiting time, from receipt of referral to patient being seen in clinic, should be identified.

6 Non-urgent referrals should normally receive a minimum period of notice (allowing for short notice appointments to fill cancellations).

7 Patients should be made to feel that it is acceptable to change their offered appointment.
Referral letters should contain instructions, including a telephone number, on how to do this.
Departments may wish to have particular regard to ethnic background and festivals/religious occasions which affect patients' wish to change appointments.

8 Attention should be given to controlling the numbers of 'Do Not Attends', including, for patients given more than a specified period of notice, the sending of reminder letters.

9   All communications should reflect the diversity of language of the local community and allow for specific disability.

All new referrals should receive information on:
a) directions to the hospital
b) public transport
c) ambulance services
d) car parking
e) disabled access
f) amenities inc. for
    — people with disabilities
    — mothers and babies
    — children
g) what to bring to the clinic including ...
h) samples
i) reception arrangements
j) clinic procedure, including anticipated delay.
k) arrangements for diagnostic tests.
l) who they can expect to see.
m) information on translation/interpreter services.
n) how to contact the hospital for advice or further information (inc. telephone number).

10 Once notified, the majority of patients should be able to expect their appointment to remain unchanged.

The Visit

11 The views of patients on aspects of the service should be sought regularly and mechanisms exist for ensuring that the views expressed are communicated to all staff.
Special arrangements should be considered to ensure that services meet the needs of children, elderly people, people with disabilities and people for whom English is not their first language.

12 Staff should receive patients in a sensitive and appropriate manner. If necessary, training should be given, especially where patients may come from a culturally diverse background.

13 All clinics should start in time.

14 All diagnostic tests known to be required before consultation should be completed and the results available before the consultant appointment time. (This may not be practical for new patients, but should be standard for return patients).

15 All medical notes should be available before the consultant appointment time.

16 Patients should be able to expect to be seen at their appointment time.

17 Patients should expect to be kept informed of any delays. It may be appropriate to ensure patients understand why some 'queues' move faster than others.

18 A mechanism should exist to ensure access of patients, if required, to the

consultant. Where possible, this should be able to take account of an expressed wish on the part of the patient.

19 Patients should understand the reasons for inviting them to a follow-up appointment.

20 Where practicable, patients should have further diagnostic tests carried out on the same day.

21 Waiting times for diagnostic tests to be carried out should be kept to a minimum. These departments should ensure that appointment systems are structured to allow for 'unplanned' referrals from outpatient clinics.

22 Where an appointment is required for further tests, this should be linked when possible to any future consultant appointment requirements.

23 A prompt report should be sent to the GP.

24 Patients should be given either a supply of any medication prescribed in a clear, appropriate instructions on use (and disposal of surplus) or clear instructions on how to report to GP.

25 Where appropriate, medication should be dispensed as promptly as possible.

26 Patients feel confident they have been/are being dealt with properly both administratively and clinically.
    The patient's visit should be as comfortable as possible.
    Environmental standards should apply not only to the main waiting areas but to all sub-areas, support departments etc.

Environment

27 Every effort should be made to ensure adequate car parking space is available to patients or that, as a minimum, patients are informed of problems and encouraged to travel by other means.

28 All staff should wear labels/have badges and be readily identifiable to patients.

29 Signposting should be clear, in appropriate languages, illustrative symbols should be used for signposting whenever possible. Patients should be given clear directions and, in appropriate case, escorted by staff.

30 Efforts should be made to identify sources for the supply of reasonably up-to-date reading material which reflects local cultural/linguistic mix.

31 Patient refreshment facilities, adequately signposted and within easy reach of waiting areas, will be open throughout clinic opening times.

32 Patients should have access to pay phones.

33 There should be an adequate number of toilets, including those for people with disabilities, within easy access of waiting areas and adequately signposted.

This was later endorsed by the National Audit Office review of NHS OP services (1991) which outlined areas to consider and measure:

Appendix 1

National Audit Office value for money study of outpatient services: Audit criteria

To guide their investigation of outpatient services, the National Audit Office developed at the outset audit criteria, drawing on work carried out by the King's Fund Centre for Health Service Development and the Scottish Health Management Efficiency Group. While they should be applicable to most outpatient services they are not intended to be prescriptive.

Service Planning

Districts and Hospitals should plan outpatient services based on an assessment of the health needs of the population. This may be achieved by:

(1) preparing district purchasing plans which identify the need for outpatient services across the full range of specialties;

(2) incorporating in contracts targets for waiting times for first non-urgent appointment for each specialty or condition;

(3) preparing hospital plans which set out the outpatient services which they provide; and

(4) subjecting plans to review.

Hospitals should establish arrangements for making cost effective use of outpatient services. They could do so by:

(5) ensuring that responsibilities for the cost-effective use of outpatient services are clear to all staff; and

(6) where practicable, developing local protocols and guidelines agreed between hospital clinical staff, and with general practitioners. The protocols should include referral criteria, and the guidelines should additionally include arrangements for the discharge of patients.

Managing the service

Hospitals should make sound arrangements for day-to-day management and review of performance. This may be achieved by:

(7) making a single individual (Outpatients Manager) or clearly identifiable group responsible and giving them the necessary authority for the management of those services which are common to two or more clinics, either across the hospital or within specialties; and

(8) monitoring routinely the operation of outpatient services.

Managers should ensure use of the most appropriate and cost-efficient mix of clinical staff and support services. They should achieve this by:

(9)   assessing tasks to be performed in outpatient departments to decide which staff should undertake them.

Hospital managers should ensure that support staff and other resources are employed efficiently. They could achieve this by:

(10)   making patient records available at minimum cost by
— maintaining efficient filing systems
— ensuring that where practicable records are called for well in advance;

(11)   identifying reasons for patients' failures to attend, and taking appropriate action to minimise this; for example by sending reminders where there is a long time (3 months or more) between booking time and actual appointment, by putting instructions on the appointment card on how to change or cancel appointments, or providing information on the hospital's policy on non-attendance;

(12)   Minimising the incidence of cancelled clinics; for example by ensuring that consultants and junior doctors notify management of their proposed absences well in advance so that they are planned as far as possible; and requiring that patients affected by cancelled clinics are seen as soon as possible;

(13)   scheduling appointments to minimise the impact of non-attendance and urgent appointments.

(14)   regular reviewing the clinic timetable to assure themselves that it permits the most efficient use of accommodation, clinical staff and support services; and

(15)   making efficient use of information technology to minimise the burden of administrative and clerical work.

Quality of service

District health authorities should incorporate quality standards in their contracts. And hospital management should plan and review quality aspects of patients' needs. They could do so by:

(16)   clearly stating staff responsibility for meeting and monitoring quality objectives.

(17)   giving continuing customer service training to all staff; and

(18)   setting quality objectives and standards, and monitoring performance by routinely collecting and reviewing information about important aspects of

the delivery of the service, including and obtaining continuous feedback, including regular sampling, from patients.

Hospital managements should ensure that acceptable standards of service are maintained. They could do so by:

(19) minimising patients' waiting times in clinics:
   — making booking arrangements which give individual appointments spread throughout the clinic session
   — adhering to booking arrangements by, for example, seeing patients in appointment order
   — ensuring, where possible, that clinics start and finish on time;

(20) where practicable offering patients choice over appointment times;

(21) issuing patients with clear instructions (in the languages of the local community) in regard to their clinic attendance, indicating:
   — date and time of appointment
   — name of consultant
   — name and location of clinic
   — an indication of whether the visit is expected to be particularly long
   — procedure if not able to attend
   — transport and parking arrangements
   — whether medical students are likely to be present, and the action the patients should take if they do not want such a presence
   — specific instructions for any investigations, such as fasting, or provision of specimens
   — the person to whom complaints should be directed.

   And, in the case of first appointments, by sending instructions three or four weeks in advance, in order to enable patients to make necessary arrangements; and

(22) creating an environment which will make the patient's wait as pleasant as possible and minimise anxiety; and include aspects as:
   — clear signposting and, where necessary, guides for patients
   — privacy for consultations and changing
   — sufficient seats for the number of patients attending the clinic
   — informing patients about any delays which arise while they are waiting
   — facilities for nursing mothers
   — facilities for patients with disabilities
   — play facilities/area for children
   — clean toilet and washroom facilities located within easy reach of the clinic
   — reading material
   — access to other facilities, such as shops, where practicable.

Mental health services

A multidimensional approach to measuring adequacy of mental health services is provided by face-functional analysis of care environment and consists of a framework shown in Figure 4.9 and a hierarchical classification and coding system as in Figure 4.10 which allows different levels of aggregation of data (Clifford, 1991).

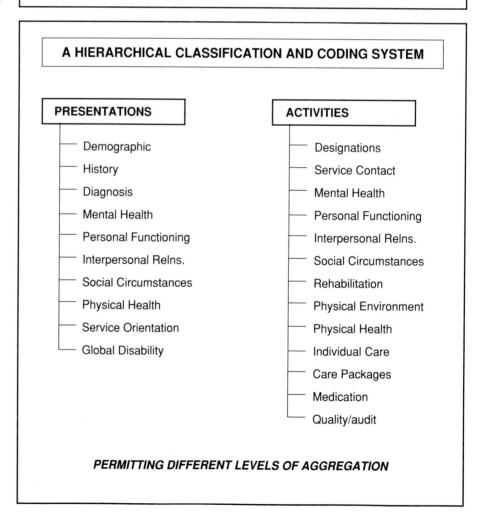

MENTAL HEALTH	PERSONAL FUNCTIONING	REHABILITATION	SOCIAL CIRCUMSTANCES	INTERPERSONAL RELATIONSHIPS	PHYSICAL ENVIRONMENT
Mental state	Self-care	Self-care	Housing	Family	Design
Containment	Domestic activities	Daily living activities	Income	Significant others	Comfort
Problem behaviour	Community activities	Budgeting	Employment	Social networks	Location
Therapeutic understanding	Personal finance	Structured activities	Legal	Social support	Privacy

INDIVIDUAL CARE

Flexibility   Autonomy   Philosophy   Consultation   Advocacy

Figure 4.9. The Face Care Grid — a Framework for Health and Social Care

A HIERARCHICAL CLASSIFICATION AND CODING SYSTEM

PRESENTATIONS
- Demographic
- History
- Diagnosis
- Mental Health
- Personal Functioning
- Interpersonal Relns.
- Social Circumstances
- Physical Health
- Service Orientation
- Global Disability

ACTIVITIES
- Designations
- Service Contact
- Mental Health
- Personal Functioning
- Interpersonal Relns.
- Social Circumstances
- Rehabilitation
- Physical Environment
- Physical Health
- Individual Care
- Care Packages
- Medication
- Quality/audit

PERMITTING DIFFERENT LEVELS OF AGGREGATION

Figure 4.10 Main Heading of the Face Classification System

Community care

In managing the *cascade of change* towards integrated, cross-agency community care, quality service has never been more important. In the Audit Commission's recent community care review (1992), they itemised from a managing service point of view aspects of acute hospital discharge and resettling people with learning disabilities which need to be assessed:

Probe 1
ACUTE HOSPITAL DISCHARGE

The first probe focuses on reception arrangements in the community for people discharged from acute hospitals with particular emphasis on the preparation for 1 April 1993 when local authorities will assume additional responsibilities for people currently going directly to residential and nursing homes.

Objectives:
1. Are authorities jointly assessing the present and future need for nursing and residential home places?
   Have they agreed on the size and nature of the problem and the opportunities presented by community care?
2. Are there plans setting out how the numbers of people going into homes can be reduced? Are both authorities putting in place arrangements (staff, administration, procedures) for implementing the changes on 1 April 1993?
3. Are the resource implications for both sides set out and agreed?
   Is the local authority satisfied that the health authority will make available any extra resources needed for community health services? Is the health authority satisfied that its beds will not become blocked?

Needs:
Are health and social services authorities mapping the current pattern of people discharged from hospital who need support — particularly those who go to residential and nursing homes direct from hospital?

Objectives:
Are authorities reviewing the potential for reducing flows to residential and nursing homes by substituting domiciliary care?

Plans:
Have the roles and responsibilities of health and social services been agreed?

Policy

Coordinating care:
Who coordinates care for people ready for discharge? What is the role of the hospital social workers?

Service delivery:
How are services coordinated? Are there dedicated staff or some other arrangement? How does liaison and cross-referral work between community health and social services?

Information:
Are systems in place to record hospitals'/wards' referral patterns; numbers placed in nursing homes or who required help on discharge; current patterns of deployment of staff in support of discharge?

Quality Assurance:
Are patients given sufficient useful information? How are observations from community staff fed back to the hospital? How do authorities evaluate whether discharge arrangements have gone smoothly?

Operational Arrangements

Probe 2

REPLACING LONG STAY HOSPITALS FOR PEOPLE WITH LEARNING DISABILITIES

The second probe focuses on arrangements for resettling people with learning disabilities from old long stay hospitals into facilities in the community.

Objectives:
1. Are authorities jointly planning arrangements for people with learning disabilities?
2. Have they a common approach to the estimation of needs and operational arrangements?
3. Are financial provisions appropriate with capital and revenue cash flows set out in the plans, showing how the gradual transfer of responsibility from health to social services is to be matched financially?
4. Are authorities introducing common monitoring systems and arrangements?

Needs:
How are local needs being measured? Jointly? What information is held about the current hospital population?

Objectives, priorities:
What are the principles which shape the policy? How have priorities and target groups been defined?

Plans:
Has a plan been introduced for learning disabled services? Is the plan joint or separate in each authority?

Policy

Coordinating care:
How do the staff of the different agencies plan and work together? How are individual needs to be assessed? Who will hold budgets, at what levels?

Service delivery:
How are services to be financed in future? Is there devolution of responsibility, authority and budgets?

Information:
Management information should be shared between authorities. What information systems are in operation/planned?

Quality Assurance:
What are the arrangements for monitoring the achievements of the policy against it aims? How are standards to be maintained (and improved) in the hospital as it runs down?

Operational Arrangements

Large and small hospitals

Hospitals have been under considerable scrutiny in recent years with the aim of measuring their quality — two major initiatives are worthy of mention:

- Small hospital project (SWRHA); and
- Organisational audit (Kings Fund).

Both have provided considerable structure to measuring quality of service pre-TQM. Shaw et al (1988), developed a guide to assessing quality in small hospitals which is extensively used in the South Western region to good effect.

The scope of this tool covers many aspects including: general hospital organisation; medical specialities; clinical support services; and non-clinical support services:

CONTENTS

Of particular interest are the medical specialities' checklists covering:

- General medical;
- Maternity; and
- Surgery and anaesthetics.

SURGERY AND ANAESTHESIA

	Yes	?	No

1. District has agreed plans for current and future surgical services in the hospital ___ ___ ___

2. There is a policy on the selection of surgical patients:
   a) it is in writing ___ ___ ___
   b) it is agreed between staff locally and at the district hospital(s) ___ ___ ___

3. Agreed procedures are used:
   a) for identification of patients undergoing general anaesthesia ___ ___ ___
   b) for the identification of limbs, digits ___ ___ ___
   c) for the supervision of consent ___ ___ ___

4. All patients have a local doctor responsible for general care ___ ___ ___

5. There is regular and effective review of policies, procedures and complications. ___ ___ ___
   How is this done?

   _____

   _____

   _____

6. Physical facilities in theatre are consistent with the level of surgery undertaken ___ ___ ___

7. Medical and nursing staff are trained in current equipment and procedures for resuscitation ___ ___ ___
   How is this done?

   _____

   _____

   _____

8. Clinical assistant anaesthetists are clinically accountable to a named consultant ___ ___ ___

9. All anaesthetists are skilled in current techniques appropriate to the procedures performed ___ ___ ___
   How is this done?

   _____

   _____

   _____

10. There is regular contact with the anaesthetist coordinator or other consultant responsible for general organisation of anaesthetic services ___ ___ ___

MATERNITY

	Yes	?	No

Policies and Procedures

1. Admission, transfer and discharge policies have been clearly defined and agreed between staff at local and district level _____ _____ _____

2. a) Written clinical policies covering indication for procedures such as enemas, pubic shaving, artificial rupture of membranes etc are available on site and have been agreed between the professional groups concerned _____ _____ _____

   b) The most recent amendment was in

   _____

3. A mechanism exists to ensure that all staff give consistent information and advice to patients _____ _____ _____

Records

4. The standard format of the obstetric notes used is the same in the consultant obstetric unit _____ _____ _____

5. a) Separate clinical records are begun for each baby _____ _____ _____

   b) A baby's notes are always cross-referenced with the mother's notes _____ _____ _____

6. The following records are retained after discharge:

   a) obstetric notes _____ _____ _____

   b) nurse's cardex _____ _____ _____

   c) booking and birth registration _____ _____ _____

7. Obstetric and babies' records are retained for 21 years _____ _____ _____

8. The following statistics are recorded:

   a) number of women initially booked for GP unit or GP care _____ _____ _____

   b) number of women transferred to consultant care during pregnancy _____ _____ _____

   c) number of deliveries in GP unit or under GP care _____ _____ _____

   d) number of live and still births _____ _____ _____

   e) perinatal mortality figures _____ _____ _____

   f) number of transfers to consultant care during labour _____ _____ _____

   g) postpartum transfers to consultant care for maternal reasons _____ _____ _____

   h) perinatal mortality in cases transferred to consultant care _____ _____ _____

   i) number of babies transferred to consultant care _____ _____ _____

   j) number of neonatal deaths up to 7 days after discharge from unit _____ _____ _____

The statistics recorded were last formally reviewed by clinical staff in

_____

Facilities and Equipment

Efforts have been made to create a nonclinical atmosphere in the delivery suite _____ _____ _____

The areas for first stage of labour meets the following standards:
a) there is space for the woman and a companion to move around, and an easy chair _____ _____ _____

b) washing and toilet facilities of a suitable size for a pregnant woman are nearby   _____ _____ _____

c) a call system is available   _____ _____ _____

d) doors are wide enough for moving beds or trolleys through   _____ _____ _____

e) privacy is achievable for the woman and her companion   _____ _____ _____

12. The following equipment is available within the delivery suite:

   a) a delivery table which can be quickly turned to the Trendelenburg position   _____ _____ _____

   b) equipment for inhalation analgesia   _____ _____ _____

   c) an anaesthetic machine with emergency oxygen supplies   _____ _____ _____

   d) drugs and intravenous equipment   _____ _____ _____

   e) oropharyngeal airways, laryngoscopes, cuffed endotracheal tubes, suction catheters   _____ _____ _____

   f) an incubator, with temperature adjustable for normal infants or for sick or premature infants   _____ _____ _____

   g) infant suction equipment   _____ _____ _____

   h) a separate oxygen supply to the incubator and infant resuscitation equipment   _____ _____ _____

   i) cardiac resuscitation equipment (or readily available to delivery suite)   _____ _____ _____

13. Lighting is versatile enough to provide a restful environment and allow clinical procedures to be performed   _____ _____ _____

14. Hot and cold running water, heating, and an emergency power supply are provided for the delivery area   _____ _____ _____

15. The postnatal ward provides sufficient room for babies to room-in with mothers   _____ _____ _____

16. Privacy for mothers is possible, eg when breast feeding   _____ _____ _____

17. Nursery facilities with an even temperature and humidity are available, and are adequate for teaching mothers about caring for their babies   _____ _____ _____

Staffing

18. The hospital receives 24-hour cover from registered midwives   _____ _____ _____

19. All GPs attending confinements at hospital are on the obstetric list and hold an individual contract with the health authority for admitting patients to the hospital   _____ _____ _____

20. A mechanism exists among medical staff to ensure that all doctors attending confinements have had sufficient recent practice to maintain competence   _____ _____ _____

21. Active encouragement is given to doctors to attend refresher courses and participate in other educational activities   _____ _____ _____

22. A consultant obstetrician last visited the hospital to review policies with local staff in _____

23. A consultant paediatrician last visited the hospital the review policies with local staff in_____

24. Clearly defined arrangements exist for sharing ante-natal care with consultant obstetricians   _____ _____ _____

GENERAL MEDICINE, CARE OF THE ELDERLY

	Yes	?	No
1. Referring doctors have clear guidelines about the types of conditions appropriate for referral to hospital	_____	_____	_____
2. Senior nursing staff are involved in arranging the admission of patients to the hospital	_____	_____	_____
3. A regular review of admissions is held by clinical staff	_____	_____	_____

Personal Identity

	Yes	?	No
4. The way in which a patient would prefer to be addressed is noted and used	_____	_____	_____
5. Patients wear their own clothing at all times	_____	_____	_____
6. The staff demonstrate knowledge of the past life of patients	_____	_____	_____
7. Patients are encouraged to choose:			
— the time they get up	_____	_____	_____
— their clothing	_____	_____	_____
— their bed time	_____	_____	_____
— their meals from a menu	_____	_____	_____
8. Chairs in the dayroom are arranged in compatible groups, rather than around the walls	_____	_____	_____
9. Patients have			
— space for their own possessions	_____	_____	_____
— their own toiletries, flannels, etc	_____	_____	_____
— regular access to professional hairdressing	_____	_____	_____

Privacy

	Yes	?	No
10. Catheter tubes and bags are concealed from sight	_____	_____	_____
11. Personal mirrors are available	_____	_____	_____
12. Patients can bathe, wash and use the toilet in privacy	_____	_____	_____
13. Visitors can talk privately to patients	_____	_____	_____

Dependence

	Yes	?	No
14. Most of the dependent patients are given time and equipment to feed themselves	_____	_____	_____
15. Patients control their own money and can spend it as they wish	_____	_____	_____
16. Patients are allowed alcohol	_____	_____	_____
17. There is an area where patients who wish to are allowed to smoke	_____	_____	_____
18. Non-smokers do not have to suffer a smoky environment	_____	_____	_____

Contact:

18. Patients who wish regularly attend Sunday service in the hospital or in church

19. Visiting hours are flexible and visitors are welcomed at all times

20. The majority of patients do have visitors

21. Up-to-date newspapers and magazines are available

22. There are simple arrangements for patients to use the telephone

23. There is an accurate clock and calendar which is kept up-to-date in each of the sitting areas

24. Call bells are answered promptly

Activities:

25. Playing cards or board games are available and complete

26. If there is a piano it is playable and in tune

27. Patients choose the programmes they watch or listen to

28. A programme of planned diversional and occupational activities is in evidence; patients participate in its development where feasible

29. Patients have easy access to a library service. Large print books are available

30. Transport is provided for outings. Patients are encouraged to plan and go on outings

Environment:

31. The ward is free of unpleasant smells

32. Decor is clean and bright and the ward is well lit

33. Patients can easily see the garden or street

34. If patients wish, pets are kept in the hospital, and patients' own pets can be brought in to visit them

Health Care

35. A programme of continence training is undertaken for all patients who require it

36. Few patients require regular laxatives or sedation (including night sedation)

37. Deaf patients have functional hearing aids

38. No patient should have dental problems which affect their ability to eat or speak

39. Patients have had vision checked (and spectacles provided if necessary) in the past year

40. Treatable foot problems which cause discomfort or limited mobility are promptly managed

The organisational audit unit at the Kings Fund has developed a self assessment and external audit approach which helps managers and clinicians extend and improve their standards by first assessing their current quality status in a clear and useful ways. See Figure 4.11.

The format which is followed for each service covers:

1. Philosophy and objectives;
2. Management, staffing and records;
3. Staff development and education;
4. Policies and procedures;
5. Facilities and equipment; and
6. Evaluation and quality assurance.

Figure 4.1. Radiology sample assessment form cont'd

RADIOLOGY SERVICE

The self-assessement forms have been included in the main body of the document. Their purpose is to provide each of the participating hospitals with an opportunity to give feedback on their progress towards meeting standards. The 'mirror image' page includes the main headings and numbers of each standard, a column for YES/NO as appropriate. Where the response is NO, please comment and/or indicate whether there is an intention to comply. If the space for comments is insufficient, please continue on a separate sheet.

The remaining half of the page is to be completed by the survey team member.

Completion of the document serves two main purposes:

1. It will greatly assist the King's Fund in the task of developing and improving the standards. The comments will be included in the re-draft of the Organisational Audit Manual.
2. A copy of the completed document is sent to each member of the survey team. This will provide the team, in advance of the survey, with some indication of the hospital's progress towards meeting the standards, and will assist them in the planning of the survey.

The completed form MUST be returned to the King's Fund six weeks prior to the survey date for your hospital.

1.   PHILOSOPHY AND OBJECTIVES

The aim of the radiology service is to provide the hospital with a high quality of service and to ensure safe and efficient patient care which complies with the relevant statutory instruments (currently the Ionising Radiation Regulations 1985, 1986, 1987 and 1988).

Standards				comment
1.1	❑ Y ❑ N			
1.2	❑ Y ❑ N			
1.3	1.3.1	❑ Y ❑ N		
	1.3.2	❑ Y ❑ N		
	1.3.3	❑ Y ❑ N		
	1.3.4	❑ Y ❑ N		
	1.3.5	❑ Y ❑ N		
	1.3.6			
	(a)	❑ Y ❑ N		
	(b)	❑ Y ❑ N		
	1.3.7	❑ Y ❑ N		

HOSPITAL

		comment
❑ Y ❑ N		
❑ Y ❑ N		
❑ Y ❑ N		
❑ Y ❑ N		
❑ Y ❑ N		
❑ Y ❑ N		
❑ Y ❑ N		
❑ Y ❑ N		
❑ Y ❑ N		
❑ Y ❑ N		

SURVEYOR

		HOSPITAL					SURVEYOR	
1.3.8	❑ Y	❑ N			❑ Y	❑ N		
1.3.9	❑ Y	❑ N			❑ Y	❑ N		

1.4

1.4.1	❑ Y	❑ N		❑ Y	❑ N
1.4.2	❑ Y	❑ N		❑ Y	❑ N
1.4.3	❑ Y	❑ N		❑ Y	❑ N
1.4.4	❑ Y	❑ N		❑ Y	❑ N
1.4.5	❑ Y	❑ N		❑ Y	❑ N

1.5

1.5.1	❑ Y	❑ N		❑ Y	❑ N
1.5.2	❑ Y	❑ N		❑ Y	❑ N
1.5.3	❑ Y	❑ N		❑ Y	❑ N
1.5.4	❑ Y	❑ N		❑ Y	❑ N
1.5.5	❑ Y	❑ N		❑ Y	❑ N

2. MANAGEMENT, STAFFING AND RECORDS

The radiology service is organised, managed and staffed to provide a safe environment for patients and staff and a safe, efficient and effective service to patients.

Standards   comment   comment

2.1	❑ Y	❑ N		❑ Y	❑ N
2.2	❑ Y	❑ N		❑ Y	❑ N
2.3	❑ Y	❑ N		❑ Y	❑ N
2.4	❑ Y	❑ N		❑ Y	❑ N
2.5	❑ Y	❑ N		❑ Y	❑ N
2.6	❑ Y	❑ N		❑ Y	❑ N

2.7

2.7.1	❑ Y	❑ N		❑ Y	❑ N
2.7.2	❑ Y	❑ N		❑ Y	❑ N
2.7.3	❑ Y	❑ N		❑ Y	❑ N
2.7.3	❑ Y	❑ N		❑ Y	❑ N
2.7.4	❑ Y	❑ N		❑ Y	❑ N

2.8

2.8.1	❑ Y	❑ N		❑ Y	❑ N
2.8.2	❑ Y	❑ N		❑ Y	❑ N
2.8.3	❑ Y	❑ N		❑ Y	❑ N

2.9	❑ Y	❑ N		❑ Y	❑ N
2.10	❑ Y	❑ N		❑ Y	❑ N
2.11	❑ Y	❑ N		❑ Y	❑ N
2.12	❑ Y	❑ N		❑ Y	❑ N

HOSPITAL   **SURVEYOR**

cont'd. Figure 4.11

Personnel

2.13

2.13.1	❑ Y	❑ N				❑ Y	❑ N
2.13.2	❑ Y	❑ N				❑ Y	❑ N
2.13.3	❑ Y	❑ N				❑ Y	❑ N
2.13.4	❑ Y	❑ N				❑ Y	❑ N
2.13.5	❑ Y	❑ N				❑ Y	❑ N

2.14   ❑ Y   ❑ N   ❑ Y   ❑ N

2.15   ❑ Y   ❑ N   ❑ Y   ❑ N

2.16   ❑ Y   ❑ N   ❑ Y   ❑ N

2.17   ❑ Y   ❑ N   ❑ Y   ❑ N

Staffing

2.18   ❑ Y   ❑ N   ❑ Y   ❑ N

2.19   ❑ Y   ❑ N   ❑ Y   ❑ N

2.20   ❑ Y   ❑ N   ❑ Y   ❑ N

2.21   ❑ Y   ❑ N   ❑ Y   ❑ N

2.22   ❑ Y   ❑ N   ❑ Y   ❑ N

2.23   ❑ Y   ❑ N   ❑ Y   ❑ N

2.24   ❑ Y   ❑ N   ❑ Y   ❑ N

2.25   ❑ Y   ❑ N   ❑ Y   ❑ N

2.26

2.26.1	❑ Y	❑ N			❑ Y	❑ N
2.26.2	❑ Y	❑ N			❑ Y	❑ N
2.26.3	❑ Y	❑ N			❑ Y	❑ N

2.27   ❑ Y   ❑ N   ❑ Y   ❑ N

Records

2.28   ❑ Y   ❑ N   ❑ Y   ❑ N

2.29   ❑ Y   ❑ N   ❑ Y   ❑ N

2.30   ❑ Y   ❑ N   ❑ Y   ❑ N

2.31   ❑ Y   ❑ N   ❑ Y   ❑ N

2.32   ❑ Y   ❑ N   ❑ Y   ❑ N

2.33   ❑ Y   ❑ N   ❑ Y   ❑ N

2.34   ❑ Y   ❑ N   ❑ Y   ❑ N

HOSPITAL   **SURVEYOR**

cont'd. Figure 4.11

3. STAFF DEVELOPMENT AND EDUCATION

The radiology service provides in-service and continuing education programmes for all levels of staff to encourage training and development on issues relevant to the needs of individuals and to the objectives of the service and the hospital.

Standards		comment		comment
3.1 ❑ Y ❑ N			❑ Y ❑ N	
3.1.1 ❑ Y ❑ N			❑ Y ❑ N	
3.1.2 ❑ Y ❑ N			❑ Y ❑ N	
3.1.3 ❑ Y ❑ N			❑ Y ❑ N	
3.1.4 ❑ Y ❑ N			❑ Y ❑ N	
3.1.5 ❑ Y ❑ N			❑ Y ❑ N	
3.1.6 ❑ Y ❑ N			❑ Y ❑ N	
3.1.7 ❑ Y ❑ N			❑ Y ❑ N	
3.1.8 ❑ Y ❑ N			❑ Y ❑ N	
3.1.9 ❑ Y ❑ N			❑ Y ❑ N	
3.1.2				
3.2.1 ❑ Y ❑ N			❑ Y ❑ N	
3.2.2 ❑ Y ❑ N			❑ Y ❑ N	
3.2.3 ❑ Y ❑ N			❑ Y ❑ N	
3.3				
3.3.1 ❑ Y ❑ N			❑ Y ❑ N	
3.3.2 ❑ Y ❑ N			❑ Y ❑ N	
3.3.3 ❑ Y ❑ N			❑ Y ❑ N	
3.3.4 ❑ Y ❑ N			❑ Y ❑ N	
3.3.5 ❑ Y ❑ N			❑ Y ❑ N	
3.4 ❑ Y ❑ N			❑ Y ❑ N	
3.5 ❑ Y ❑ N			❑ Y ❑ N	
3.6 ❑ Y ❑ N			❑ Y ❑ N	
3.7 ❑ Y ❑ N			❑ Y ❑ N	

4. POLICIES AND PROCEDURES

There are written policies and procedures for all activities of the radiology service which reflect current knowledge and principles, the relevant regulations, statutory requirements and objectives of the service.

Standards		comment		comment
4.1 ❑ Y ❑ N			❑ Y ❑ N	
4.2 ❑ Y ❑ N			❑ Y ❑ N	
4.3 ❑ Y ❑ N			❑ Y ❑ N	
4.4 ❑ Y ❑ N			❑ Y ❑ N	
4.5 ❑ Y ❑ N			❑ Y ❑ N	
4.6 ❑ Y ❑ N			❑ Y ❑ N	
HOSPITAL			**SURVEYOR**	

cont'd. Figure 4.11

	HOSPITAL		SURVEYOR

HOSPITAL column:

4.7   ❏ Y   ❏ N

4.8   ❏ Y   ❏ N

4.9   ❏ Y   ❏ N

4.10
  4.10.1   ❏ Y   ❏ N
  4.10.2   ❏ Y   ❏ N
  4.10.3   ❏ Y   ❏ N
  4.10.4   ❏ Y   ❏ N
  4.10.5   ❏ Y   ❏ N
  4.10.6   ❏ Y   ❏ N
  4.10.7   ❏ Y   ❏ N
  4.10.8   ❏ Y   ❏ N

4.11   ❏ Y   ❏ N

4.12   ❏ Y   ❏ N
  4.12.1   ❏ Y   ❏ N
  4.12.2   ❏ Y   ❏ N
  4.12.3   ❏ Y   ❏ N
  4.12.4   ❏ Y   ❏ N

4.13
  4.13.1   ❏ Y   ❏ N
  4.13.2   ❏ Y   ❏ N
  4.13.3   ❏ Y   ❏ N
  4.13.4   ❏ Y   ❏ N

4.14   ❏ Y   ❏ N

4.15   ❏ Y   ❏ N
  4.15.1   ❏ Y   ❏ N
  4.15.2   ❏ Y   ❏ N

4.16   ❏ Y   ❏ N

SURVEYOR column:

❏ Y   ❏ N

❏ Y   ❏ N

❏ Y   ❏ N

❏ Y   ❏ N
❏ Y   ❏ N
❏ Y   ❏ N
❏ Y   ❏ N
❏ Y   ❏ N
❏ Y   ❏ N
❏ Y   ❏ N
❏ Y   ❏ N

❏ Y   ❏ N

❏ Y   ❏ N
❏ Y   ❏ N
❏ Y   ❏ N
❏ Y   ❏ N
❏ Y   ❏ N

❏ Y   ❏ N
❏ Y   ❏ N
❏ Y   ❏ N
❏ Y   ❏ N

❏ Y   ❏ N

❏ Y   ❏ N
❏ Y   ❏ N
❏ Y   ❏ N

❏ Y   ❏ N

5. FACILITIES AND EQUIPMENT

The radiology service is provided with facilities, equipment and supplies for the safe, effective and efficient performance of all services provided.

Standards   comment   comment

5.1   ❏ Y   ❏ N   ❏ Y   ❏ N

5.2   ❏ Y   ❏ N   ❏ Y   ❏ N

5.3   ❏ Y   ❏ N   ❏ Y   ❏ N

5.4   ❏ Y   ❏ N   ❏ Y   ❏ N

5.5   ❏ Y   ❏ N   ❏ Y   ❏ N

5.6   ❏ Y   ❏ N   ❏ Y   ❏ N

HOSPITAL   **SURVEYOR**

cont'd. Figure 4.11

	HOSPITAL			SURVEYOR	
5.7	❏ Y ❏ N			❏ Y ❏ N	
5.8	❏ Y ❏ N			❏ Y ❏ N	
5.9	❏ Y ❏ N			❏ Y ❏ N	
5.10	❏ Y ❏ N			❏ Y ❏ N	

5.11

	HOSPITAL		SURVEYOR	
5.11.1	❏ Y	❏ N	❏ Y	❏ N
5.11.2	❏ Y	❏ N	❏ Y	❏ N
5.11.3	❏ Y	❏ N	❏ Y	❏ N
5.11.4	❏ Y	❏ N	❏ Y	❏ N
5.11.5	❏ Y	❏ N	❏ Y	❏ N
5.11.6	❏ Y	❏ N	❏ Y	❏ N
5.11.7	❏ Y	❏ N	❏ Y	❏ N
5.11.8	❏ Y	❏ N	❏ Y	❏ N
5.11.9	❏ Y	❏ N	❏ Y	❏ N
5.11.10	❏ Y	❏ N	❏ Y	❏ N

	HOSPITAL		SURVEYOR	
5.12	❏ Y	❏ N	❏ Y	❏ N
5.13	❏ Y	❏ N	❏ Y	❏ N
5.14	❏ Y	❏ N	❏ Y	❏ N
5.15	❏ Y	❏ N	❏ Y	❏ N
5.16	❏ Y	❏ N	❏ Y	❏ N
5.17	❏ Y	❏ N	❏ Y	❏ N
5.18	❏ Y	❏ N	❏ Y	❏ N
5.19	❏ Y	❏ N	❏ Y	❏ N
5.20	❏ Y	❏ N	❏ Y	❏ N
5.21	❏ Y	❏ N	❏ Y	❏ N
5.22	❏ Y	❏ N	❏ Y	❏ N
5.23	❏ Y	❏ N	❏ Y	❏ N

6. EVALUATION AND QUALITY ASSURANCE

The radiology service ensures the provision of high quality care by its involvement in evaluation activities of the hospital in line with the quality assurance plan for the hospital and the service.

Standards		comment			comment
6.1	❏ Y ❏ N			❏ Y ❏ N	
6.2	❏ Y ❏ N			❏ Y ❏ N	
	HOSPITAL			**SURVEYOR**	

cont'd. Figure 4.11

6.3

6.3.1	❏ Y	❏ N	❏ Y ❏ N
6.3.2	❏ Y	❏ N	❏ Y ❏ N
6.3.3	❏ Y	❏ N	❏ Y ❏ N
6.3.4	❏ Y	❏ N	❏ Y ❏ N
6.3.5	❏ Y	❏ N	❏ Y ❏ N

6.4

6.4.1	❏ Y	❏ N	❏ Y ❏ N
6.4.2	❏ Y	❏ N	❏ Y ❏ N
6.4.3	❏ Y	❏ N	❏ Y ❏ N
6.4.4	❏ Y	❏ N	❏ Y ❏ N
6.4.5	❏ Y	❏ N	❏ Y ❏ N

6.5   ❏ Y   ❏ N   ❏ Y   ❏ N

6.6   ❏ Y   ❏ N   ❏ Y   ❏ N

6.7   ❏ Y   ❏ N   ❏ Y   ❏ N

6.8   ❏ Y   ❏ N   ❏ Y   ❏ N

6.9   ❏ Y   ❏ N   ❏ Y   ❏ N

6.10 ❏ Y   ❏ N   ❏ Y   ❏ N

6.11 ❏ Y   ❏ N   ❏ Y   ❏ N

6.12 ❏ Y   ❏ N   ❏ Y   ❏ N

6.13 ❏ Y   ❏ N   ❏ Y   ❏ N

6.14 ❏ Y   ❏ N   ❏ Y   ❏ N

6.15

6.15.1	❏ Y	❏ N	❏ Y ❏ N
6.15.2	❏ Y	❏ N	❏ Y ❏ N
6.15.3	❏ Y	❏ N	❏ Y ❏ N
6.15.4	❏ Y	❏ N	❏ Y ❏ N
6.15.5	❏ Y	❏ N	❏ Y ❏ N
6.15.6	❏ Y	❏ N	❏ Y ❏ N

SURVEYOR'S COMMENTS

Standard Number

Recommendation

cont'd. Figure 4.11

Day surgery

With increasing emphasis being placed on shortening length of stay of patients in hospital, a key component of health care delivery to measure is the provision of day surgery. In the *NHSME VFM Unit Study* (1991), the range and extent of day surgery in NHS hospitals was examined:

CONTENTS

In particular a checklist of key functions of an integrated day surgery unit was produced as in Figure 4.12.

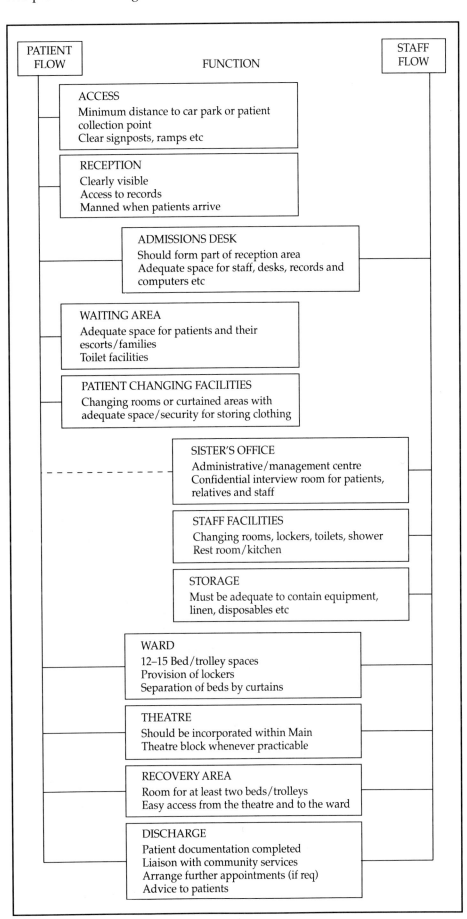

Figure 4.12. Checklist of key functions for integrated day surgery units

An assessment checklist for type/range of day surgery currently offered with the implied recommendation for improved quality and increased day surgery was also given as in Figure 4.13.

MANAGEMENT

EXECUTIVE

VFM Unit

On completion, please return via your Unit General Manager to: VFM Unit, Room 1322a, Euston Tower, 286 Euston Road, LONDON NW1 3DN.

QUESTIONNAIRE ON THE PROVISION OF DAY SURGERY FACILITIES

GUIDANCE ON COMPLETING THE QUESTIONNAIRE

Please read all instructions carefully before completing each stage of the questionnaire.

Please note:

❑ **Sections 1, 2 and 3** should be completed by all hospitals with an **operating department**.

❑ **Section 4** should be completed only by those hospitals that do not have **an integrated day unit.**

❑ **Section 5** should be completed only by those hospitals that do have **an integrated day unit**.

DEFINITION OF TERMS

❑ **Day Surgery:** An operation or procedure performed on a patient who is admitted on a non-residential basis. It will include minor and intermediate procedures carried out under local and general anaesthesia or sedation, for which a period of recovery is generally necessary, as well as procedures involving special equipment, such as endoscopies, where they are performed in operating theatres.
This definition excludes, however, minor procedures which can be carried out on a day basis in A & E Departments and in Outpatients.

❑ **Integrated Unit:** This will usually comprise a distinct operational entity where ward and theatre(s) are run as a combined unit. It will generally have self-contained theatre(s), ward(s), admission and recovery room and may or may not include an endoscopy room. The unit will generally (although not always) have its own staff working exclusively within the unit as distinct from main theatre or general ward staff.

❑ **Whole-time Equivalent:** This should be calculated by dividing the total number of hours worked by the number of hours in the standard working week for that grade of staff.

❑ **Funded Establishment:** This should include all posts in that grade, including any vacancies, for which funds have been committed.

❑ **Staff in Post:** Include all staff, with the exception of those from an agency, on the payroll for the unit, irrespective of whether they were on annual, maternity or sickness leave, or training courses.

Figure 4.13. Assessment checklist
cont'd

cont'd. Figure 4.13

Section 1 — PLEASE GIVE DETAILS OF YOUR HOSPITAL

Hospital ....

Contact Name (for queries) ....

Tel No. & Ext ....

District ....

Region ....

Section 2

2.1 Please identify all specialties within the hospital carrying out day surgery as defined on the front page.

General Surgery   ❑

Gynaecology   ❑

Urology   ❑

Orthopaedics   ❑

Dental/Oral   ❑

ENT   ❑

Ophthalmology   ❑

Plastics   ❑

Pain Relief   ❑

Others — Please specify below   ❑

....

2.2 Please state the (approximate) percentage of Paediatric procedures carried out on a day case basis.

[   ] %

cont'd. Figure 4.13

Section 3

3.1 Please indicate below (by ticking the appropriate box) which of the following best describes the general arrangements for carrying out day surgery in your hospital.

Where arrangements vary (eg between specialties), please tick one box only which best describes the arrangements for the majority of procedures, and then go on to complete Section 3.2:

a) Self-contained Day Surgical Unit — including dedicated theatre(s), ward(s), admission and recovery room, and including endoscopy room. ☐

b) As at (a) above, but excluding endoscopy room. ☐

c) Day surgery carried out in the main operating suite in theatre(s) dedicated exclusively to day procedures. ☐

d) Day surgery carried out in the main operating theatre on lists which are dedicated exclusively to day cases, but in theatres which are not. ☐

e) Day surgery carried out in main operating theatre incorporated as part of the routine list. ☐

f) Other — please give brief details

....

....

....

3.2 If specialties or surgical firms vary from normal arrangements for day surgery please identify the specialty and give brief description of the arrangements, using categories (a) to (e) above where appropriate:

Specialty   Arrangements

....

                                             ....

....

                                             ....

....

                                             ....

NOTE. If you have ticked box (a) or (b) at 3.1 above please proceed to section 5.

Organisational/management quality

Moving from actual delivery of care to management of service delivery, key elements to measure include:

- Organisational culture;
- Management team effectiveness;
- Organisational communication;
- Integration of; and
- Development of QM techniques.

An approach is outlined below for auditing each of these areas:

1. **Organisational culture**
   This is not a comprehensive checklist, more a preliminary discussion tool aimed at raising awareness of the initial culture experience on entering hospital.

A PRACTICAL GUIDE TO DISCOVERING ORGANISATIONAL CULTURE

GOING INTO HOSPITAL/CENTRE

1. As you approach it, what does it look like — an office block, a factory, a school? or what?

2. What is the outside environment like — industrial, crowded, green?

3. Has there been an attempt to improve the appearance, if so how?

4. What kind of notices are there outside?

5. What signs tell you the way to the entrance?

6. What does the main entrance look like?

7. What do you experience immediately on entering the hospital/centre?

8. What is the nature of your reception?

9. What are the surroundings like where you will spend more of your time?

THE VISUAL MESSAGES OF THE INSIDE OF THE HOSPITAL/CENTRE

There are many ways in which the interior can be treated. In a row of identical semi detached homes or on a vast anonymous housing estate, every one will be very different from the others as soon as we go inside. Institutions have enormous choices as to what they do. So have a look around your hospital/centre as an interior designer might.

1. How are the walls and ceilings decorated? What messages does that give?

2. What textiles and fabrics are used (curtains, carpets etc)?

3. What kind of furniture is provided? What state is it in?

4. What pictures, or other works of art are displayed?

---

2. **Management team (MT) effectiveness**
   Mathew (1990) states that it is possible to assess MT effectiveness at any level.

3. **Organisational communication**
   The questionnaire refers to the nature of interpersonal communication in a provider unit and is simple to use. See Figure 4.14.

Organisational Communication Climate Survey

Directions: This brief questionnaire refers to the nature of interpersonal communication in your work unit or organisation. Answer each question in terms of the extent to which the people with whom you interact in your work unit or organisation — employees, peers, and higher-level managers — typically display the behaviours described. You are not trying to evaluate any particular person; the aim is to get a 'picture' of the overall 'climate' of interaction in the work unit or organisation.

Answer Key:		
VG	=	To a Very Great Extent
C	=	To a Considerable Extent
M	=	To a Moderate Extent
S	=	To a Slight Extent
LN	=	To Little or No Extent

Circle the letter(s) that best represent the extent to which you think the behaviour described is common in your work unit or organisation.

To what extent do people in this work unit/organisation. ...

1. show that they listen to one another; try to understand others' viewpoints? VG C M S LN

2. 'pick up on' and verbally describe the feelings another member has and tries to express? VG C M S LN

3. ask others to repeat or clarify what they have said in order to better understand? VG C M S LN

4. restate for clarification what another person has said before going on to make their own points? VG C M S LN

5. share their own feelings in clear non-threatening ways? VG C M S LN

6. provide support and encouragement in a discussion in order to really explore an issue in depth? VG C M S LN

7. give others a chance to talk; 'opening the door' for others to contribute to a discussion? VG C M S LN

8. help explore an issue in depth without trying to push their own ideas? VG C M S LN

9. say clearly, 'up front', what their expectations of one another really are? VG C M S LN

10. face disagreements directly; try to understand the reasons underlying differences? VG C M S LN

11. give one another feedback that is concrete and specific without being evaluative? VG C M S LN

12. when talking, care about another as a person and colleague? VG C M S LN

Figure 4.14. Climate of communication

Quality of nursing care

One of the most utilised tools in the NHS to measure quality of nursing care, is *Monitor*. It is an adaptation for the UK of the Rush Medicus Nursing Process Methodology, which was based on in depth examination of a variety of tools and studies measuring quality of nursing care.

Monitor, developed by Goldstone et al, consists of four separate patient based questionnaires, each related to a different category of patient dependency, and a further wardbased questionnaire. It is complete and self contained. The backup documentation is extensive. An example of the monitor form for *planning nursing care* is shown in Figure 4.15.

Figure 4.15. Sample from Monitor

MONITOR

DEPENDENCY CATEGORY II PATIENTS
INSTRUCTIONS: Please tick one answer per question.

Assessor Name _____   Ward Name _____   Study Start Date _____

or Assessor Code _____   or Ward Code _____   Stop Date _____

Source of information _____   Patients Code or Initials

SECTION A : PLANNING NURSING CARE

1. Assessing Patient on Admission

Records   a   DOES THE NURSE INTERVIEW/OBSERVE THE PATIENT FOR ASSESSMENT OF PROBLEMS *WITHIN* 6 HOURS AFTER ADMISSION? Look at chart/records for evidence of assessment. May ask patient 'When you were admitted, did a nurse come to talk with you about your illness or any special problem?' 'How long after you were admitted did the nurse talk to you?'

No
Yes
Not available/ Not applicable
1
SCORE

Pursue for time only if evidence that assessment was made. Answer 'yes' only if there is evidence of a comprehensive assessment *and* it was done with 12 hours of admission.

'Assessment' means that the nurse interviewed and observed the patient to identify his habits and problems.

'Comprehensive' refers to mention of psychological, sociological and physical needs of patient.

Records/   b   IF THE PATIENT HAS PHYSICAL DISABILITIES, (eg IMPAIRED HEARING, VISION, SPEECH, etc) ARE THEY RECORDED WITHIN 24 HOURS OF ADMISSION?
Check or ask patient

No
Yes
Not applicable
2
SCORE

If nothing recorded, check patient. If patient *has* physical disabilities, code as 'No'. If patient *does not* have physical disabilities code as 'Not applicable'.

Integration of quality management

A key theme already alluded to in Chapter 3, is the need to fully integrate quality planning and management with the other strands of management within the unit. With this in mind, certain key variables need assessment pre-TQM implementation:

- Is there a link between business planning and TQM?
- Do managers have QI objectives in their IPR objectives?
- Is performance measured in the unit?
- Does performance gap analysis take place?
- Are the functions of the quality department clearly understood by other departments?
- Are quality indicators firmly in place in contracts?
- Is there a comprehensive standard setting strategy?

As regards the last question, a further checklist is provided in Figure 4.16.

**STANDARD SETTING AND MONITORING
CHECKLIST**

	YES	WORKING TOWARDS	NO

1   Has the department written standards
which are;
   (a) Descriptive (ie prose not usually
       measurable)
   (b) Measurable (ie specific, often
       numerical, can be measured)

2   Are the measurable standards:
   (a) Comprehensive (ie covering all
       aspects of service)
   (b) Covering between 1-10 major areas/
       topics

3   Does the department have clear idea/
plan of areas/topics which should
eventually be covered by standard
setting?

4.   Do all staff in the Department:
   (a) Know a little about this process
   (b) Know and agree all these standards

5   Is there clear monitoring process for
accessing current performance against
these standards?

6.   (a) Does a quarterly report get
       prepared?
   (b) Is this discussed with staff?
   (c) Does the Senior Manager receive a
       copy?
   (d) Does 'Non-conformance' which gets
       identified get acted on?

*Figure 4.16. Standard setting and
monitoring checklist*

Measuring costs of quality

Talking to senior managers in many industries who have implemented TQM, one frequently hears that the main, if not only, way in which quality is measured, is via the organisation's *quality costs* — the cost of achieving and maintaining quality is a true measure of the quality effort (Oakland, 1989). Effective health care management, *doing the job well*, is based on a balance between quality and cost factors. This objective is accomplished by analysis of the cost of quality.

Analysing quality costs are an important measurement tool for managers and clinicians and provide a way of:

•   Measuring the overall effectiveness of health care delivery;
•   Monitoring change as a result of TQ; and
•   Determining particular problems and, partly via their cost implications, decide on priorities for intervention.

Introducing quality costing management systems can meet, initially, with considerable resistance due to fear amongst managers that it is a means of *reapportioning blame* for *poor* management (Davies, 1992). It is also sometimes seen as a negative approach, ie measuring cost of *failure*. However, it allows a unit to identify and understand its main *cost drivers*. Readers are referred to Koch (1991) and Koch and Higgs (1991) for descriptions of quality costs.

Developing a quality culture within a provider unit and implementing a quality management tool and techniques will result in greater consistency of care and service, improved standards, increased 'customer' satisfaction and raised staff morale. But what happens to 'cost'?

Investment in quality training, team building, leadership and other quality improvement projects should result in reduction of operating and other revenue costs and ultimately in improved 'market share'. The model of 'quality costing' which has been so successful in the manufacturing and service industries, can help identify and quantify these costs. The usefulness and limits of quality costing to prioritise quality management efforts and focus quality improvement teams to achieve real financial benefits, is also discussed.

Existing studies on quality costs in the NHS

Several provider units have detailed information on their quality costs. Preliminary projects have been undertaken in Acute services (Cheltenham, 1990) and priority services (Aylesbury, 1992) as an integral part of both their TQM projects.

Why Measure Quality Costs?

The measurement of health care quality costs is inextricably linked to the health care business and the developing business plan. Quality costs measurement focuses attention on areas of high expenditure and helps to identify potential cost-reducing opportunities and is the first step towards control.

Context

It is impossible to describe a 'typical' provider unit. However, to place the ensuing discussion on quality costing in some form of context, two 'caricature' units — a District General Hospital and a Community Unit — are described in Figure 4.17. They are for outline purposes only.

	District General Hospital	Community Unit
Number of staff (WTE)	1,000	750
Revenue budget	£19,000k	£10,000k
Main activities	*Revenue costs %*	*Revenue costs %*
Accepting patients	2-3	1-2
Caring for patients	30-35	35-40
Diagnostic/assessment	15-25	10-15
Treatment	30-35	35-40
Discharge actions	3-5	2-4
Nonclinical support services	7-10	4-6
Management	3-5	3-5

Figure 4.17

Quality-related Costs

Three main categories of quality costs in the delivery of health care can be defined:

• **Prevention Costs**

Time and costs incurred trying to keep 'failure' costs and 'appraisal' costs to a minimum (see below). Time and revenue spent on training, planning, staff awareness raising, quality improvement projects, quality management are included here (salary, costs of quality officers, plus part of staff supervisory positions).

• Appraisal Costs

Time and costs incurred in determining conformance to an agreed or implicit quality of care/service standard setting and monitoring, clinical and management audit, implicit everyday inspection (eg by ward sisters or their staff), testing equipment.

• Nonconformance Costs

These fall into three important sub-categories:

— *Internal 'failure' costs* — associated with failure to provide the appropriate service to the patient or internal customer before they have received it (eg missing medical records lead to cancelled outpatient appointments).

— *External 'failure' costs* — associated with failure of care/service after the patient has received it, eg inappropriate medication information, poor directions to X-ray department, inaccurate appointments information. (Both internal and external failures involve work not being done properly 'first time' requiring additional resources to put right.)

— *Cost of 'exceeding requirements'* — paradoxically, some elements of care and service can be unnecessary and not related to the desired outcome, eg excessive diagnostic testing, overabundance of information, inappropriate/unnecessary follow up by junior medical staff.

The Methodology of Quality Costing

Costs need to be collected by activity and put into the categories of quality-related costs given above — namely prevention costs, appraisal costs and nonconformance costs.

Utilising the main activities identified above ('The Context'), further inspection and investigation is necessary to identify more accurately:

- The key 'customers' and 'suppliers' of care/service in each activity and at each level.
- The awareness by staff of prevention, appraisal and failure activities, and time spent on each.
- The major problems, 'effective issues' or nonconformance and the effect they are having on the running of the unit.
- The costs in terms of time and/or actual revenue being expended in these activities.

The main activities of a hospital or community unit can be analysed and defined using a 'Patient Trail' model backed up by the Structured Analysis and Design Technique (SADT). This methodology, termed IDEF by its originators, was first used to model activity in the USAF. This is, briefly, based on the notion that any activity can be modelled as illustrated in Figure 4.18.

In summary, the inputs and outputs show what is done by the health care activity, the control shows why it is done and the mechanism shows how it is done by whom. This allows rules or structure for gradually introducing further detail during quality costing analysis. Different levels of health care delivery and service can be identified relating to, for example, the whole hospital, managing the hospital and the clinical directorate (Figures 4.19, 4.20, and 4.22). (Note these are not complete examples.)

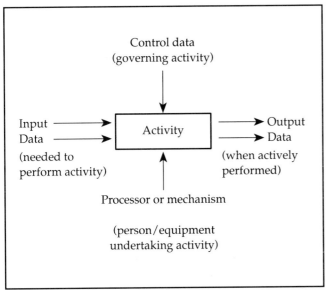

Figure 4.18. IDEF(O) Structure

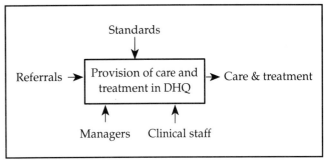

Figure 4.19. The Whole Hospital

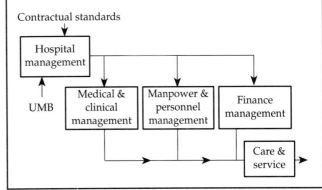

Figure 4.20. Managing the Hospital

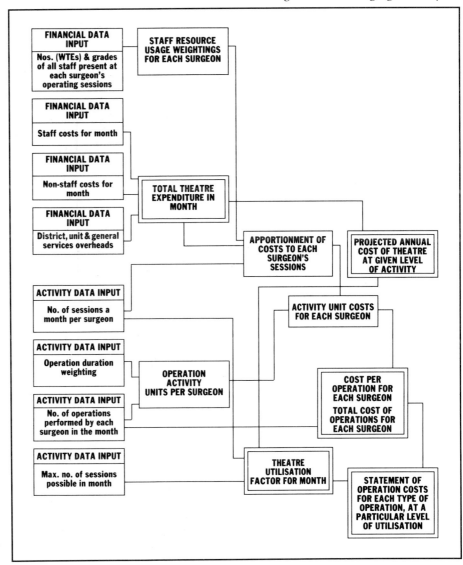

Figure 4.21. Financial and activity
data: theatre model

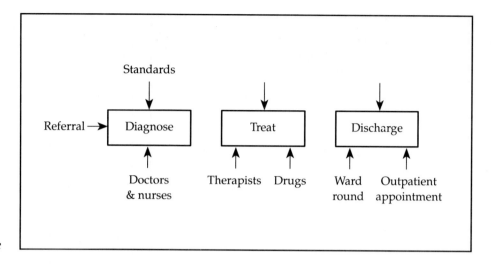

Figure 4.22. Clinical Directorate

Quality costing methodology

Aims

1. To raise staff awareness of costs and services and particular costs of poor quality;
2. To assess the level of quality costs within the unit (internal/external failures, inspection, prevention); and
3. To establish a quality improvement team (QIT) approach to releasing resources (cash or non-cash — releasing).

Methodology

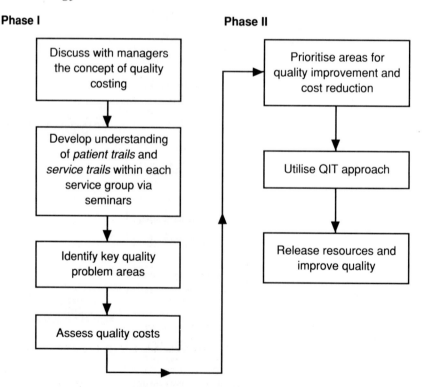

Further levels can be identified and described and quality costs attached using the IDEF structure more exhaustively.

The methods by which this information can be obtained are interview, survey, questionnaire and direct observation. Each gives information of a different reliability, validity and usefulness. See Figures 4.23 and 4.24.

PROBLEM AREA	TIME INCURRED	OPPORTUNITY COST	REMEDIAL	TIME NEEDED	COST OF ACTION	RELATIVE PAY OFF
PHYSIO OPD (CH)						
RECORDS DEVOLUTION (CH)						
DIETETIC ACCOMMODATION						
COSHH FUNDING (CH)						
MANAGING/ SUPPORTING SENIOR SECRETARIES (LK)						
RECRUITMENT AND SELECTION						

Figure 4.23. Problem area table.

Problem Area	Outcomes or Effects	Time/Wastage/staff overtime incurred (per annum)	Opportunity Costs NCR CR	Remedial Action	Time Needed	Cost of Action	Relative Pay Off
1. Inadequate reception 'customer care'	Lack of call screening Nurses answering calls Poor 1st impressions by clients Inspection time by secretary Complaints	3hrs per sister shift					
2. Admin & clerical duties carried out by nurses	Telephone Activity figure preparation	4hrs per shift					
3. Use of external laundry services	Unreliable service Expensive Need for additional sheets		Service £6000 p.a. Sheets £6,100				
4. Wasted catering	Poor food Not portioned Unattractive Limited choice Staff making additional meals	Food Nursing time	Food £3600 p.a. Staff £12000 p.a.				
5. Inappropriate use of McMillan nurses	Assessing patients Meetings in unit Late referrals Poor planning	Wasted nurse time 75% of 2 Nurses	£20,000 NCR				Improved patient care; Improved throughput; More patients seen in community
6. Inappropriate day place scheduling	Inappropriate referrals Blocking of places Lack of review care			12 wk contract			More people seen

Figure 4.24. Palliative care

Staff have difficulty in approving time for appraisal activities

As a result of surveying staff at one or more levels in the unit, the analysis of information received will show that:

- Non-conformances are many, and can, in some instances, lead to considerable costs (typical examples are shown in Figure 4.25).
- Time spent in prevention and appraisal activities (especially the latter) is not always explicit and clear and varies considerably from unit to unit.
- Insufficient explicit investment of time occurs in prevention and to a certain extent, appraisal activities.

- Staff have difficulty in approving time for appraisal and prevention activities, especially if it appears to detract from direct care or service activity.
- Appraisal activity time varies considerably depending how explicit an activity is.

From the identified non-conformances, some decision is required as to how to proceed to analyse costs further. The major nonconformance items need further analysis (see Figures 4.26 to 4.28) as regards:

- More precise measurement of frequency of nonconformance
- Staff group involved
- Main effect of nonconformance/quality problem
- Time incurred/number of staff/grade
- Likely cost implications.

Car parking
Outpatient clinic — DNAs

Meal requirements (inpatient)
Maintenance response times

Theatre/portering liaison
Availability of theatre drugs/instruments
TTO drug scripts
Use of antibiotics
Poor internal communications
Inappropriate financial information
Catering for staff at nights
Incorrect use of diagnostic services
Delays transporting specimens
Delay in X-ray portering
Lost health records
Inefficient appointments systems
Hospital-acquired infections
Pressure sores in hospital

Inefficient ward stocks
Discharge delays
High turnover of managers
Nurse skill mix
Excessive pathology on-call
Complaints
Litigation
Iatrogenic disease

Figure 4.25. Typical Nonconformance Activities

Figure 4.26. Problem analysis

Problem	Staff involved	Main effect	Time incurred	Cost
Pressure sores acquired in hospital	Nurses	Length of stay increased	Equivalent of 150-200 pressure sores per annum resulting in four days extra in-patient care per care	£3.5k on average for extra treatment

QUALITY 'FAILURE COSTS'

ELDERLY MENTAL HEALTH

PROBLEM AREA	OUTCOME/EFFECT	OPPORTUNITY COST (per annum)		COMMENTS
		NCR	CR	
1. Excessive length of stay (due to social placement problem)	Wasted resources. a) Waiting or Part III/private accommodation. 1 patient per Ward constantly 0.5 per patient per relief ward			
2. Inappropriate hospital admission (due to inadequate support in the community)	Wasted resources. 0.5 admission bed			
3. DNA at day hospital (25 places) (10-28%)	Wasted sessions. Disruption of programmes. Increase in admissions. CPN time. Ambulance time. Catering costs.			
4. Duplication of assessment by members of CMH Team				
5. Clerical Duties by Nurses	1 hour per day per unit.			
6. Inflexible Nursing patterns	Reduced continuity of care and Key Worker. Reduced staff satisfaction.			

Figure 4.27. Quality 'failure costs' – elderly mental health

QUALITY 'FAILURE COSTS'

GENERAL COMMUNITY SERVICES

PROBLEM AREA	OUTCOME/EFFECT	OPPORTUNITY COST (per annum)		COMMENTS
		NCR	CR	
1. Use of Community Hospital a) 7 additional funded beds (currently not in use)	Unit likely to be paying excessive capital charges, as compared to helping District to save 'full charge' on these beds rather than our marginal charge			
b) Low use of Day Hospital	Currently 2 day use, marketable to 3 days – 2 days (40%) wasted resource			
2. D.N.A. & cancellation	Disrupted clinical time			
3. Poor car parking arrangements	Wasted staff time Patient dissatisfaction			
4. Information gathering	Wasted time Lowered staff motivation			
5. Less than optimal profiling of staff/skill mix	Duplication of 'wasted' time			
6. Poor post-discharge Use of District Nurses				
7. Multi-disciplinary Team Working & Time Management (Clinical & Non-clinical)	'Wasted' time and less focussed action			

Figure 4.28. Quality 'failure costs' – general community services

Preliminary studies in several provider units in the UK are indicating that approximate quality costs, ie costs of poor or failed quality run at between 10-20 per cent of the operating revenue budget. This is within the limits often found in other large companies. It should be added however that total non-conformance costs will probably be approximately twice the total of those major non-conformances easily identified. At this stage in the application of quality costing models to health units, it is wise to be cautious over possible savings in cash releasing terms. However, conservative targets are 1-5 per cent with greater savings in staff time, currently less than efficiency used, should be possible.

Quality Costing: The Action Plan

The following steps needed to be followed by any provider unit to ensure maximum benefits in quality and cost terms are achieved through application of the quality costing approach.

- Analyse patient flow of care and service.
- Identify key non-conformances.
- Analyse and detail each major nonconformance.
- Attach costs to each area (time lost/revenue used).
- Analyse real cost as percentage of revenue in that area.
- Develop quality improvement teams (QIT) to reduce non-conformance and costs.
- Develop quality costing information systems.
- Communicate information of seven steps above to appropriate staff.
- Seek staff ideas for improvements.
- Identify investment costs (if any) in achieving improvement.
- Appoint and train QIT facilitating in structured problem solving: cause/effect analysis, etc.
- Split costs into prevention, appraisal and failure and look for ways to concentrate on prevention in order to reduce appraisal and failure costs.
- Allocate responsibilities for measuring quality costs, setting improvement goals and monitoring progress.
- Recognise and reward success in reducing non-conformance and releasing staff time and/or resources.
- Use of the first quality costing report and subsequent reference.

Conclusions

Quality costing and consequent cost reduction should only be seen within the context of an overall management commitment to quality improvement and the processes of total quality management. As a result of adapting and utilising some of the ideas inherent in quality costing, realistic targets for savings must be set and met. The inclusion of quality costing training is essential to enable staff to understand the financial implications of training.

Quality costing is an essential part of improving health care service

The relative costs of gradually increasing prevention and appraisal activities of quality management, standard setting and monitoring, audit and customer care training must be taken into account and related to current or reducing 'failure' or non-conformance costs.

At this stage, early in the development and application of quality management tools, techniques and culture to the NHS, quality costing is an essential part of maintaining and improving an excellent health care service.

One danger in going into quality costing in too great detail is that managers become over concerned with accuracy rather that the quality/conformance issues themselves. It is likely that 20 per cent of the variables account for 80 per cent of the quality costs. Therefore focusing on the major items of non-conformance gives the best return for effort. The average quality costing figure of 10-20 per cent operating revenue, means that in the average unit there is about one tenth spare capacity devoted to producing waste and inefficient practice. Therefore a direct link exists between QI and throughput. Hence to convert this 10-20 per cent quality cost to productive use — via TQM — is an appropriate goal.

It has been mentioned that in many hospitals the majority of quality time is spent correcting problems that have occurred, ie acting within *failure mode*. Major cost savings, ie reduction of failure costs, can materialise if prevention is taken more seriously. Clinical and medical audit and other TQM techniques, aim to prevent problems occurring by;

- Just-in-time management;
- Reducing and eliminating redundant processes; and
- Eliminating defects.

Inspection and prevention costs

To recap there are three categories of Quality Costs:

- Prevention Costs
- Appraisal Costs
- Non-conformance Costs

The last of these three, which usually accounts for the greater proportion of costs, has been dealt with.

Prevention costs

Interviews with managers often indicate an awareness of a need for Prevention/ Quality Improvement activity. However, it is fairly typical within the NHS to find that time is not easily made available for this activity. With Middle Managers and Heads of Departments the notion of Prevention is understood but again little time made available for this.

It is clear that Prevention costs are not great. They include time spent on the following activities:

1. Total Quality Strategic planning
2. Implementation of key TQ initiatives
   a) Quality Improvement Teams: Training and Meetings
   b) Establishing Standard Setting and Monitoring Mechanisms
   c) Quality Costing
   d) Customer Feedback
   e) Training (for Quality Improvement)
3. Medical, Nursing and Clinical Audit
4. External Consultancy Advice

Inspection and appraisal costs

Understanding exists but, lack of time at Senior and Middle Manager/HOD level and an ambivalence to the concept (and hence practice) of 'inspecting and monitoring one's professional staff'. This ambivalence will hopefully decrease as the general idea and practice of standard setting and monitoring and contract management becomes more common.

The main activities, see Figures 4.29 to 4.35, under this heading are:

1. Specific clinical area audits
2. Supervision of hotel-type contracts
3. Control of infection activities
4. Checking and measuring staff performance
5. Health and safety checking

STANDARD	CONSULTANT			
	A	**B**	**C**	**D**
4) Acknowledgement was sent an average of	9 days	2 days	N/A	N/A
5) Waiting times for non-urgent appointments	3 weeks	14 weeks	4 weeks	11 weeks
6) Notice given for non-urgent appointments	3 weeks	14 weeks	4 weeks	11 weeks
8) Non-attenders at clinics	5%	7.5%	7.9%	5.4%
9) Appointment changed by hospital	10%	2.4%	10%	16%
13) Average delay in start of clinic	22 mins	10 mins	15 mins	9 mins
14) Percentage of unavailable test results	2.8%	0%	0%	0%
15) Percentage of unavailable casenotes at start throughout clinic	2% 1.5%	4% 2.5%	0% 0%	2% 0.5%
17) Average delay in clinic finishing	24 mins	35 mins	5 mins	35 mins
18) Percentage of patients seen by consultant	28%	47%	100%	50%
23) Clinic letters were typed within an average of	6 days	5 days	3 days	4 days
fictitious data				

Figure 4.29. Results of monitoring of all surgical clinics which were held during the pilot period

DELIVERY AND COLLECTION TIMES:

	TARGET	MON.	TUES.	WED.	THURS.	FRI.
<u>TO LOCATION X</u>						
No. of patients delivered (0%) before 09.15 hours.	0%	(1) 9.1%	(6) 31.6%	(1) 5.9%	– –	– –
No. of patients delivered (78%) between 09.15 – 10.15 hours.	78% or more	(9) 82%	(13) 60%	(12) 70%	(11) 73%	(13) 92.9%
No. of patients delivered (22%) after 10.15 hours.	22% or less	(1) 9%	– –	(4) 23.5%	(4) 26.6%	(1) 7.1%
<u>FROM LOCATION X</u>						
No. of patients collected (44%) before 15.15 hours.	44% or less	(3) 27.2%	(15) 80%	(5) 29.4%	(8) 50%	(6) 40%
No. of patients collected (48%) between 15.15 – 16.15 hours.	48% or more	(5) 45.5%	(4) 20%	(6) 35.3%	(8) 50%	(7) 33.6%
No. of patients collected (8%) after 16.15 hours.	8% or less	(3) 27.2%	– –	(6) 35.3%	– –	(2) 11.76%
No. of patients *not* delivered to location X.						
No. of patients *not* collected from location X.						

Figure 4.30. Transport survey

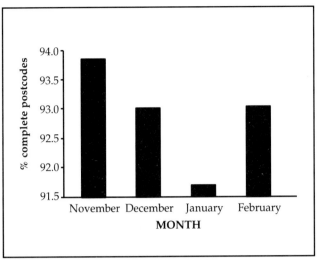

Figure 4.31. % complete postcodes

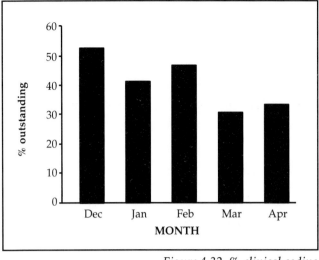

Figure 4.32. % clinical coding

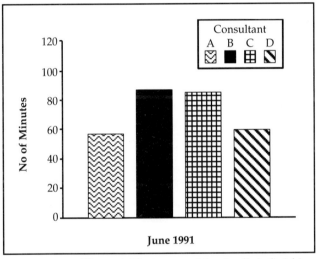

Figure 4.33. Average delay in clinic finishing

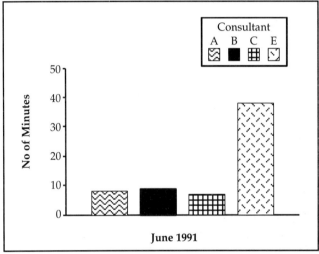

Figure 4.34. Average delay in start of clinic

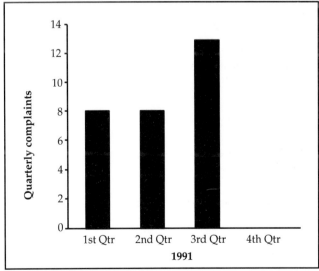

Figure 4.35. Quarterly complaints

Chapter 5   Quality planning and identifying quality indicators

Quality planning framework: part I: Maxwell model

In Northwick Park Hospital (NPH), Harrow, with the development of a clinical directorate structure (Koch & Chapman, 1991), which is the most common management structure now operating in the NHS, quality planning implementation and monitoring was seen as providing the most constructive framework within which clinical directorates, nursing and business managers could operate.

An initial seminar involving key senior managers and clinicians led to the development of a framework to look at quality throughout the unit. Simultaneously it addressed issues that the main purchasers, Harrow Health Authority, wished to see on the Local Quality Agenda:

1. Appropriateness of treatment and care;
2. Effective services;
3. Acceptable service;
4. Accessible service;
5. Recognition of staff;
6. Safe environment;
7. Management capability;
8. Medical and clinical audit;
9. Adherence to external policies, statutes and accepted practices; and
10. Minimum waiting times and lists.

It was incumbent on Harrow's main provider, NPH, to ensure its quality plan provided for activity and validating information to assure Harrow's ability to provide high quality care.

Framework for the Northwick Park Hospital quality plan

Northwick Park Hospital is dedicated to providing demonstrably high quality clinical services which meet requirements of patients and other *customers*, as specified within the contracts given to the hospital by its main purchaser(s).

To achieve this *mission*, a structured and organised approach towards quality was required. This approach also had to satisfy the expectations of the Harrow Health Authority *Purchaser Specifications*.

What does this mean in practice? As a result of internal seminars with senior staff it was decided that *high quality service* could be thought of as including the following complementary ideas with each defined practically. See Figures 5.1 and 5.2.

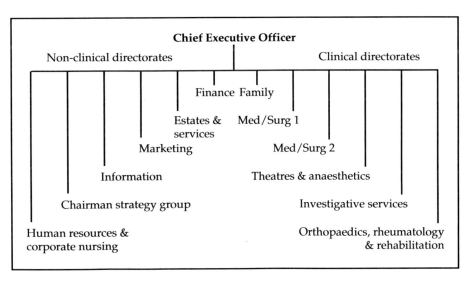

Figure 5.1. Directorate Structure

1.   Services must be:
   • Accessible;
   • Effective;
   • Acceptable; and
   • Appropriate: to patients, purchasers, and the Department of Health;

2.   Services must be organised with the appropriate quality input for:
   • Clear management commitment, leadership and capabilities;
   • Optimum team work and recognition of staff value;
   • Implementation of quality techniques: clinical audit; standard setting; information/monitoring; communications;
   • Monitoring and identification of performance against contract specification and reduction of *nonconformance*;

3.   Service quality must be considered at four levels:
   • Hospital-wide
   • Directorate-wide
   • Specialty/clinical area-wide; and
   • Individual member of staff.

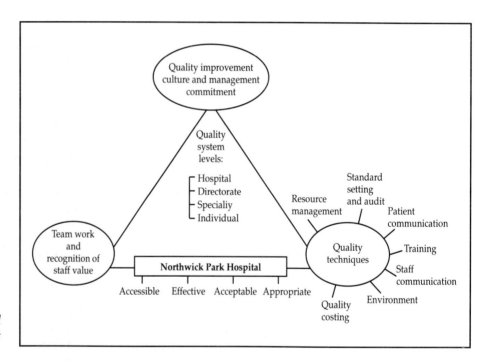

Figure 5.2. A model for Total Quality Management

The *quality plan* identifies a number of specific components of service delivery which the hospital and each directorate need to assure itself it is addressing and where appropriate providing to defined and acceptable standards. These components have been grouped under three headings:

1.   Delivery of patient care;
2.   Techniques/systems; and
3.   Teamwork and staff values:
   • Culture and commitment; and
   • Specialty based excellence

See Figures 5.3, 5.4 and 5.5.

Hospital-wide Quality Plan (Clinical Care)

Section 1: Delivery of Patient Care/Services

Appropriateness	Acceptability	Accessibility	Effectiveness	Statutory and non-statutory requirements	Quality systems and techniques	Teamwork and Staff recognition
OPD policies Admission policies Discharge policies Communication with GPs Communication with the public Special needs policies Departmental operational policies Department staffing levels Use of locum/agency/bank staff	Patient feedback systems Complaint systems Customer relations and customer care Confidentiality of patient information	OPD waiting time IP waiting time Access for disabled	Clinical protocols Identification of medical litigation issues Audit reports Documentation of patient episodes Individual care planning	Compliance with statutory requirements 1. Health and safety 2. Environmental health 3. Fire precautions and emergency procedures 4. Radiation protection 5. COSSH 6. DOH safety notices 7. Employment policy 8. Data Protection Act 9. Childrens Act 10. MHA Act Compliance with non-statutory requirements including: 1. Confidentiality of patient information 2. Infection control 3. Major accident planning 4. Childrens Act 5. Discharge policy 6. Accidents to staff 7. Complaints 8. Policies for • smoking • healthy eating • alcohol, etc 9. COSHH 10. Health and safety 11. Employment law	Quality management strategy and implementation plan Standard setting plan Communication plan Customer relations plan Patient feedback plan Quality specification for contracts plus monitoring plan Quality cost reduction plan Directorate quality planning plan Clinical audit systems: 1. Multidisciplinary clinic audit 2. Medical audit 3. Nursing audit 4. Clinical services audit Non-clinical audit systems 1. Hotel services 2. Management	Communication with staff Staff development Team development Induction programme Directorate quality planning

Figure 5.3. Hospital-wide quality plan (clinical care)

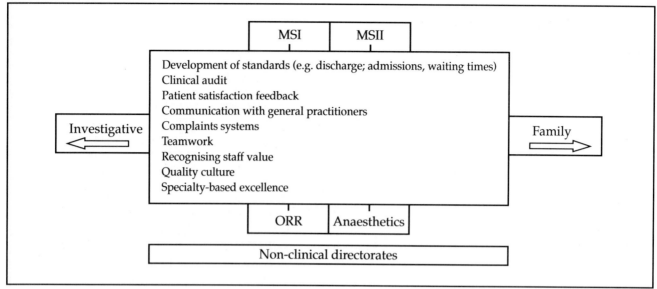

Figure 5.4. Non-clinical directorates

Topics from One Directorate Plan

Section I: Delivery of service			Section II: Quality systems and techniques	Section III: Team work and staff value
Appropriateness	Acceptability	Effectiveness		
Outpatient policies	Patient feedback system	Multidisciplinary clinical protocols	Standard setting	Team work
Admission policy			Staff communication	Quality plan
Day care	Complaints system	Shared care protocols		Speciality-based excellence
Discharge policy	Verbal and written information for patients			
Communications with GPs				
Extent of "open access" to GPs	Response to social groups			
	Physical environment			
	Waiting time for OP consultation			
	Waiting time for IP consultation			

Figure 5.5 . Topics from one directorate plan

Quality planning: part II: flow chart model

With the experience of the developing model using Maxwell dimensions and management/TQM variables, Quality Planning has developed to not only encompass these essential variables, but to place them in the context of a *patient trail flow charting* approach.

In the systematic planning, and investment in clinical and non-clinical clarification of care processes and management, it is useful to record/itemise the series of events and activities that take place accurately, clearly and concisely. Flow charts of the main trails of clinical and managerial activity are a useful way of looking at the quality of health care processes. If a trail cannot be explicitly drawn, then the process is not fully understood. For many, especially in some complex clinical fields, eg psychotherapy, counselling, terminal care, it is an uncomfortable but rewarding experience to try and draw the patient trail that epitomises the activity being undertaken. The act of flow charting helps individual teams to understand the processes better and leads to team cooperation to identify service improvement. The main trail for health care delivery is shown in Figure 5.6 as *(AO) unit function:*

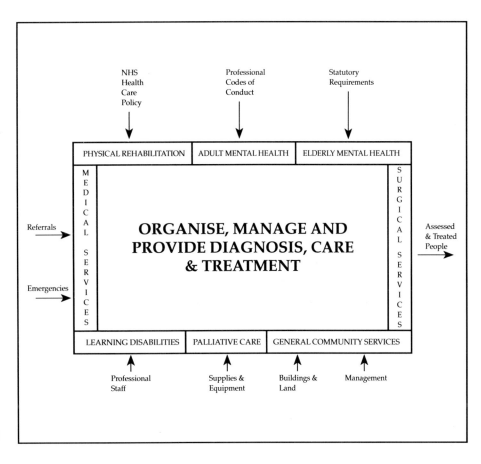

Figure 5.6. A0 Unit function

Patients *enter* the system (eg hospital, clinic) as a routine or emergency referral from a GP and *emerge* with their problem assessed and, hopefully treated.
The next stage of clarification *A1 clinical activity* is shown in Figure 5.7.

Figure 5.7. A1 Clinical activity

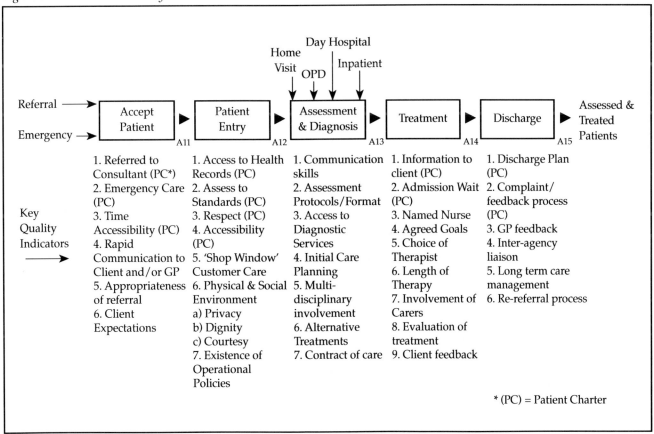

The trail epitomises and describes almost all clinical processes in outline and in the main *factory trail* in an NHS facility.

Faced with this trail the question is begged as to what issues, topics or indicators reflect the quality debate in a particular unit. This will be informed by several sources:

1. Unit staff experience of quality issues;
2. Purchasers' requirements;
3. DoH initiatives eg *Patient Charter*; and
4. Professional bodies' codes of conduct.

Within the staffs' own experience, *quality issues* may relate to:

1. Key processes eg admission, discharge;
2. Problematic processes eg multidisciplinary agreement or clinical decisions; and
3. Variable problems eg protocol for hip replacement and time taken.

Identification of these *quality indicators* is essential to developing a *quality management programme* to allow both comprehensiveness and focusing to occur.

Figure 5.7 indicates how many of the indicators shown in Fig 5.6 referring to NPH can be reformatted into the Clinical Activity Patient Trail (Unit wide) and for particular service areas, eg adult mental health (Fig 5.8) learning disabilities (Figure 5.9) and elderly mental health (Fig 5.10). These are working/ operational sheets and not meant to be exhaustive and comprehensive. The notions (Aylesbury Vale Community Health Care NHS trust, 1992) used are as follows:

PC	Patient charter;
P	Main purchaser requirements; and
U	Unit requirement: generated by service itself.

Figure 5.8. A.M.H. clinical activity

Each of these *clinical activity trails* can be further explored in greater detail as shown in Diagrams 5.12 to 5.16.

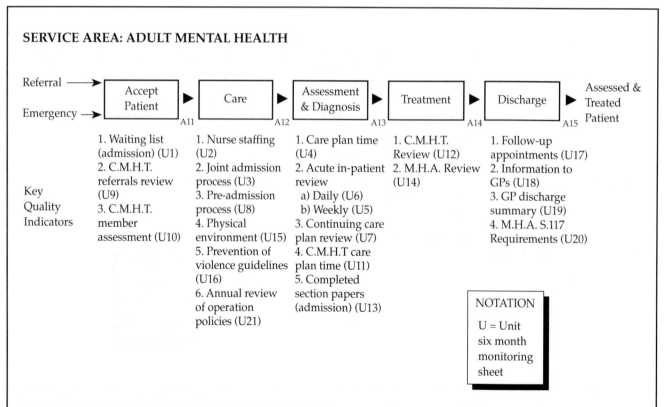

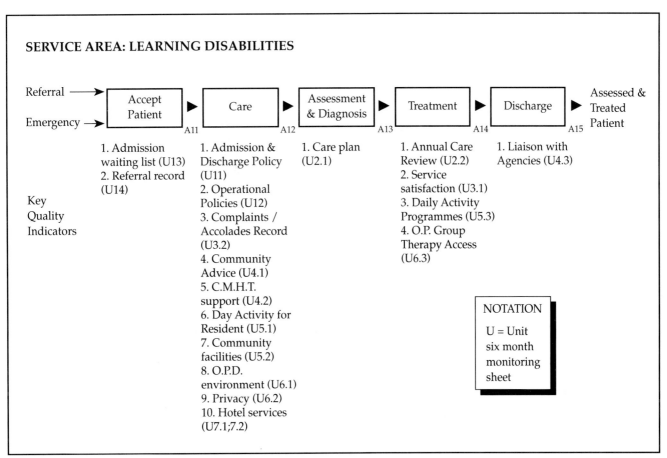

Figure 5.9. A1 L.D. — clinical activity

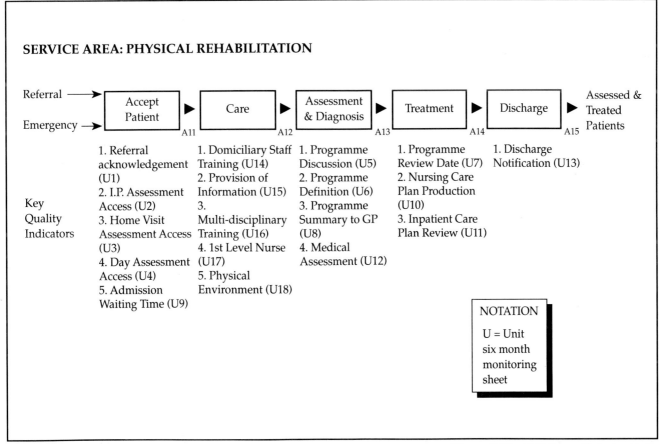

Figure 5.10. A1 P.R. — clinical activity

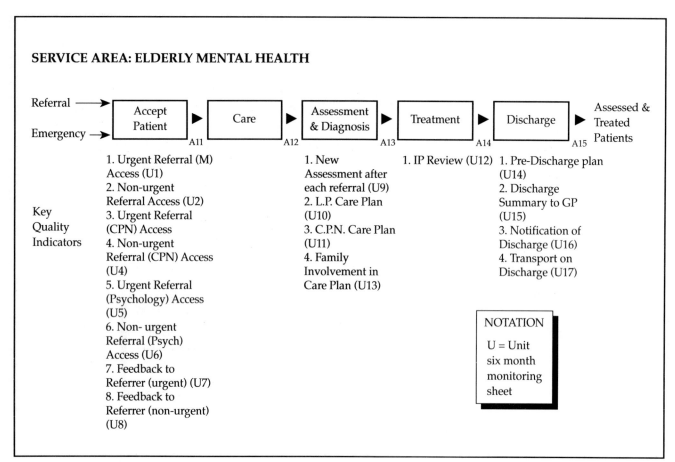

Figure 5.11. E.M.H. — clinical activity

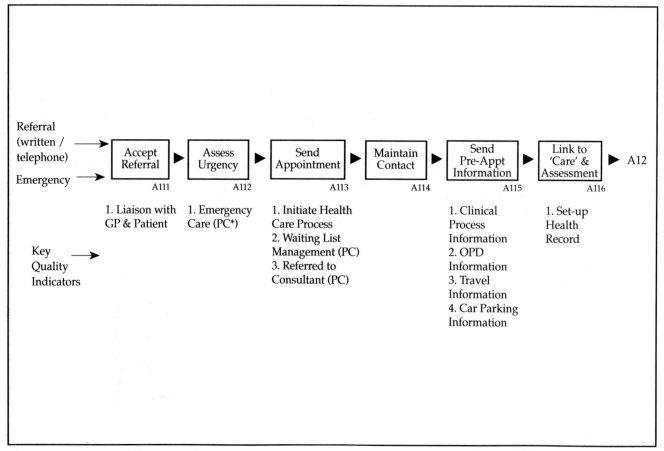

Figure 5.12. A11 — Accept patient

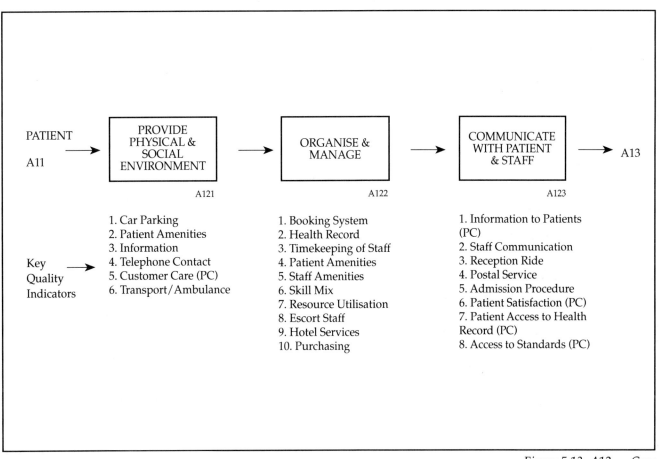

Figure 5.13. A12 — Care

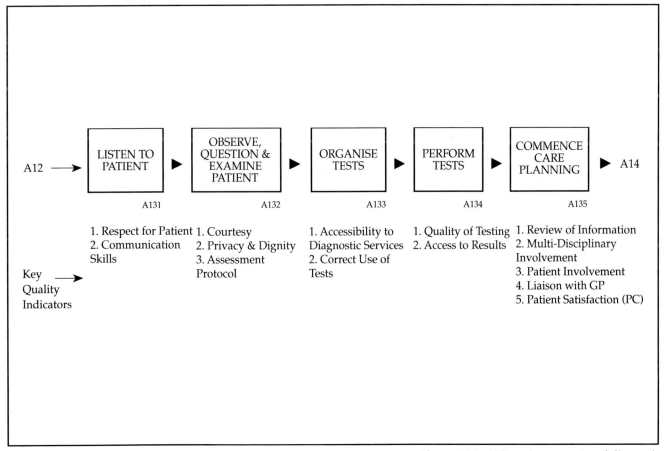

Figure 5.14. A13 — Assessment and diagnosis

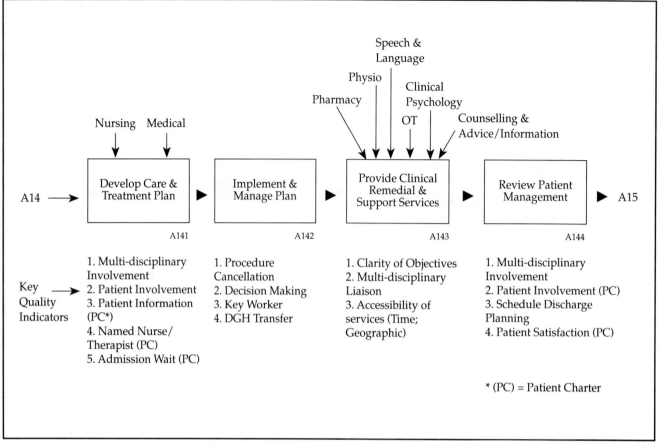

Figure 5.15. A14 — Treatment

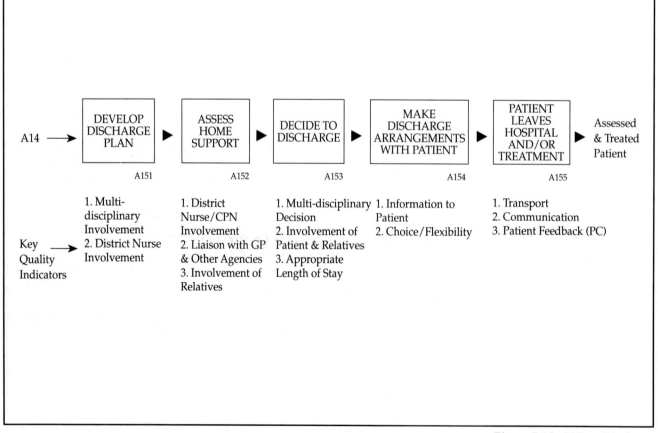

Figure 5.16. A15 — Discharge

To explore non-clinical support services and management functions in a similar way is not really applicable or practical, as most support functions apply to the *patient episode* or patient stay in total, although of course key aspects can be associated with a *patient trail*. However, although not strictly a trail, management functions can be identified and the associated *quality indicators* identified as in Fig 5.17.

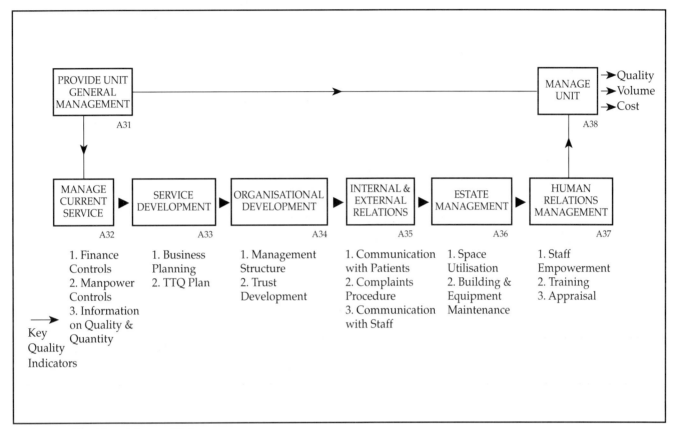

Figure 5.17. A3 — Manage Unit

Moving into medical/clinical care in greater detail, two models have been developed which are useful to consider:

- Clinical pathway analysis; and
- Collaborative care planning.

The analysis management of a medical or surgical process is referred to by Lowenhaupt (1991) as a *clinical pathway*. It includes all aspects of the clinical process under investigation — eg preadmission assessment — operative technique — rehabilitation service. The aim of any *clinical pathway* is to:

- Optimise care; and
- Return the patient home as soon as possible.

Clinical pathways use the tools of TQM with medical staff to increase productivity or *quality of health care*. It is an ideal mechanism/approach to enlist medical staff into the TQM process.

Measurement of *clinical processes* is a complex task — an example of a clinical pathway is shown in Figure 5.18. It arose from a noted significant variation in hospital costs between physicians in a USA hospital. Initial analysis revealed significant problems:

- Appropriate gathering/handling of pretreatment sputum culture;
- Gram stain specimen;
- Timely administering of first dose of antibiotic; and
- Consistent guidelines for physician to change to oral therapy etc.

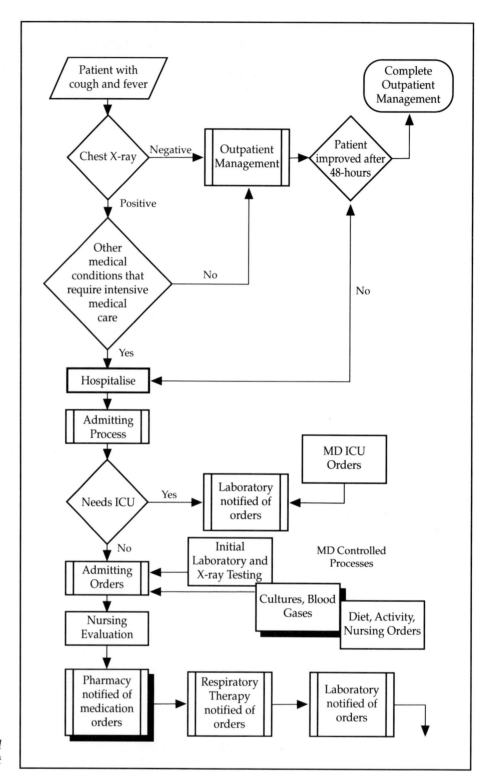

Figure 5.18. Pneumonia clinical pathway flow chart

Solution:

- User trail for emergency room and floor nurses in obtaining and handling sputum sample;
- Training for junior doctors in management of pneumonia; and
- Written set of guidelines for each firm.

Result:

- Cut in costs; and
- Increase in quality medical care.

This generalist example of analysis of determinants of poor quality at work can be adapted and applied to many different types of health care delivery problems — clinical and nonclinical.

It is difficult to draw flow charts or clinical pathways for even simple processes that are:

- Correct;
- Not oversimplified; and
- Comprehensive.

A variation on this is to show specific flow of an individual activity via a map (Oakland, 1991) which allows a critical examination of purpose/place/sequence/people/method of a certain activity leading to elimination/combination/rearrangement/simplification of this activity.

The second model is collaborative care planning (CCP) developed in W. Midlands and specifically written about by Hewitson. This is a patient centred, multidisciplinary approach to care planning which is tailored to meed individual patient needs. It required each member of staff to review current practice and determine care intervention required to achieve desired outcomes. Examples are given in Figures 5.20 and 5.21.

Further in depth planning of quality problems can be obtained in any of the above approaches using the *fishbone analysis* tool as in Figure 5.19. It is well known in problem solving in the manufacturing industry for greater clarity and understanding of why problems occur.

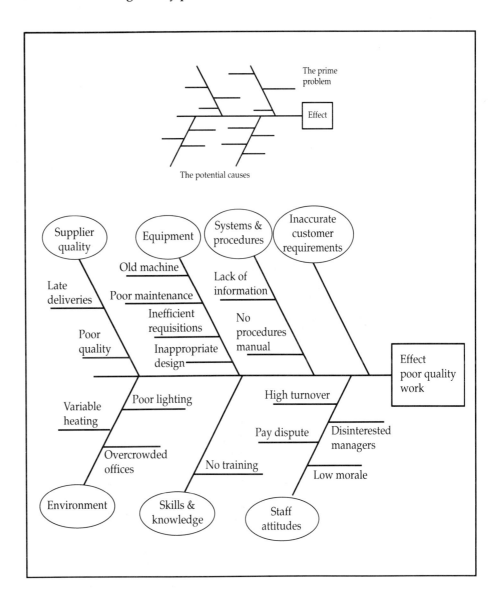

Figure 5.19. Fishbone diagram

Figure 5.20. Collaborative care plan: myocardial infarction

Collaborative Care Plan - Myocardial Infarction

Date of Admission _____
Time of Admission _____

* DELETE AS NECESSARY
** "A" = "LOOK AFTER YOURSELF"
"B" = "WEIGHT CONTROL LEAFLET"

PATIENTS' DETAILS

Surname _____   Unit No. _____
Forenames _____   Date of Birth _____
Address _____   Consultant _____
  Ward _____

DAY	MEDICAL TEAM	SIGNED/DATED	NURSING TEAM	SIGNED/DATED	PHYSIOTHERAPY	SIGNED/DATED	PHARMACOLOGY	SIGNED/DATED	DIETICIAN	SIGNED/DATED	OTHER REFS.	SIGNED/DATED
Day 1	**Admission** Document time of admission Document time of onset of chestpain IV Access Analgesia E.C.G. & Commence Cardia Mon. Aspirin } Document if thrombolysis } not indicated Consider – G.T.N. IV Beta Blocker Review with RMO & Consultant CXR (on call if indicated or weekend) Blood: Cardiac Enzymes U & E F.B.C. Glucose Random Cholesterol		As Care Plan Admit patient Start Discharge Checklist Meet patients/relatives Observational/physical/ psychological needs as identified on assessment Continue throughout hospital stay		Bed rest Breathing Exercises } x 1 hourly Circulatory Exercise		Visit Evaluation and prescription chart		Consider dietary referral for patients with specific needs, eg Diabetes Hyperlipo-protein-aenemia Evidence of Emaciation Referred Seen All patients told their ideal weight as soon as is convenient			
Day 2	Review by H.O. E.C.G. Cardiac Enzymes		As Care Plan Start Education Package		Bedrest/sitting out Breathing Exercs. } x 1 hourly Circulatory Exercs.		Visit Evaluation of presc. chart		Ensure patient referred as Day 1			
Day 3	Review by H.O. E.C.G. if indicated Discontinue cardiac monitor Enzymes if an doubt Transfer to Ward 6 Ward 6 staff to remove IV cannula		As Care Plan Prepare ward transfer		Mobilising around bed Breathing Exercs. } x 1 hourly Circulatory Exercs.		Visit Evaluation of presc. chart		Advice given Nurse/Dietician Leaflets to all patients 'A' plus 'B' (if overweight)			
Day 4	Review by H.O. E.C.G. if indicated		As Care Plan Continue rehab. programme and discharge plan		Mobilising on way to toilet and around own bay Continue above exercs. hourly plus add excerts. in In-patient Activity sheet		Visit Evaluation of presc. chart		Advice given Nurse/Dietician			
Day 5	Review by H.O. E.C.G. if indicated		As Care Plan		Fully mobilising around ward Inpatient Activity Sheet exercises		Visit Eval. of presc. chart		Advice given Nurse/Dietician			
Day 6	Review by HO E.C.G. if indicated Discuss medical condition prior to discharge		As Care Plan Ensure patient has understanding of condition		Fully mobilising around ward In-patient Activity Sheet exercises Walk up stairs		Visit Evaluation of presc. chart		Advice given Nurse/Dietician			
	Discharge letter T.T.O.s E.C.G. Refer to Cardiac Rehab.		Discharge Checklist		Continue exercises for one week x 3 daily Progress to Outpatient Activity Sheet		Discharge Drug Counselling		Advice given Nurse/Dietician Refer to Dietician as per plan Seen by Dietician			

Discharge
M.I.   YES/NO
Thrombolysis   YES/NO
Reason for no thrombolysis _____

Any Complications _____

Planned Discharge Date _____

Actual Discharge Date _____

Figure 5.21. Community care plan

Coventry Community Care Unit

COLLABORATIVE CARE PLAN FOR CHOLECYSTECTOMY

Name _____ No _____ Discharge Date _____

Address _____ DoB _____ GP _____

_____ Consultant _____

Post-Operative Day	DNS	Patient	General Practitioner	Social Services
1st Visit (Day after discharge)	9) Arrange with patient date of next visit	9) i) Aware of contact numbers ii) Contact GP if needed iii) Demonstrate knowledge of condition, confident to respond to problems arising		
2nd Visit (as arranged)	1) i) Evaluate general condition ii) Evaluate wound iii) Evaluate pain level iv) Evaluate diet fluid intake v) Evaluate bowel activity vi) Evaluate mobilisation	1) Report to DNS any change or any problems present re: i) wound ii) pain level iii) diet fluid take iv) bowel activity v) mobilisation	Inform GP of any problems presenting	
10th Day Post-Op	1) Evaluate general condition. Evaluate wound — discuss & explain suture removal if wound satisfactory 2) Discharge patient if condition satisfactory Complete Outcome Objective Form and forward to: Mrs M R Mitchell Community Liaison Sister H2 Phase IV Walsgrave Hospital	1) Reporting any problems presenting Demonstrate able to respond to problems arising and take appropriate action		

Collaborative Care Plan — Cholecystectomy

Outcome Goals

- All patients will have attended a pre-admission screening clinic and given an admission date.

- By discharge the patient will display minimal or no signs of potential complications:

    pain, cellulitus, bruising around the wound, chest problems, leg problems and will be ready for discharge on third post-operative day.

- By discharge the patient/family will be fully conversant with the care plan and will have the opportunity to discuss with the multidisciplinary team as appropriate:

    the surgery and possible risks, prior to theatre

    wound healing, possible complications and actions to take

    pain relief

    diet modifications

- By discharge physical and psychological needs will be met

cont'd. Figure 5.21

DAY	MEDICAL	NURSING	DIETICIAN	PHYSIOTHERAPY	THEATRE	DISTRICT/SW
Pre-admission Clinic Date Signature	1) History and Examination 2) Assessment of risk factors 3) Arrangements for discharge 4) FBC/U & E 5) CXR 6) ECG 7) Allocate admission date	1) Urine test 2) Record weight and height 3) Discuss worries and problems 4) Start Kardex 5) Nurse contact telephone no. 6) Show patient ward 7) Visiting times				1) Assess suitability for early discharge 2) Assess the extent of social services and home nursing back-up required 3) Initiate arrange-ments for back up as required
Pre-op Admission Day Date Signature	1) Assessment 2) Theatre list 3) Refer to Anaesthetist 4) Explain operation and consent forms 5) Medication • Heparin • TEDS • Prophylaxia • Antibiotics • Pre-medication • Sedatives	1) Welcome to ward – introduction to staff & patients 2) Baseline observations 3) Complete Kardex 4) Confirm social circumstances and discharge arrangements 5) Pre-operative talk 6) Skin preparations if necessary 7) Fast from ... 8) Safe custody of valuables	Low fat diet for lunch & evening meal	1) Introduction 2) Explain physiotherapy role 3) History – Assess mobility and listen to chest 4) Teach breathing and circulatory exercises and demonstrate supported coughing	Pre-op visit	1) If suitable for early discharge give notice to district nurse

DAY	MEDICAL	NURSING	DIETICIAN	PHYSIOTHERAPY	THEATRE	DISTRICT/SW
Pre-Admission Clinic Date Signature	1) Operation Notes 2) IV Rota 3) Analgesia	1) Bath and toilet 2) Check notes 3) Theatre check-list procedure 4) Check airway, position vital signs 5) Monitor pain — analgesia 6) Check wound and drain 7) Care IVI 8) Wash hands and face 9) Sit up in bed 10) Breathing exercises		Remind post-op exercises		
First post-op Day Date Signature	1) Check chest, legs, wound, drain 2) Assess fluids 3) Review 4) Discuss operation with patients and relatives	1) Analgesia 2) Bed Bath 3) Mobilise 4) Care of IVI 5) Elimination 6) Check wound RVAC 7) 4 hourly TPR		Breathing & circulation exercises	Post-op visit	

cont'd. Figure 5.21

DAY	MEDICAL	NURSING	DIETICIAN	PHYSIOTHERAPY	THEATRE	DISTRICT/SW
Second post-op day Date Signature	1) RVAC out if still in 2) Review analgesia 3) Check wound, neck, chest, legs	1) Discuss plan of care with patient 2) Mobilise for bath 3) Check wound 4) Light diet 5) 4 hourly TPR		1) Breathing & circulation exercises 2) Assess mobility and encourage mobilisation		
Third post-op day Date Signature	1) Check wound 2) Check intestinal function 3) Assess mobility 4) Check suitability for discharge 5) Check patient understands meaning of Cholecystectomy	1) Encourage self-care 2) Check wound 3) Check TPR 4) TTOs 5) Confirm transport & district nurse 6) Discharge time				
Forth post-op day Date Signature						1) Up.ad.lib. 2) Self caring 3) Check wound 4) Post-op Education

Chapter 6   Designing and specifying service excellence

Introduction   If the NHS were planned and developed to start afresh operating in 1994, would it be different from the NHS we know now? Undoubtedly, yes. It would include redesign to cater for ease of operation and change in specification to improve patient (and staff) requirements. However, like most established organisations the *luxury* of 'let's start again' is not possible. Instead periodically we have to update the quality of care and services provided.

In many industries companies can opt to:

1.   Retain existing services, maintaining *they know best*;
2.   Search for new markets — still providing the same products;
3.   Update services; and/or
4.   Develop new products and services.

In health care, although for much of the time option 1. is where the unit often is; option 2. is now becoming more relevant as the contracting process becomes more significant; and options 3. and 4. relate to real *quality improvement* at both clinical /professional and managerial levels.

The design function in health care is the responsibility of several roles — decisions made within this function will and should have significant and long term effects on a hospital or community service. The common location of these functions are within the:

1.   Quality/business planning/contracting/marketing directorate (each of these functional labels is often found used)
     - General *Quality Management* expertise is developed and quality management actually organised and coordinated.
     - Needs of customers (Patients, Purchasers and GPs) are identified and collated.

2.   Service operational management (service manager, clinical director/ coordinator)
     - Responsibility for implementing and delivering high quality services which meet an explicit specification or set of standards, is their responsibility.

3.   Medical and clinical audit — separate from the first location
     - Specialist skills in medical/clinical audit (doctors, nurses, PAMs) are developed, including medical audit assistants/facilitators.

As with all aspects of multilocation problem solving management, close liaison is needed between these three departments to ensure design and operational functions work well in tandem.

Through commitment of senior managers and clinicians to the design/ audit/improvement process, quality of care and service improves and patient satisfaction increases. This chapter outlines issues of design and specification. This does not necessarily guarantee quality: a service must be *capable* of conforming to this design and reproducing it every time. These issues of capability and control will be dealt with in Chapter 7.

Proper design of care and service is a crucial component in the fight to reduce and eliminate errors, waste and image action. If the design of a service is *right* to begin with, there will be less, or no need, to experience time consuming modifications at a later stage.

Much has already been written about design and standard setting (Koch 1991). Some of the issues, in general, are shown in Figure 6.1.

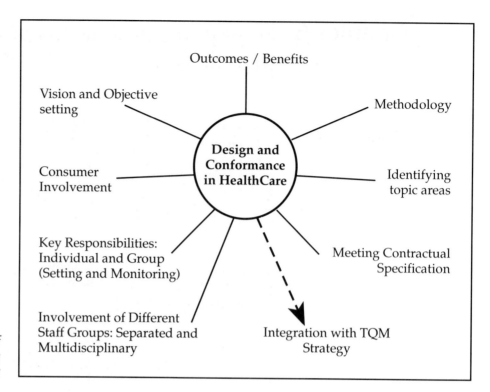

Figure 6.1. Dimensions of standard setting and monitoring strategy

The benefits of good design are:-

• Increased consistency;
• Patient satisfaction;
• Better resource use;
• Reduced errors; and
• Staff satisfaction.

In general these issues concern the audit loop shown in Fig 6.2.

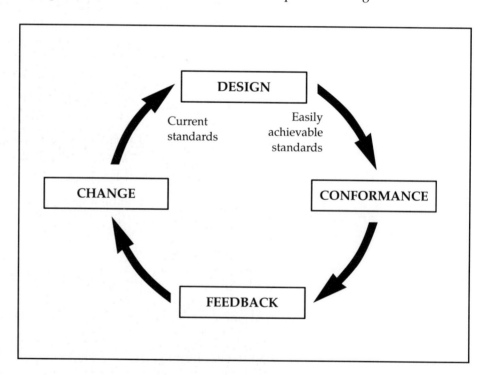

Figure 6.2. Audit loop

This should be applied in a *total* way to a provider unit — for example, within a DGH the design and specification process should be applied to each operation area as in Figure 6.3.

MANAGEMENT			
		Theatres	Paramedical Services
Outpatient Services	Wards	Investigative Services	Non-clinical Support Services

Figure 6.3. Main service areas of DGH

Before progressing much further you might use the *design framework* in Figure 6.4 to consider what aspects should be examined in your own unit to establish a comprehensive design/standard setting approach:

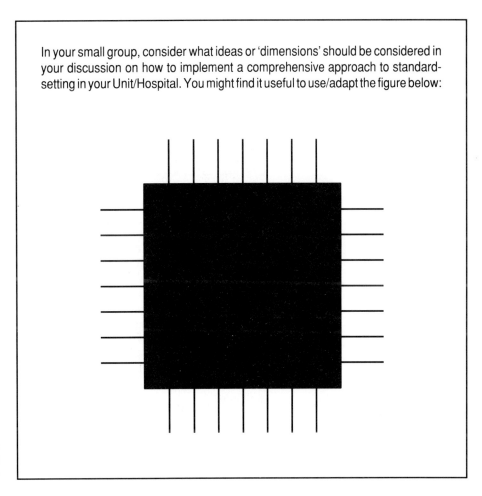

In your small group, consider what ideas or 'dimensions' should be considered in your discussion on how to implement a comprehensive approach to standard-setting in your Unit/Hospital. You might find it useful to use/adapt the figure below:

Figure 6.4. Exercise: Design framework for comprehensive standard setting

What do the words *design* and *specification* mean and entail?

In this chapter, we shall be discussing:

- Standard setting in the context of meeting purchaser/contracting requirements;
- Tools and techniques for standard setting and health care design;
- Control and management of design and standard.
- Systems for organising standards; and
- Documentation.

Contract specifications and standards

This subtitle implies a strong relationship between explicit standards and standardisation of health care services and their specification within contracts. This should not, as some think, lead to stultification and reduced innovation — quite the opposite in fact.

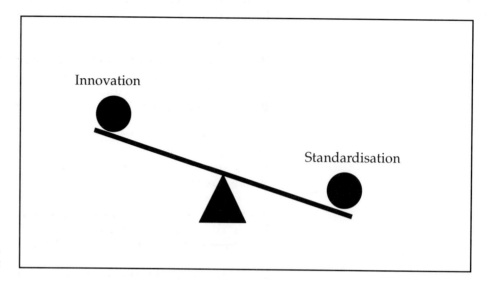

Figure 6.5. Innovation v. standardisation

Figure 6.5 illustrates the tension between standardisation and innovation. On the basis of clear, explicit description of what is currently delivered, innovation and creative development can take place.

The specification and associated standard is the main way, backed up by appropriate documentation, for attaining and maintaining quality and its control. In time we may see hospitals meeting the *International Standards Organisation (ISO) ISO 8402 (1986)* document for prescribing requirements to which the hospital has to conform.

The basic requirements of a specification are that it gives:

- What performance/activity is required by a service, eg a surgical team;
- Variables, such as access times, length of stay parameters, which describes the service adequately and in a quantitative way;
- Where appropriate, consumable materials used;
- Clinical and non-clinical processes involved;
- Inspection/monitoring requirements; and
- Appropriate reference to other quality assurance/specification documents.

Close links are necessary between provider units' approach to standard setting and design and their main (and other) purchasers' requirements within the contracting framework. Regions and purchasing agencies have been deliberating what their role should be in this respect — *Hands on or Hands off* (Spiby and Griffiths 1991).

Taking an example of an ENT service, the following key issues and standards were considered appropriate by the South West Thames Regional Health Authority:

Key issues
- What standards are applicable to ENT?
- How might the relevant importance of each category of standards be determined?
- If no agreement about the relative importance of different categories of standards can be achieved, how should differences be resolved? What sanctions can be brought into play and how can they be enforced?
- How will consumers' priorities be taken into account?
- Having agreed standards for services which are acceptable to all parties, who will be responsible for ensuring that the actual pattern of service across the region's provider units enables those standards to be achieved?

Standards

The panel decided that there are four mandatory standards on which the RHA should be prepared to monitor and intervene if necessary. These are based on the belief that the main business of the 'how' and the 'what' of service delivery should occur between the purchaser and the provider. The primary purpose is to provide high quality service.

This service should:
- provide effective treatment to the appropriate people;
- provide sufficient care in an equitable way;
- provide care in a humane way;
- ensure that these objectives are met in the most efficient way.

The primary focus of the RHA should be:
- quality of service;
- expected outcomes of the services;
- costs of the service.

The following four mandatory standards should be set:
- Purchasers will be expected to know the characteristics of their population and the implications of the epidemiology of the diseases for which ENT services are to be provided.
- Cover for ENT inpatients should be provided on a 24-hour basis by resident ENT trained medical staff of at least senior house officer status.
- All medical staff providing ENT services should participate in a regular systematic medical audit. Other staff should participate in a clinical audit.
- Purchasers will be expected to define outcomes. These should be both clinical and service related.

An outline monitoring checklist and key questions to be asked is given in Figure 6.6. In general, purchasers and providers need to develop a co-operative partnership in delivering the service, as illustrated by Smith (1991) in the list below.

Checklist

STANDARD 1
- Is there a demonstrable understanding of the epidemiology of ENT diseases and their implications for the population?
- Have other factors that influence the assessment of need been considered?
- Is there a profile of services currently provided for the population?
- Is there a strategy for matching identified needs of appropriate services to produce measurable health gain?

STANDARD 2
- Is there a system by which the postgraduate dean will monitor the placement of ENT senior house officers and report unsatisfactory situations to the RHA?

STANDARD 3
- Has the Regional Committee for Medical Audit developed and monitored the implementation of ENT audit regionwide?
- Are all clinicians involved?
- Are all staff participating in clinical audit?

STANDARD 4
- What outcome measures have been developed for ENT services?
- How has consumer input been sought in this process?
- How has information gained from this process been used to inform developments of future ENT services?

Key questions

MONITORING AREAS OF CONCERN
The RHA should seek to clarify the issues raised as concerns for each purchasing authority. The following checklist summarises key examples.

BREADTH OF SERVICE
❑ Does the purchasing policy consider the wider range of services such as: screening; paediatric audiology; hearing aids?
❑ Are there agreed protocols between primary and secondary care for referral and management by GPs?

ACCESS TO SERVICES
❑ What is the balance between day surgery and inpatient provision?
❑ Are outpatients accessible locally?
❑ What other services, eg. hearing aid maintenance and battery replacement, are available locally and can these be provided within the community?
❑ Have consumers been consulted on this aspect of provision?

DIALOGUE WITH CONSUMERS
❑ What processes are in place for gaining the consumers' and GPs' opinions?

SPECIFIC SERVICES FOR CHILDREN
❑ What is the incidence of ENT disease locally in children?
❑ What information is collected to ensure that the needs of the child population inform your decisions on purchasing ENT services?
❑ How are the outcomes of ENT treatment for children used in your district?
❑ From whom are surveillance services for the specialty areas purchased?
❑ Are there protocols on the management of hearing loss in children between the primary and secondary units?
❑ What is the waiting time for referrals to: paediatric audiology; ENT consultant outpatients; inpatient treatment?

ENT RELATIONSHIPS
❑ Has the inter-relationship between ENT services and other services, eg. accident and emergency, paediatrics, anaesthetics, been considered and dealt with satisfactorily?

SMALL CASE-LOADS
❑ What information is collated on casemix and case load for ENT?
❑ What are the agreed sub-optimal standards?
❑ Are junior doctors being trained appropriately?
❑ Is there adequate experience available to provide wider staff training?

EDUCATION AND RECRUITMENT RESEARCH, DEVELOPMENT AND AUDIT
❑ What programmes of postgraduate education exist for hospital and GPs in ENT?
❑ Are there recognised opportunities for research and innovation?
❑ What areas have been identified for operational research?

PRIVATE PRACTICE
❑ What is the view on the impact of private practice on the market and its influence on need for ENT services in your population?

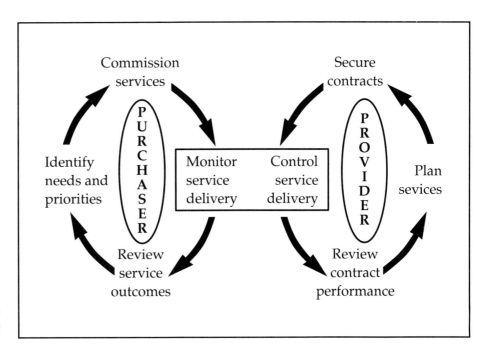

Figure 6.6. The quality partnership: delivering the service

Appropriate documentation and information to ascertain the levels of:

- Clinical and Service Quality
- Customer/patient satisfaction; and
- Resource use per case.

are available as illustrated by Upson below:

PURCHASER TOOLS TO ANALYSE AND MONITOR PROVIDER RESPONSIVENESS

Clinical quality
Quality Managment Data
Mortality Data
Continuous Quality Improvement Process (TQM)
Small Area Analysis & Pre-authorization of High Variance or High Cost Care
Appropriateness, Outcome, Efficiency

Customer Quality
Gallup Surveys
Link to All Levels of Management & TQM Teams

Resource Use per Case
Comparative Analysis of Cases by DRG or similar category
All Cases, Inliers & Outliers

Techniques and tools for health care design

Standard setting and health care design within a provider unit must be seen as a *Total* and *Managed* process:

- Total: all operational parts of the unit must be included
- Managed: this type of explicit design, standard, specification has not been done before and requires coordination of what is a huge multifarious set of *operations*.

To develop this, a set of tools and techniques, known collectively in industry as *quality function deployment* (QFD) (Oakland, 1989) can be used to address many, various aspects of the design/standard setting process. The tools of relevance to health care design are:

1. **Affinity diagram;**
2. **Interrelationship diagram;**
3. **Tree diagram;**
4. **Matrix diagram;**
5. **Matrix data analysis;**
6. **Process decision programme chart; and**
7. **Arrow diagram — similar to patient trailing and clinical pathway already discussed.**

These tools are all simple and interrelated, more or less in the order given above, starting with the creative brainstorming activity and ending with highly ordered, topical and practical subtask scheduling and describing.

1. Affinity diagram

This is grouping, basing on naturally, or apparently natural!, relationships between items via brainstorming. It is used to generate ideas and categories to *order* or organise apparently unconnected or various aspects of a task or problem.

It is especially useful if and when:

• Ideas are *chaotic, disordered,* and complex;
• New thinking is required; and
• Solutions are *not* simple!

Four main processes to generate an affinity diagram are:

1. Brainstorming *untidily* all the issues/topics relevant to the task under review;
2. Write this on one or more sheets of paper;
3. Look for one or more sets of five – ten categories or headings which *explain* or include 80–90 per cent of the topics generated in points 1. and 2.
4. Review these sets and agree on the best set *for now*

The output is an ordering of a large number of ideas under a small, limited number of headings for further analysis (see example below):

**What is good
Clinical Assessment
and Diagnosis?**

Clear assessment protocols	Initial care planning	Awareness and discussion of alternative treatments
Access to diagnostic services	Multidisciplinary involvement	Clear specification in contracts
Effective team communication	Involvement of patient	Leads to clear treatment plan and positive outcome

2. Interrelationship diagram

This follows the affinity diagram, using greater logical or sequential linking among categories or factors identified. It allows previously anticipated ideas and links to emerge in discussion and can be applied to specific clinical and non-clinical operational issues and also general management issues. It is used when:

- An issue is complex and relationships are not immediately obvious; and
- Quality requires correct linking and sequencing and includes, once the affinity diagram has been produced:
  1. Further generation of related issues, by brainstorming or addressing relevant available documentation;
  2. Use of arrows to indicate linked items; and
  3. Use of a double box to denote a key factor or cause as in Figure 6.7.

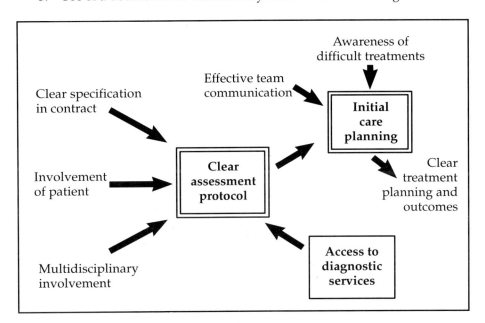

Figure 6.7. Interrelationship diagram

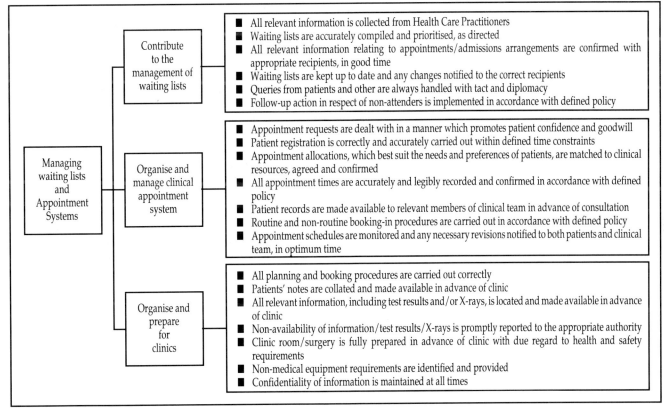

Figure 6.8. Tree diagram: management of waiting lists

3. Tree diagram

This systematically arranges a range of activities needing to be accomplished to reach a desired goal or outcome. It requires examination of topical and sequential links between tasks. It is an antidote to the quick, superficial, albeit action orientated method of finding a quick fix solution! It is used when:

* Chaotic understanding of a process exists;
* More comprehensive analysis is needed;
* Moving from one task to a broad set of goals; and
* The issue is complex.

  It involves:

* Starting with one task or operation statement on the left hand side of a paper/board;
* Ask what is needed to accomplish this task — generate 1–5 points;
* Ask, of each of these, the same question.

  An example is shown in Figure 6.8 for the management of waiting lists:

4. Matrix design

The purpose of this important tool is to outline the interrelationships between subtasks and to identify relative importance. It is typically presented in Figure 6.9 as an L-Matrix, and shows the intersection of two related sets of items. An example looking at *patient* reception quality and *surgeon* perception of quality is shown in Figure 6.10.

  This can be adapted in a T-shaped matrix which is a combination of two L-shaped matrices. An example involving unitwide quality training is shown in Figure 6.11.

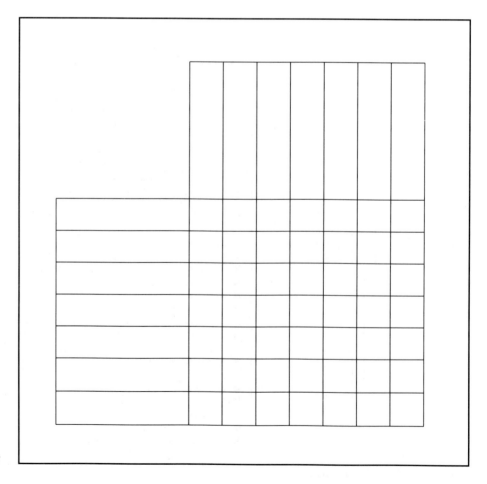

Figure 6.9. L - matrix

	Length of stay	Bed availability	Theatre availability	Junior medical staffing	Speed of procedure	Team work	Rapport with patient
Access to admission							
Reception							
Hotel Services							
Staff attitudes							
Information							
Post operative pain							
Discharge arrangements							

Surgeon Perception / **Patient Perception**

Figure 6.10. Patient/surgeon perception

Who needs training?

| Doctors |
| Nurses |
| PAMs |
| Hotel services |
| Senior managers |
| Middle managers |
| Secretaries |
| Support services |

Training in what?: What is TQM? / Cultural values / Team Work / QITs / Business plannng / RMI / Customer care / Design & standards / Training / Quality costing

Who provides training?

| Senior managers |
| Quality managers |
| Senior clinicians |
| Business managers |
| Trainers |

Figure 6.11. Unitwide quality training

5. Matrix data analysis (MDA)

MDA helps to arrange information from the matrix diagram so that it is easier to inspect and shows relationships between variables. It can be complex to develop, sometimes using sophisticated statistical techniques (eg components analysis). It allows presentation of key topics/ issues/behaviours in at least a two-dimensional way. Readers are referred to the training diagram in Koch (1991) P.111 which is reproduced again in Figure 6.12.

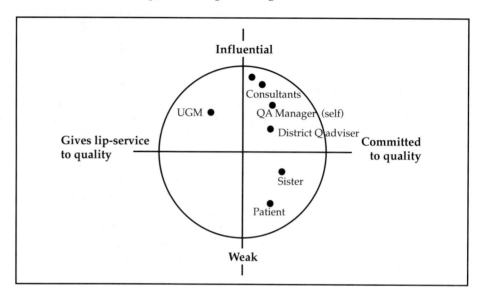

Figure 6.12

6. Process diagram programme chart (PDPC)

This is used to identify each event, expected and unexpected, in a clinical and / or non-clinical process. It helps to plan for it, and plan counter measures for deviations from it. It is similar, in structure, to the tree diagram and involves:

- Specifying one part of the process under scrutiny;
- Asking the question; 'What could, or does go wrong at this particular point?';
- Listing action and counter measures that could be taken;
- Continuing until process (or you) is/are exhausted; and
- Repeating with other parts of the process.

An example below relating to the provision of psychotherapy is given in Figure 6.13.

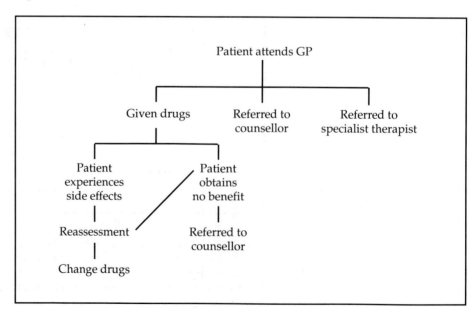

Figure 6.13. Process diagram chart

7. Arrow design

This is very similar to the patient trailing methodology outlined in an earlier chapter and is used to plan a task specifically and in detail. It is useful in understanding important but repetitive jobs and is similar to critical path analysis.

Many, if not all, of these approaches, which collectively are called *quality function development* are relatively simple and yet provide structure and organisation to the analysing and design of complex processes.

Management of design and setting standards

It is important in this major area of *quality management* to ensure that this process is controlled; checked for completeness; involves the appropriate people; and is adequately resourced in terms of time and expertise.

It is important to realise that:

- No health care set of standards will ever be comprehensive and complete — improvement will always be possible;
- Any provider unit, or set of staff, can learn from what other units have developed — in no way does this counteract the ownership issues, ie staff developing their own standards; and
- Design is nearly always limited by patients or purchaser constraints, and financial constraints.

Key elements of the standard setting process are shown in Figure 6.14.

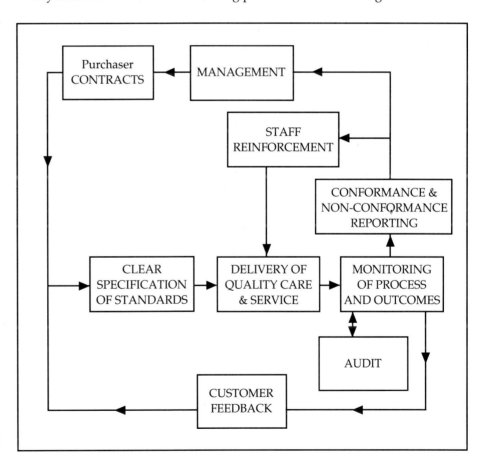

Figure 6.14. Key elements in standards setting

In a previous section the key initial checklist for standard setting was shown. An example of the results of such an initial audit are shown in Figure 6.15, and indicate considerable activity but the need to develop further. An example of an implementation plan and timetable for standard setting (and monitoring) is shown in Figure 6.16.

PROFESSIONS ALLIED TO MEDICINE
STANDARD SETTING AND MONITORING CHECKLIST

Has the department written standards	Dept A	Dept B	Dept C	Dept D
(a) Descriptive (i.e. prose, not usually measurable)	✓	✓	✓	✓
(b) Measurable specific, often numerical, can be measured)	Some	Some	Some	Some
(c) Mission statement / service objectives?	?	✓	✓	✓
Are measurable standards				
(a) Comprehensive (i.e. covering all aspects of service)	90%	99%	80% clinical 75% Admin	75% clinical 95% Admin / Service
(b) Covering between 1–10 major areas/topics	No	✓	✓	✓
(c) 6 Monthly Review dates	?	To be decided	No	✓
Does the department have a clear idea/plan of areas/topics which should eventually be covered bystandard setting?	Yes	Under review	Under review	✓
Do all Staff in the department				
(a) Know a little about this process	✓	✓	✓	✓
(b) Know and agree all these standards	✓	✓	✓	✓
(c) Is this linked to Audit	?	In two areas	Being developed	✓
(d) Is this linked to customer feedback	?	In outpatients	?	Annual report goes to referrers
Is there a clear monitoring process for assessing current performance against these standards?	1. Cards audited 2. Needs Development	1. Waiting times audited 2. Needs Development	1. Needs Development 2. Possible External Audit	1. Annual Output Report 2. Fortnightly Peer review to link to Standards 3. Individual Patient Discharge checklist Audit 4. Link to Staff
6 (a) Does a quarterly report get prepared?	No	No	No	Annual report
(b) Is this discussed with staff?	No	No	No	Yes
(c) Does the senior manager receive a copy?	No	No	No	Yes
(d) Does 'Non-conformance' which gets identified get acted on?	Informally	Not formally	Not formally	Yes

Figure 6.15. Professions allied to medicine: standards setting and monitoring checklist

---

QUALITY OF HEALTH CARE DESIGN: STANDARD SETTING AND MONITORING

IMPLEMENTATION PLAN AND TIMETABLE

Introduction

Considerable discussion and work has taken place in many departments throughout the District on developing measurable standards. The reasons and objectives of standard setting were described in a recent document when the 'Total Quality' Strategy was developed earlier this year. The difficulty of identifying key service issues/topics was also discussed. It follows a series of workshops on this issue. It also dovetails with the wider Directorate Quality Planning process now nearing completion. This briefing paper outlines a straightforward implementation plan and timetable to achieve a comprehensive approach.

Implementation Plan

The following steps will be required, if they have not been achieved already:

(a) Audit current Standard Setting process, using checklist attached. An example of how this has been used is attached.

(b) Establish Departmental Plan to achieve:
    1   Topics to be considered in standard setting for 1991/92
    2   'Operationalizing' Topics into:
        (a) Measurable standards
        (b) Clear Monitoring mechanisms
    3   'Conformance Reporting' Format and timetable
    4   Use of Information from (3) to:
        (a) improve service
        (b) reinforce staff

It is suggested that a single form of paperwork is used unless a compelling reason exists otherwise. This will then be consistent with the Directorate Quality Planning initiative.

Timetable

Step (a) Standard Setting Audit   End October 1991
Step (b) Department Standard Setting   End December 1991

Figure 6.16. Implementation plan and timetable for standard setting

The patient trail model, previously described, in *Quality Planning* is a very useful way of ordering the development of standards in that each *topic* or *quality indicator* identified can be translated into one or more standards (see Figure 6.17). Further examples of written standards and formats used are shown in Figs 6.18 — 6.21.

Indicator	Descriptive standard / objective	Measurable indicator(s)	Target(s)	Monitoring method, frequency and responsibility
(1) Quality of service delivery (1.1) Appropriateness	1.1.1 Patients are waiting in clinic for the minimum possible time	Waiting time	75 per cent seen in 30 mins 100 per cent seen in 45 mins at least	Business manager to review waiting times for each clinic monthly
	1.1.2 Patients are "welcomed" on the ward and shown their bed as quickly as possible. "Welcome" to include patient and family understanding the reason for the admission	Time between entering ward and being shown bed	80 per cent in 10 mins 100 per cent in 20 mins	Ward sister to review weekly. Directorate nurse manager to check 10 per cent of ward admissions fortnightly
	The ward environment be pleasing and hygenic	Weekly visual inspection and weekly ward cleaning checklist	No complaints by either *any* staff member or patient	Ward sister and domestic supervisor weekly. Control of infection sister and directorate nurse manager monthly
	Patient valuables and property to be safe during patient's admission and all staff are aware of policies	Documentation is completed when necessary and patients are aware of policies	No losses	Monthly random checks of knowledge of policies by staff and patients. Business manager to monitor any losses
	Dedicated rheumatology and CRC ward to ensure high quality of specialist care similarly dedicated elective orthopaedic and dedicated beds	Diagnosis of patients admitted	Refuse entry if not under directorate consultant	Directorate nurse manager (or her nominated deputy) to inform business manager of outliers daily
	1.1.3 Increase number of patients treated in day care trauma	Number of patients seen in day care and number of elective admissions	25 per cent for orthopaedics	Monthly via theatre computer by business manager
	1.1.4 To implement the policy	Discharge date set within 24 hours where possible	90 per cent	Directorate nurse manager to perform random documentation checks: 5 per ward per fortnight. Ward sister to keep list of all patients who leave before the discharge letter is signed and send numbers to B.M. monthly
		Number of patients who are discharged without the discharge letter signed by the relevant houseman	98 per cent	
		Number of patients who are passed fit for discharge by doctor but cannot leave	2 per cent	
	1.1.5 Orthopaedics: Timely communication with GP	Out-patient clinic letters posted	Within 1 week	Senior secretary to monitor weekly and report
	Rheumotology	Out-patient clinic letters posted	Within 2 weeks	Senior secretary to monitor weekly and report
	All consultants are available to talk to GPs on the telephone. Registrar/senior registrar available 24 hours on bleep	Number of complaints oral and written	Availability at least 2 x 1 hr/week	Business manager monthly spot check

Figure 6.17. Directorate: Quality plan of service delivery: appropriateness (Koch and Chapman, 1991)

- To receive health care on the basis of clinical need, regardless of ability to pay;
- To be registered with a GP;
- To receive emergency medical care at any time, through your GP or the emergency ambulance service and hospital accident and emergency departments;
- To be referred to a consultant, acceptable to you, when your GP thinks it necessary, and to be referred for a second opinion if you and your GP agree this is desirable;
- To be given a clear explanation of any treatment proposed, including any risks and any alternatives, before you decide whether you will agree to the treatment;
- To have access to your health records, and to know that those working for the NHS are under a legal duty to keep their contents confidential;
- To choose whether or not you wish to take part in medical research or medical student training;
- To be given detailed information on local health services, including quality standards and maximum waiting times;
- To be guaranteed admission for treatment by a specific date no later than two years from the day when your consultant places you on a waiting list; and
- To have any complaint about NHS services — whoever provides them investigated and to receive full and prompt written reply from the chief executive or general manager.

Figure 6.18. Patient Charter Standards (DoH 1992)

Children and their parents have a right to express things in their own way and to be involved in decision making. We have a responsibility to preserve these rights within the operational constraints of this hospital.

Children should have impartial access to treatment and facilities which are available within the hospital for them.

Children have a right to considerate and respectful care, which maintains their dignity at all times.

Children have the right to be treated in a safe environment.

Communications should be clear and in plain language. An understanding by the child as well as the parent is important. Help should be given to those with communication difficulties.

Parents are welcome to participate in the care of their children where appropriate. We have the responsibility to provide adequate support.

Parents have the right to stay with their child during the hospital stay. Accommodation or sleeping facilities will be provided.

Children have the right to appropriate education and play facilities during their stay in hospital.

Children and parents are entitled to know the name and professional status of each person providing a service for them.

Children and their parents have a right to be consulted about care being given or involvement in teaching and research.

Children and their families are entitled to expect effective communication, and liaison between hospital, community health services and the caring agencies.

Figure 6.19. Children's charter (Nottingham 1991)

Figure 6.20. Psychologist Case Management

	ACCESSIBILITY AND PARTICIPATION	BREADTH OF FUNCTIONS	INDIVIDUAL PLANNING	CONTINUITY	RESPONSIBILITY AND ACCOUNTABILITY
REFERRAL / IDENTIFICATION	• Does the service have an appropriate image?	• Does the service fulfil an appropriate range of functions and is this reflected in the type and source of referrals?	• Is enough information gathered at referral to properly plan assessment?	• Is referral made to the agency that will perform the assessment and coordinate service delivery?	• Is it clear who is responsible for assisting people that do not fulfil eligibility criteria?
ASSESSMENT	• Is effective communication promoted, (e.g. through using advocates, interpreters, fitting false teeth)?	• Does the overall assessment address the full range of needs and strengths that users and their carers are presenting?	• Does the location of assessment, choice of assessors and style of assessment take account of characteristics of the individual referred?	• Can others already involved, such as other workers and carers, take part in the assessment?	• Is responsibility for coordinating assessment clearly apportioned?
PLANNING	• Does the process of decision-making allow the views of users and carers to be heard?	• Is planning actually based on assessment of needs and strengths?	• Do workers have access to budgets which might increase the flexibility of the individual service plan?	• Does planning build on existing supports without increasing burden?	• What influence does the agency concerned with individual planning have over other providers (e.g. does it have a purchasing role)?
IMPLEMENTATION/ SERVICE DELIVERY	• Are the services provided physically accessible, non-stigmatising, culturally sensitive and used by people who do not have disabilities?	• Do the services provided address the full breadth of the needs of users and carers and build upon strengths and assets?	• Does service delivery reflect the individual tailoring of the plan?	• Is the same person or team always available during crises or periods of transition?	• Who is accountable if one agency involved in implementing a plan fails to deliver?
REVIEW	• How are users and carers involved in decisions about how well the help provided is fulfilling the user's needs and building on their strengths?	• Does the review process query the range of functions that the service (and other services with which it liaises) should be fulfilling for users?	• Is the review based upon the specifics of the plan or gross judgements of outcome?	• Is one person continuously monitoring progress?	• Are lines of accountability for service short-falls clearly specified?

Out-Patient Standards		
PRINCIPLES	**QUALITY STATEMENTS** GENERATION OF LOCAL STANDARDS	**POSSIBLE DATA COLLECTION** **METHODS**
Access		
1 GPs should be provided with information on out-patient and in-patient waiting times for each consultant and indicating areas of special expertise (which might include, where appropriate, knowledge of further languages). GPs should be provided with a protocol, where necessary by specialty or individual consultant and including advice on diagnostic tests required, for making an urgent referral. GPs will be consulted about the quality of presentation of information.	Information to GPs will be updated and sent to GPs every ...... months.	Check that GPs receive the information. Discuss with LMC.
2 All patients should receive a prompt acknowledgement that their GP's referral has been received.	All non-urgent first referrals will be sent an acknowledgement, offering an appointment date or indicating anticipated waiting time, within...... days of hospital receipt of referral.	Regular sampling of time gap between receipt of referral letters and date on which acknowledgement sent.
3 A maximum desired waiting time, from receipt of referral to patient being seen in clinic, should be identified.	...... % of non-urgent first referrals will be offered an appointment date which means they will be seen in clinic within ...... weeks of hospital receipt of referral.	What are current waiting times (see GP information) for a new appointment? Regular sampling of time gap between date referral received and appointment date.

Figure 6.21. Outpatient Standards
(Trent)

The reader is referred to the previous description of the standard setting process in Koch (1991) for further detail in the writing of standards.

Whatever style, method, and process undertaken to plan, specify, and standardise a service, a design *review* is important to ensure the process moves towards the desired objective(s) of clear specification or services provided. The aim of this design (standard setting) review is to establish:

- Service design/standards meet *all* the explicit performance criteria laid down in:
    1. Contracts;
    2. Statutory requirements; and
    3. Professional requirements (agreed by the unit);
- Design/standard can be produced in a way that is satisfactory to the patient and the unit;
- Viable alternatives have been considered; and
- Design/standards are documented adequately.

One key issue currently being addressed by the author is how to collate and organise this design process with the implication of many hundreds of written *active* standards into a computer aided system so that it is manageable.

Quality management system design

To ensure a *consistently* high quality health care service is provided, the unit must *manage* this consistently ensuring that the design/standards predict the use of one process which involves the same equipment, method/procedure in exactly the same way every time. The process must be *under contract* and is the aim of a health care quality management system. A fully documented quality management system (Oakland, 1989) will ensure that two major requirements are met:

- Customers' requirements (purchaser and patient) — confidence that hospital and community services deliver the service consistently; and
- The Unit's requirements — by using resources optimally and to best effect

Objective evidence must be produced from information supporting the existence of quality management system activities.

Requirements for a quality management system fall into several general categories and are similar to those detailed under *ISO 9000/BS5750* now being considered by some provider units and specific services for certification as operating under approved quality management systems (McDonald 1991, Grimsby Health Authority; Hopkinson 1991, 1992 Ambulance Services; McCarlty and Hicks 1991, Dialysis Technical Services)

These categories are:

1.	Quality policy	The organisation of a unit's quality strategy, either stand alone or integrated with its business plan, should be clear, unambiguous, understood and implemented throughout the unit.
2.	Organisation	Organisational relationships and accountabilities in general and specifically for quality management should be clear and unambiguous.
3.	Quality system	A quality manual setting out the general quality policies, procedures and practices of the unit relevant to delivering health care to the purchaser's specification. The unit must answer: <ul><li>It is capable to meet these procedures as designed;</li><li>Staff have appropriate and requisite skills;</li><li>Procedures are carried out, not just given lip service by staff, supervisors and managers;</li><li>Measurement is accurate and precise;</li><li>Quality inspection and monitoring (quality control) is accurate, precise and documented;</li><li>Ambiguity is minimal; and</li><li>Customers', both purchasers' and patients', requirements are understood and regularly established.</li></ul>
4.	Control review	Each purchaser contract and in a different way each patient *episode*, should be documented and monitored to ensure requirements are: <ul><li>Clear and written; and</li><li>Met.</li></ul> Appropriate discussions with both purchasers, at contract management meetings, and patients, in consultations, should exist to ensure clear understanding of the adequacy of what is being provided.

5. Design/standards control

There should be procedures which control and monitor the relevant aspects of service delivery to ensure these have been translated into standards and customer requirements are being met.

6. Document control

All documentation relating to quality should be up to date, reviewed and systematically organised and controlled, manually or with computer assistance. This should include:
(a) Quality manual;
(b) Directorate specific standard;
(c) Departmental operating manuals;
(d) Procedures and policies; and
(e) Purchaser contracts.

7. Purchasing

Mechanisms should exist to ensure that purchased products and services necessary to health care delivery and service conform to the requirements set and expected.

8. Identification and traceability

The many processes involved in delivering health care and service must be explicit, understood and traceable. If process control is to be effective, problems, when they occur, can be identified, traced and solved at source. This is of particular relevance when reviewing *clinical pathways*.

9. Processes control

Fully documented instruction must be available for any member of staff required to carry out complex tasks for which his/her initial training may be adequate but which are often performed with variable proficiency.

10. Inspection, measuring and monitoring

Any standard or specification worth stating must be followed by appropriate monitoring of staff performance as to conformance to the standard. Different levels of monitoring exist:
•   Individual's own monitoring of own performance;
•   Supervisor's/manager's monitoring;
•   Quality managers auditing; and
•   External auditing
    — Patient Group (CHC)
    — Purchaser Group
    — National Group (eg HAs)

11. Non-conforming services

Ways of dealing with care and service which occasionally does *not* conform to the desired, agreed and required specification should be clearly identified. (Use of results of complaints procedure, need for readmission due to error, iatrogenic complaints)

12. Corrective action

Procedures by which corrective action as a process which has gone wrong must be explicit and hence can lead to continuous/never ending quality improvements. This will usually be initiated when:
(a) Quality failures are identified by staff;
(b) Patients complain; and
(c) Purchasers complain.

13. Quality records

Health records (and non-clinical service records) provide the ongoing evidence that care and service is provided as per standard. Record collection, filing and retrieval should be explicit.

14. Training

Appropriate procedures to include all staff:
• Identification of training need;
• Training activity; and
• Record of Training.

15. Use of ongoing information

Information and methods of analysing it should be kept and regularly used to monitor the ongoing trends in quality of health care and service provided.

16. Quality system audits & review

A provider unit should arrange to self-audit its quality system by internal (within unit) and external (use of outside bodies).

17. Structure documentation

In order to record and show that the activities implemented in the previous sections are alive and well, a quality manual is necessary to explain how the unit carries out its quality policy. Very few provider units, at the time of writing this book, have such a manual. In many units, alongside an unclear view of Total Quality Management, is a reluctance to back up its staff's professionalism with documented proof of its Quality Management system, explicit or otherwise. The following points are useful in preparing a manual:
• It should be concise (20-40 pages);
• There is no standard format; and
• Sections should reflect the preceding categories insofar as they are relevant to the particular service provided.

A contents list to start any provider unit in discussing and developing its own *quality manual*
1. Unit quality policy/strategy including mission statement;
2. Responsibilities for unit and quality (organisation chart);
3. Quality system description;

4. Contract management and review;
5. Design/standards control including indicators covered;
6. Document control;
7. Purchasing control;
8. Identification and traceability;
9. Process control;
10. Inspection, measuring and monitoring;
11. Control and non-conformance;
12. Corrective action;
13. Quality records;
14. Training;
15. Use of information; and
16. Internal quality audit.

Chapter 7   Capability for and control of quality care

Introduction

Throughout this text, and its predecessor, *Total Quality Management in Health Care*, it has been suggested that quality of health care and services is the responsibility of senior managers, consultants *and* operational staff. For all those involved to take this responsibility, in its fullest sense, they must have the information and skills needed to:

1. Know what standards of care and service are expected;
2. Know clearly and unambiguously what the desired clinical or non-clinical process to achieve these standards is;
3. Know whether this process is *capable* of meeting or conforming to these standards;
4. Know if this is occurring at any point in time; and
5. Be able to make adjustments to the process if it is not meeting the standards required.

In chapter 5 on Quality Planning, the patient trail model was used to begin to describe, in general terms, the many clinical processes tied up in the overall patient trail. It is still difficult, in a service which combines human, mechanical, technical, and social processes every step of the way, to define the patient care process rigorously, unambiguously, and reliably. Without it, however, quality management is very difficult. In defining health care processes, various inputs need to be identified such as:

* People (skills, training, knowledge, experience);
* Methods, procedures, instructions;
* Information;
* Materials;
* Equipment; and
* Records and paperwork.

Outputs which are likely also need to be identified such as:

* Assessed and treated patients;
* Discharge summary to GP;
* Typed letters;
* Completed drug prescriptions;
* Delivery of goods; and
* Wage slips.

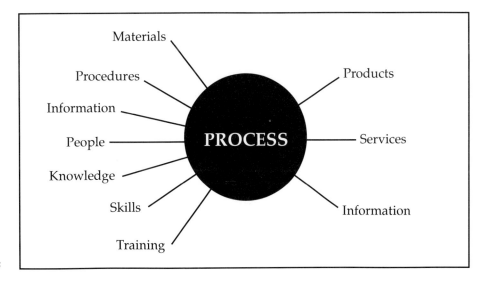

Figure 7.1. Process

The classification and documentation which reflects a clear process between inputs and outputs is likely to prevent failure. Process documentation involves:

- Data collection;
- Clarity of thought;
- Analysis of problems in process; and
- Action to improve the process.

The aim throughout quality control in health care is the total avoidance/ reduction of *failure* ie the zero defect model in health care. Any process can be monitored and brought 'under control' (Oakland, p. 180). It involves measuring performance and repeatedly being open to feedback leading to possible corrective action where appropriate.

Process control, often called *statistical process control* in the manufacturing sector, is a strategy for reducing variability and hence improving quality, by increasingly providing health care which is reliable and consistent.

Question   What processes or variables in *your* work are regularly monitored, measured and *charted* graphically?

This simple bar chart might appear in *your* service — what variable could it be measuring?

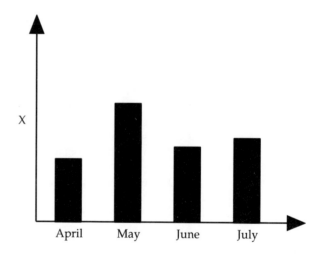

Systematic process control

The importance of information has been reinforced in the NHS ever since the introduction of firstly *general management*, then *resource management* (and *information technology*). However, it has been difficult to get data and information as a basis for action and process control. Several simple methods have been found useful in measuring process in any organisation and are applicable to health care. They are:

- Health care process flow charting — describing what is being done;
- Check sheets/activity sampling — how often it is done;
- Histograms/graphs — what variation takes place over time or between similar processes;
- Pareto analysis — which problems explain the most variance in a situation; and
- Cause and effect/fishbone analysis — what are the likely causes of problems.

1. Health care process charts

These were examined in Chapter 5 and help to develop a clear understanding of a particular process, eg:

Anaesthetic process:

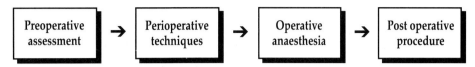

Further examples are shown in Figures 7.2 to 7.4. Unless there is this clear understanding, analysis of quality and problems will be incomplete; vary between *investigations*; and be unreliable.

Figure 7.2. Case management critical path: primary total hip arthroplasty

START ----→	DAY 1 (SURGERY)	1st PO DAY	2nd PO DAY	3rd PO DAY	4th PO DAY	5th PO DAY	6th PO DAY
TESTS				Sed. Rate Hgb & HCT			
		Daily problems x 7 days – →					
ACTIVITY	Bedrest – Turn▶	PT @ bedside▶ Sit in chair – ▶ and/or dangle BID	To PT for Ambul.▶ (parallel bars) Commode activ. ▶ Elev. toilet seat	PUW – – – ▶ Crutches – – – – – – – – – – – – – – → Ambulation if appropriate Stairwalking In and out of car Ambul. with ▶ Ambul. in halls ▶QID or more ▶ Amb. with asst. walker to BR TID with POW with S asst. devise or crutches of staff Transfers			
MEDICATION	PCA or IM narcs or – – – – – – – – – – ▶ D/Cd IM narcs before – – – – – – – – – – ▶ Rx for pain pills Epi cath PT. PO narcs other Coumadin – ▶ Stool softners – ▶ IV antibiotics – – – – – – ▶ D/C Check on renew of home meds. – ▶						
TREATMENTS	Hemovac– – – – – – – – – – ▶ D/Cd by MD TEDS (remove BID) – ▶ Encour. cough & deep breath q 2° x 24° then QID – – – – – – – – – – – – – – ▶ Incentive Spirometer q 1° x 24° then q 2° W/A – – – – – – – – – – – – – – – ▶ Abductor pillow – – – – – – – – – – – – – ▶ @ HS only (regular pillows during day) – – – – – – – – – ▶ Eggcrate matress – ▶ VS routine PO▶ VS q 4° – – ▶ VS QID if stable– – – – – – – – – – – – – – – – ▶						
DIET	Clear liquids ▶ Full liquid– ▶ Regular – ▶ or reg. as tol.						
D/C PLANS		Soc. Service to see	Start NH referral if appropriate or alert Home Health	OT to eval ADLs	Encourage family to attend Pt. sessions		

TEACHING	PT teaches – ▶
	exercises
	
	No abduction
	or internal
	rotation of hip
		Continuous encouragement – – – – – – – – ▶ Home exercises given – – – – – – – – – – – ▶
		and reinforce exercises by to Pt.
		staff Reinforce use – ▶
		                                of walker
		Pivot transfers
		Reinforce restrictions – ▶ D/C Instruction
		                                            sheet & antibiotic
		                                            sheet given to Pt.
		                                            F/U in 4 wks.
		                                            PRN narcotics					

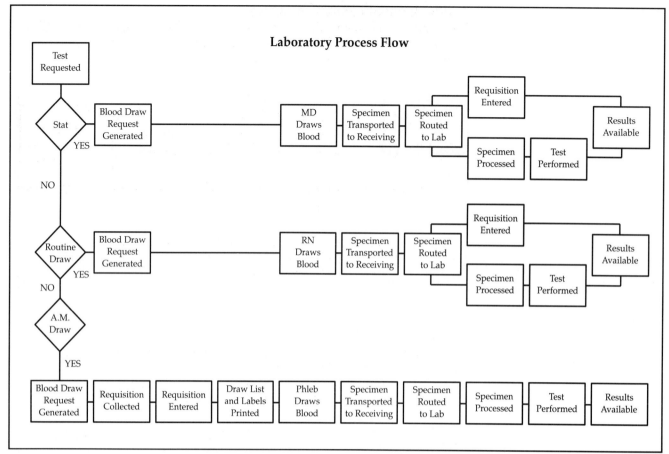

Figure 7.3. Operations improvement

| | SURGERY DAY | POST-OPERATIVE DAYS | | | | | |
		1	2	3	4	5	6
TESTS							
ACTIVITY							
MEDICATION							
TREATMENTS							
DIET							
DISCHARGE PLANS							
TEACHING							

Figure 7.4. Example of a general surgical path

2. Check sheets/activity sampling

To counteract the inevitable vagueness at the outset of problem solving, check sheets are useful to quickly and easily generate data for further analysis. Simple steps in activity sampling involve:

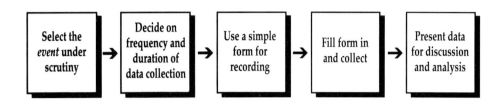

This allows a simple way of not only having information to base further problem solving and analysis on, but also, usually, involves key operation staff in identifying the extent of a particular problem.

3. Histogram/graphs

Although data gives *some* indication of the extent of a problem, or attempt of extent of successful quality control, the next crucial step is to collect the same type of data periodically to see what variation takes place over time. Histograms show clearly the frequency with which a certain problem occurs. They are also useful in communicating to staff involved the extent of the problem. An example of missing health records on admission is a good example, as in Figure 7.5.

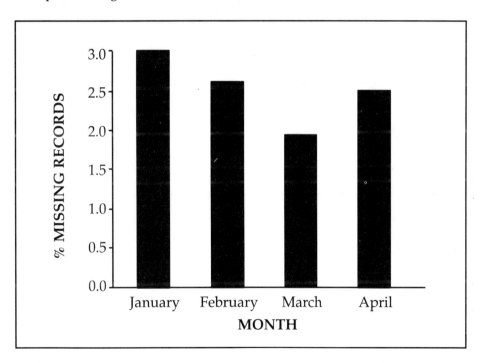

Figure 7.5. Example of a bar chart

4. Pareto Analysis

When a complex problem is analysed and several contributory causes found, it is useful to identify what variation can be attributed to each cause. Such an analysis — *pareto analysis* — can identify the main causes and prevent over-concentration on any one particular problem to the exclusion of others, due to the oversubjectivity of bias.

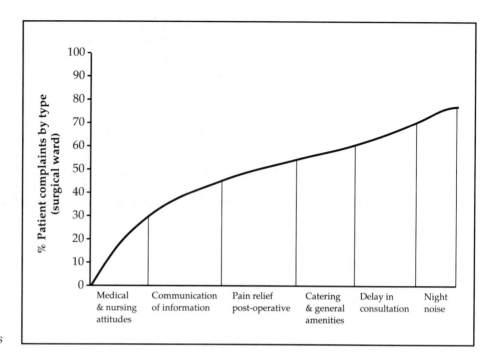

Figure 7.6. Pareto analysis

5. Cause and effect/fishbone analysis

The Ishikawa diagram is now widely used to investigate the several causes
which combine to produce a particular effect (good or bad). The use of group
discussion and brainstorming facilitate the creative production of ideas using
this format:

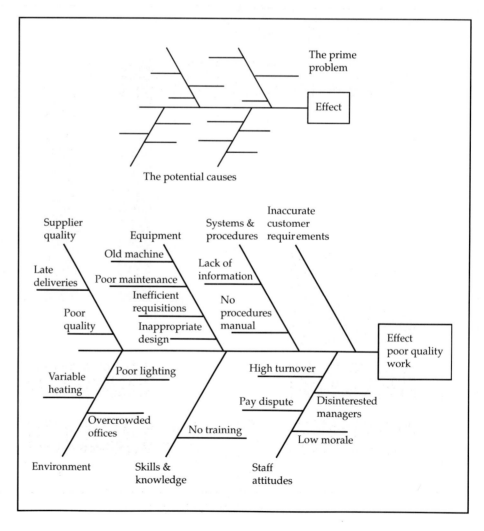

Figure 7.7. Fishbone analysis

These five different tools can be combined as a *package* to be used sensibly to tackle health care operational problems. An approach to activity/problem analysis has been used in Merton and Sutton Acute Unit and is shown in Figure 7.8 and Figure 7.9 respectively.

Acute Services Unit

REQUIREMENTS REVIEW FORM

Department

Location

Activity

Tick requirement type   Input ☐   Output ☐   Process ☐

Existing requirements	New requirements

Reasons for change in requirements

Requested   **Approved**

Date   **Date**

Figure 7.8. Acute Services Unit form

7 INPUT REQUIREMENTS
- Available 36 hours before session
- Session start time
- Legible
- Op time required
- Op name
- Patient name & no.
- Ward

6 SUPPLIER
- Theatre Sister
- Surgeon
- Med Sec
- ITU / CCU

5 INPUTS
- Theatre availability list
- Surgeons' ops list
- Operation equipment needs
- Nurse availability for special equipment
- ITU/CCU availability
- Session schedule forms

1 ACTIVITY

Scheduling a theatre session

SCOPE

Initial task: Contact Med Secs

Final task: Distribute typed schedule

2 OUTPUTS
- Typed session available

3 CUSTOMER
- Theatre Sister
- Anaesthetist
- ODA's
- Wards
- Path/Radio/Physio
- Haematology
- Porters
- Junior Doctors
- Surgeons

4 OUTPUT REQUIREMENTS
- Patient name & no.
- Operation
- Start/finish times
- Theatre no.
- Date
- Surgeon's name
- Ward name
- Legible
- Signed
- Distributed 24 hrs in advance
- Available session time filled
- Correct no. of copies

8 ACTIVITY REQUIREMENTS

Equipment	Policies/Procedures	Employee Skills
Typewriter?WP in order	Theatre allocation procedures	Hospital procedures
	Schedule distribution procedures	Theatre practice
		Knows all contact persons
		Knowledge of surgical procedures
		Scheduling priorities

Explanatory Notes

1. Activity
This should define the activity from a start point to a finish point (scope).

2. Outputs
Outputs are the materials, information and services you provide to customers.

3. Customers
Customers are the people to whom you provide the results of your activity.

4. Output Requirements
Establish requirements to which the output of the activity must conform.

Explanatory Notes

5. Inputs
Inputs are the materials or information you need in order to perform your activity.

6. Supplier
Suppliers are the people who provide you with the material and information to perform your activity.

7. Input Requirements
Establish requirements to which the inputs must conform before undertaking the activity.

8. Activity Requirements
Requirements which have to be satisfied for the process itself to operate correctly.

Figure 7.9. Acute Services Unit Activity Analysis Diagram

A second format is shown from a non-health organisation, Jaguar quality management department.

Figure 7.10

QUALITY MANAGEMENT
PROCESS IMPROVEMENT RECORD

Team Members

\#

\#

\#

JAGUAR

Team Members

\#

\#

\#

LSC	
Team leader	
PIL	

PROJECT TITLE

TQM
THE WAY
FORWARD

CONTINUOUS IMPROVEMENT

Problem Ref:

Date:

IMPROVED PROCESS

Process flow chart

Improvements adopted

Customers feedback

Statistical measures of improved process

Conclusions

Recommendations for further improvements

Date:

INVESTIGATIONS/ACTIONS TAKEN
(Supplementary pages to be attached to the Process Improvement Record)

Project Ref: ----------------

Project Title: ----------------

Supplement No: ----------------

Date: ----------------

Process flow chart
(Flow chart of partial improvement or any change from previous situation)

Observations/data collection/interpretation
(Briefly identify method of observations made including data collected. Name any dept. that made valuable contribution)

Progress made
(since last supplied)

Barriers/road blocks

Next action
(Identify the next set of actions or direction the team intends to follow)

Health care process variability

Examples: Two orthopaedic surgeons routinely carrying out standard hip replacement operations on fit adults: one takes 37 minutes, one takes 2 hours 30 minutes, with similar outcomes.

Two hospitals with similar management structures: one routinely has great difficulty making corporate decisions on any important issue on resource allocation/quality improvement: the second in most cases solves complex management problems with all senior staff feeling involved in the process and *owning* the decision whichever way it goes.

Question: How can this variability be addressed?

Process control procedures exist because of variables like the examples above; in hospital community services; in people, their practices; materials and consumables used; and services provided. Because health care is so dependent on people and *social* processes, the variability is usually even greater than in other services, such as manufacturing where machinery and instrumentation have a greater contribution to make. In most acute hospitals process control and consistency (the opposite of variation) are higher in services such as radiology, pathology, anaesthetics, medical physics, and some estates services than in other clinical and non-clinical services which rely less on scientific equipment, calibration, and ongoing maintenance and inspection.

If variability is great, it will be very difficult to predict if a service is being provided appropriately or acceptably.

However, it is important to control variability due to identifiable causes, not random variability. If a process varies in the way it is performed due to random variation, it may be impossible to reduce this.

The introduction and maintenance of *quality management systems*, which are aimed at reducing process variability and lead to continuous quality improvement have a big impact. How would (or does) your organisation achieve the following?

1.   Define procedures for *all* aspects of clinical and non-clinical services; and
2.   Ensure staff conform to these.

If a provider unit adopted these, its variation in service quality would be reduced as would its quality.

Monitoring and reporting

As a result of inspection, data on performance against explicit standards requires collation into a useful understandable format, whether for internal use at ward/directorate or unit level, or for external purposes in contract management. The simple form in Figure 7.11 was developed for this purpose. It allows a large number of quality variables to be considered (especially helpful in contract management) and three main areas of inspection of this data are:

- Areas of achievement (the majority);
- Areas of under-achievement (reasons, funding/training requirements (or improvement)); and
- Areas of over-achievement.

As part of the RCN *Standards of Care Project* (1991) two parts of the audit package covering the audit record and the audit summary are reproduced in Figures 7.12 and 7.13. They enable collation of large amounts of information and the practical consideration of action as a result of inspection.

Inter-clinician variability — always a sensitive issue — was examined in the Trent outpatient department standards project. The results of monitoring all surgical clinics held in one hospital during a pilot period are shown in Figure 7.14. They clearly illustrate the variability between consultants which needs further discussion between the consultants themselves as a first step.

This is a six month record (April – October) of performance on agreed quality standards.

	EXCEEDED	ACHIEVED	PARTIALLY ACHIEVED	NOT ACHIEVED	TARGET FOR ACHIEVEMENT

1.   Under five years of age

1.1   Every child will be offered a hearing test at the age of 8 months.

1.2   Every child will be offered development tests at the age of:

a) 8 months

b) 3 years

c) 4½ years

1.3   Every child will be offered immunisation and vaccination.

a) Diptheria, Tetanus and Polio at 18 months of age (95% target up take).

b) Pertussis vaccination (90% target up take).

c) Booster tetanus and Polio at 5 years of age.

d) M.M.R. (90% target up take).

Figure 7.11. Performance against explicit standards

AUDIT OBJECTIVE: Whether hospital environment & nursing activities enable pts/carers to understand and feel confident about caring for their plaster 24 hrs prior to discharge
PT / CARER SAMPLE: Every other pt/carer over a 4 week period
STAFF SAMPLE: Nil
WARD / ENV SAMPLE: 1 observation per week of the ward environment
AUDITORS: Nurse trained in plaster care
TIME FRAME: Apr – May 91
DATE:

KEY
Y = Yes N = No
NA = Not Applicable NR = Non-Response
E = Expected A = Actual

TARGET GROUP	CODE	1	2	3	4	5	6	7	8	9	10	Obs	Y	N	E	A	COMMENTS
Patients	O1a	Y	Y	Y	N	Y	N	N	Y	Y	Y	10	7	3	100	70	70% compliance: 20% did not understand nurse; 1 case very elderly patient, no relatives
	O1b	Y	Y	Y	N	Y	N	N	Y	Y	Y	10	7	3	100	70	
	O2a	Y	N	N	Y	Y	Y	Y	N	Y	Y	10	7	3	100	70	
	O2b	Y	Y	Y	N	Y	Y	Y	Y	Y	Y	10	10	0	100	100	
	O2c	Y	Y	Y	N	Y	Y	Y	Y	Y	Y	10	9	0	100	90	Elderly patient could not remember
	O3	Y	Y	Y	N	Y	Y	Y	Y	Y	Y	10	10	0	100	100	
	P1	Y	Y	NR	NR	NR	Y	Y	Y	Y	Y	7	7	0	100	100	Care plans not available at time of audit. No record of teaching for 1 patient transferred from another ward.
	P2	Y	Y	NR	NR	NR	N	Y	Y	Y	Y	7	6	1	100	90	
	P3	Y	N	N	N	N	Y	N	Y	Y	Y	10	5	5	100	50	Understanding of teaching programme not consistently recorded
	P5	NA	NA	Y	N	NA	Y	Y	Y	Y	Y	7	7	0	100	100	
Ward Environment	S1a	Y	Y	Y	Y							4	4	0	100	100	
	S1b	Y	Y	Y	Y							4	4	0	100	100	
	S1c	N	N	N	N							4	0	4	100	0	No trained plaster nurse around at night
	S2	Y	Y	Y	Y							4	4	0	100	100	
	S5	Y	Y	Y	Y							4	4	0	100	100	
	S6	Y	Y	Y	Y							4	4	0	100	100	
	S3a	Y	Y	N	Y							4	3	1	100	75	Facilities closed once for decoration
	S3b	Y	Y	N	Y							4	3	1	100	75	No answer once – on holiday
	S4	Y	Y	N	Y							4	3	1	100	75	Medical students in room 1 that week

Figure 7.12. Audit record

Audit Summary

AUDIT OBJECTIVE: To find out whether the hospital environment and nursing activities enable patients/carer to understand and feel confident looking after their plaster 24 hours prior to discharge

TIME FRAME: 1.4.91 – 1.5.91

SAMPLE: Every other patient/carer over a 4 week period; 1 observation per week of the ward environment

AUDITORS: Nurse trained in plaster care

DATE:

ACTIVITY	FINDINGS	CONCLUSIONS
Patient teaching and preparation for discharge	70% of patients could explain their care and possible complications. One elderly patient was unable to remember.	Find out what happens to confused/elderly with no apparent carers. The other two did not appear to understand the nurse properly.
	The teaching area was not always available.	There may be a need to negotiate for the use of the room.
	70% of patients had out-patients appointments.	There may be a problem with the distribution of cards.
Recording of care	Care plans are not readily available (30% sample).	This could be a problem when nurses start shifts. Where are the care plans?.
	50% of care plans showed evidence that the nurse checked that the patient understood the teaching programme. Other 50?!	There is a need to ensure that the patients listen and understand the teaching programme. Check programme and teaching methods.
Availability of staff	There was no nurse trained in plaster available on the night shift.	Need to do something about night cover.
	25% of time, there were no after care personnel around. On holiday.	Holiday cover?

© RCN Standards of Care Project 1991

Figure 7.13. Audit summary

STANDARDS	CONSULTANT			
	A	B	C	D
4) Acknowledgement was sent an average of	9 days	2 days	N / A	N / A
5) Waiting time for non-urgent appointments	3 weeks	14 weeks	4 weeks	11 weeks
6) Notice given for non-urgent appointments [1]	3 weeks	14 weeks	4 weeks	11 weeks
8) Non-attenders at clinics	5%	7.5%	7.9%	5.4%
9) Appointments changed by hospital	10%	2.4%	10%	16%
13) Average delay in start of clinic	22 mins	10 mins	15 mins	9 mins
14) Percentage of unavailable test results	2.8%	0%	0%	0%
15) Percentage of unavailable case notes at start throughout clinic	2% 1.5%	4% 2.5%	0% 0%	2% 0.5%
17) Average delay in clinic finishing	24 mins	35 mins	5 mins	35 mins
18) Percentage of patients seen by consultant	28%[2]	47%	100%	50%
23) Clinic letters were typed within an average of	6 days	5 days	3 days	4 days

Notes

[1] The amount of notice given reflects the average waiting time for non-urgent appointments, as waiting time is calculated from the time the appointment letter is sent out, until date of the appointment

[2] Consultant A, absent during one clinic

Figure 7.14. Results of monitoring of all surgical clinics which were held during the pilot period

Much has been written about the importance of clinical audit, integrated clinical audit, and multidisciplinary team work. Central funding in 1990-91 and 1991-92 went a long way to stimulate the collaboration of medical, nursing and PAM professionals in development models for inspecting and monitoring of care.

A more recent venture has explored how pharmacists — a clinical service specialty — can collaborate with doctors to improve prescribing as shown in Figures 7.15 and 7.16 (Eccles 1992; *A Better Pill* 16 April 92):

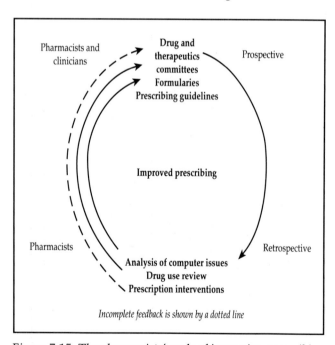

Figure 7.15. The pharmacists' cycle of improving prescribing

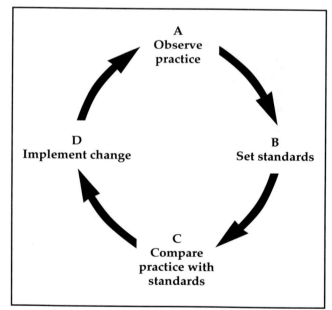

Figure 7.16. Where the pharmacist can contribute to the audit cycle

Collaborative care planning audit for cholsystectomy patients referred to in Chapter 5 is shown in Figures 7.17 and 7.18. It is an example of multidisciplinary audit (see Figure 7.19). Many of these processes are included in the clinical audit programme.

Coventry Community Care Unit

COLLABORATIVE CARE PLAN AUDIT FOR CHOLECYSTECTOMY PATIENTS

		YES	NO	WHY	PERCENT
1.	Were all patients over 65 years old seen at Pre-Admission clinic?				
2.	Was the patient's documentation completed according to the Community Nursing Service Policy?				
3.	Did the patient receive advice as Nursing Care Plan?				
4.	Did the patient have the need for pain relief considered and met?				
5.	By discharge had the patient followed the Collaborative Care Plan and been de-sutured on the 10th day where achievable?				
6.	Did the patient reach the expected level of recovery to be discharged by District Nursing Service on the 10th day?				
7.	By discharge did the patient understand the recovery period and possible complications which may arise and what actions to take?				
8.	By discharge did the patient feel confident that physical and psychological needs had been met where achievable?				

Figure 7.17. Collaborative care plan audit

Acute Unit Collaborative Care Plan for Cholesystectomy – Audit Report

Name: _____   Reg No: _____   Consultant: _____   Sex: Male / Female

Date of Admission: __/__/__

Date of Discharge: __/__/__

OUTCOME OF OBJECTIVES

	Achieved	Not Achieved	Comment
MEDICAL			
1. The patient will be admitted to hospital on the planned admission day			
2. Prior to theatre the patient and family will have had the opportunity to discuss their surgery, care and possible risks with the multidisciplinary team as appropriate			
3. In relation to the care plan the physical and psychological needs of the patient will be met			
4. The patient will be medically fit for discharge on the third post-operative day			
NURSING			
5. The patient will have attended a preadmission clinic			
6. All post-operative equipment will have been checked and prepared ready for use			
7. The patient will have had the need for pain relief considered and met			
8. By discharge the patient will understand the process of wound healing, possible complications and the action to take			
9. By discharge the patient will have followed the investigatory plan			
10. The patient documentation will be completed according to the hospital policy			
11. The patient will have had the information booklet fully explained to them			
PHYSIOTHERAPY			
12. Prior to theatre the patient will demonstrate breathing, circulatory and supported coughing exercises			
THEATRE STAFF			
13. The patient will have had a pre-post operative visit			
DIETARY			
14. The patient will receive dietary advice			

Figure 7.18. Collaborative care plan — audit report

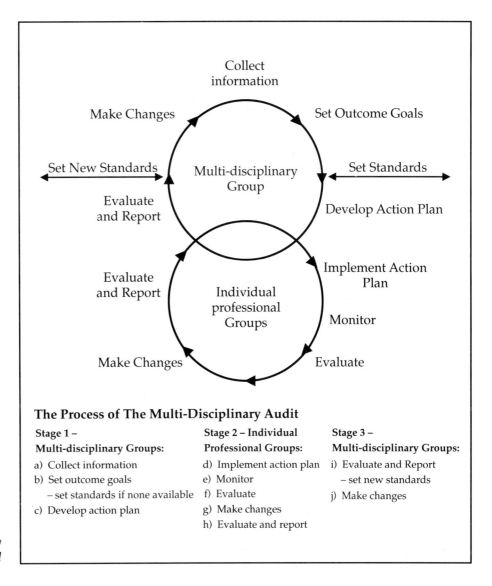

The Process of The Multi-Disciplinary Audit

Stage 1 – Multi-disciplinary Groups:	Stage 2 – Individual Professional Groups:	Stage 3 – Multi-disciplinary Groups:
a) Collect information	d) Implement action plan	i) Evaluate and Report – set new standards
b) Set outcome goals – set standards if none available	e) Monitor	j) Make changes
c) Develop action plan	f) Evaluate	
	g) Make changes	
	h) Evaluate and report	

Figure 7.19. Multidisciplinary audit model

CLINICAL AUDIT PROGRAMME

Patient Trails and Key Clinical Process Analysis

It is important to define explicitly clinical and patient care processes or 'trails' to identify weaknesses or areas for improvement in quality of care and/or service. Three related approaches are outlined here which may be of use.

They are: a) Patient Trailing & Identification of Quality Indicators
b) Standard Setting & Monitoring
c) Specific Outcome Identification

Each will be described briefly and can easily be adapted to fit particular clinical area audit requirements.

a) Patient Trailing

Here the main steps in one or more patient care processes are identified and the particular patient quality indicators labelled.

A typical overview of the patient trail is outline below with some key quality indicators already identified. These indicators come from three sources: The Government's Patient Charter (PC), the March Workshop and Dr Koch's previous experience.

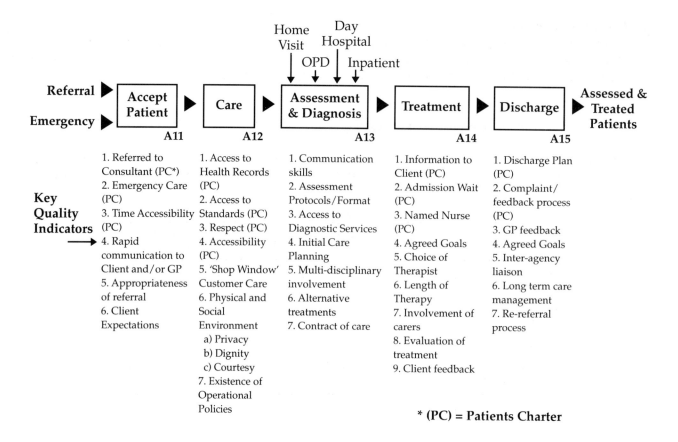

1. Referred to Consultant (PC*)
2. Emergency Care (PC)
3. Time Accessibility (PC)
4. Rapid communication to Client and/or GP
5. Appropriateness of referral
6. Client Expectations

1. Access to Health Records (PC)
2. Access to Standards (PC)
3. Respect (PC)
4. Accessibility (PC)
5. 'Shop Window' Customer Care
6. Physical and Social Environment
  a) Privacy
  b) Dignity
  c) Courtesy
7. Existence of Operational Policies

1. Communication skills
2. Assessment Protocols/Format
3. Access to Diagnostic Services
4. Initial Care Planning
5. Multi-disciplinary involvement
6. Alternative treatments
7. Contract of care

1. Information to Client (PC)
2. Admission Wait (PC)
3. Named Nurse (PC)
4. Agreed Goals
5. Choice of Therapist
6. Length of Therapy
7. Involvement of carers
8. Evaluation of treatment
9. Client feedback

1. Discharge Plan (PC)
2. Complaint/ feedback process (PC)
3. GP feedback
4. Agreed Goals
5. Inter-agency liaison
6. Long term care management
7. Re-referral process

Key Quality Indicators

* (PC) = Patients Charter

A1 Clinical Activity
Each of these 'boxes' eg. Accept Patient (A11) can themselves be developed/expanded to explore in greater detail quality indicators in that area. Two further examples are available.

Possible Local Action No 1
Use this format, either as it is, or amended for local use to identify key quality indicators for further discussion and/or standard setting.

b) Standard Setting and Monitoring

Once particular Quality indicators have been identified, an important next step is the setting up an **agreed**, **achieved** and **measurable** standard(s) for each indicator to increase **consistently** high quality care or service. A single approach is shown in the Table 7.1 with definitions and an example.

INDICATOR	STANDARD	MEASURABLE INDICATOR	TARGET	MONITORING
Definitions A short phrase identifying the topic (1–3 words)	A sentence identifying standard being achieved/aimed for	What will be measured to know the standard is being achieved	Either/both a) Numerical target to be achieved b) Date	Person, method and frequency of how performance will be monitored
Examples Individual Care Planning	Each patient admitted will have a Care Plan written within 48 hours	a) Completed Care Plan b) Time of completion from time of admission	100% within 48 hours	Nurse Manager Review of five Care Plans per area Monthly

Table 7.1

Possible Local Action No 2
Use this format, and discuss, agree and set achievable standards (one or more) for as many topics as you have time. It does **not** have to be time-consuming. Try and set a timetable for what indicators will have standards set by when. It can't all be done at once but equally does not have to take years!

c) Specific Outcome Identification and Monitoring

To ensure audit is grounded firmly in **outcome** measurements, each clinical area could identify five key **positive** and five key **negative** outcome indicators which could be regularly monitored. Examples are given below with a useful format.

Negative Indicators	Is Data Available?	Data Collected by:	Data Reported on when:
1. Violent incidents on ward 2. DNA's in day hospital or OPD 3. Deliberate self harm while in treatment 4. Complaints 5. Serious drug reactions			
Positive Indicators			
1. Patient satisfaction 2. Treatment goal attainment 3. Symptom relief 4. Return to work 5. Improved communication or relationships			

Possible Local Action No 3
Identify five positive and five negative outcomes relevant to your own clinical area and use this format to set up how to monitor these (or some of them).

Specialty Action Plan

Having considered the foregoing information, please discuss and agree an action plan for how audit can proceed in your clinical area. There is no one effective method. It will depend on what type of audit has already taken place and the nature of the clinical area. Some of the 'possible local action' suggestions may be helpful to consider. Please ensure one of your specific actions is to review quarterly the 'so what' question ie, how have we improved our service using audit?

Specific Actions	Completed Date	Responsibility

1.

2.

3.

4.

5.

6. Quarterly Review

Please return a copy of this completed back page to the Clinical Director, to help him be aware of progress being made and to provide appropriate support when necessary or requested. A follow-up workshop is being planned with Dr Hugh Koch for later this year (October/November). It is likely that progress with audit plans can be discussed at that workshop, if you want this.

Thank you.

References

Bennett J & Walshe K (1990) Occurrence Screening as a Method of Audit, *BMJ* 300, 1248-1250
Harman D & Martin G (1991) *Medical Audit & The Manager*, HSMC, University of Birmingham
Koch H C H (1991) *TQM in Health Care*, Longman, Harlow
Koch H C H (1992) *Clinical Audit: A Practical Framework*, South Warwickshire

Inspection and monitoring, in whatever service, should not be an end in itself. However, it should be a quality process itself and its own variation — the variation of the measurement/audit process — should be reduced to a minimum. This necessitates an understanding of variation in measurement due to:

- Human factors — skill and repeatability of the monitoring, — officer/manager and his/her measurement process;
- Precision of any technical or administrative technique or equipment; and
- Variation in sampling techniques.

NHS staff find this area of TQM a little difficult to accept immediately. However, experience shows that tools outlined in this chapter are potentially of great utility in controlling wasteful variation in health care.

Questions: How could you use brainstorming and cause and effect analysis? Would it help solve:
- Car parking problem?
- Waiting list management?
- Medical bed problem?

How could you use pareto analysis? Would it help with:
- Nursing health record problem?
- Errors in invoices to suppliers?

Would Histograms be useful in monitoring:
- Staff casual sickness rates?
- Percentage complete postcoding?

Provider units are beginning to understand that process control techniques are an integral and important part of TQM and a key source of *quality improvement* information.

Progress in reduction in the variability of any health care process will lead to a diminishing range of values in that process. For example the operating time of two orthopaedic surgeons will gradually converge as a result of inspecting the process with them as Figure 7.20 illustrates.

Poka-yoke (mistake-proofing) — a system developed by Skigeo Shingo — links the three aspects of quality control:

- Zero defects;
- Poka-yoke; and
- Source inspections.

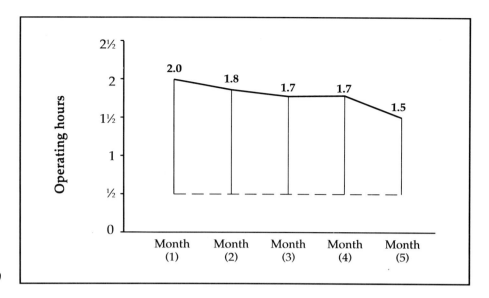

Figure 7.20

In poka-yoke, errors are examined once identified — *there and then*. In other words, the service delivery is stopped and immediate analysis of the problem occurs to identify the process problem and prevent it from happening again. For example:

Scene: Seminar in Hospital 11 am. Coffee ordered.

Action: No coffee arrives.
Catering service contacted. Apologies for omission.
Coffee arrives 11.25 am.
Trainer contacts catering manager at lunchtime who requests written information about problem. Trainer resists this prevarication and instead discusses with the catering manager the lack of process controls, supervision, and inspection of prepared *orders* within the catering department. The result is improved process and tea arrives at 3.15 pm as ordered!

Poka-yoke concept has similarities to *foolproofing* in which an operation is built into the process which can only be performed if previous aspects have also been performed. An example on a surgical ward would be to obviate many of the completion of discharge summary problems by ensuring that patients could only go home once the discharge summary had been completed by the junior medical staff!!

Conclusion

Quality is not a matter of chance — each health care episode, whether in the community or in a hospital, consists of several subprocesses and many items of clinical and non-clinical activity. These processes have been developed by professionals over many years and need to be tested, monitored, and increasingly precisely defined. This is the main, if not only way, to ensure that the patients (and other customers) have full confidence in the correct functioning of their hospital or community service.

Each process requires *cataloguing* or *documenting* with clear, explicit details of the characteristics of that process. Continuous inspection and modifications/corrective action ensures that improvement in design of health care is always being incorporated and communicated to all staff.

Meticulous compliance with specification is not a stultifying procedure stifling clinical innovations — it is the most important part of the NHS quality. Uncompromising standards are already held by doctors and nurses and others. TQM and process control have a high priority in maintaining and increasing these standards.

Chapter 8 Problem solving and Quality Improvement Teamwork (QIT)

Structure for incisive management and teamwork

Good, effective *general management* has been epitomised, in theory and practice by a *bias for action* by managers with personal accountability for their own and their staff's performance. However, good managers, like good parents if they expect 100 per cent success within resources from their organisation they are doomed to failure, not abject failure, but failure nevertheless. For even with the most clear, well thought out management structure and approach, the mere existence of a top-hierarchical approach, however beneficial to delivering health care and service, will stultify the creativity and innovations of staff. It is therefore not at all surprising that before, during, and since the introduction of *general management* into the NHS, teams of individuals often from different background/functions have spent time together in delivering *quality services* and solving ongoing operational problems as they arise. Such teams come to mind as:

- Nursing ward team;
- M/D clinical team;
- Management team;
- Clinical directorate team; and
- CMH team.

The better the function of these teams, at both the *task* level and *social/emotional/relationship* level, the higher the team performance. However, despite the best intentions of those involved in these teams and those to whom (hopefully) these teams are accountable, certain characteristics creep in which are antithetical to high performance and creative problem solving:

- Hierarchical levels of power, status and apparent importance;
- Lack of involvement of junior staff;
- Lack of involvement in *clinical* teams of non-clinical staff (and *vice-versa*); and
- Overabundance of management tasking, and less creative brainstorming and problem solving.

For this reason many organisations in general and provider health care units in particular have been ensuring that the strategy for establishing some *controlled subversion* via the introduction of *quality improvement teams* is built in to the strategy. This is either as a one-off pilot scheme or as comprehensive *quality improvement team* (QIT) per operational area plan. There are very many ways in which QITs can be built into the unit, as shown in Figure 8.1:

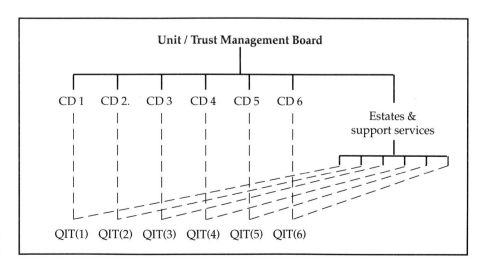

Figure 8.1. Quality improvement teams

The main advantages of these teams, some of which it must be said are apparent in line-management teams are:

- Ability to solve a large variety of problems, especially cross functional ones;
- Problems are addressed from many different standpoints/experiences; and
- Boosts satisfaction and morale of staff through their involvement.

When such teams are up and running, units find that the process of problem solving become quicker and more efficient. The word *empowerment* is frequently used on a cornerstone of TQM — the ability of an organisation to *empower* staff at every level to feel part of the *quality improvement/problem solving* approach whenever appropriate is a crucial element. QITs embody this notion of empowerment.

What does Empowerment mean to you as a Manager?

- Would you be happy for all your staff to *make* sensible suggestions for *quality improvement*? *Yes/No*

- Would you be happy for your staff to *carry out* sensible suggestions for *quality improvement*? *Yes/No/Yes, but*

- Do you *know* what suggestions your staff have made recently? *Yes/No*

- Do you show them you feel their ideas are good and well worthwhile? *Yes/No*

- How?_____

- Would you take the *risk* of letting your staff implement and learn from implementing a silly idea, once in every fifty occasions? *Yes/No*

Dramatic improvements have been made in the private sector (eg Rolls Royce, Marks and Spencer) and the public sector services (eg NHS) by the introduction of QITs in recent years. It is not *just another way* of managers getting problems solved: it is a creative, voluntary, and highly energetic dimension to solving operational problems, which are often apparently resistant to the normal management process.

What are the benefits that can accrue from setting up QITs?

- Cuts across boundaries;
- Spreads understanding;
- Generates ownership;
- Taps skills and knowledge; and
- Develops people.

QITs, drawing directly on the knowledge and skill at ward/clinical/operational *shop floor* levels — are self-directing, yet still a full part of the unit. As such it has been described as 'dramatically opposed to the received wisdom of much General Management Policy' (Hutchinson 1991). Their main claim to fame is that they empower and *involve* people.

Role of communication in teamwork

Irrespective of the existence of specific QITs, teamwork of any sort in health care delivery is based on effective communication. For in-depth coverage of this topic the reader is referred to Koch (1991). Failure to communicate properly and effectively creates unnecessary problems and leads to poor operational performance.

Perhaps the most powerful method of communication is by example: by individual members of staff's own personal commitment to *quality*, for example by:

- A positive approach and attitude to *quality improvement*;
- Our *quality* behaviour in our own area of work;
- Standards of general personal behaviour and standard of our own work; and
- Our willingness to value and reward our own staff.

Focusing this personal commitment onto communicating our interest in quality for health care delivery and service is essential. Here are some ideas:

1. Posters and poster campaigns

Before you groan, many hospitals are finding that posters, small or large, can be an important part of how they communicate the *quality* message to staff (and patients, and relatives). Small informative signs/labels appear in obvious and less obvious places.

Several companies now develop and market posters for quality improvement although they need to be customised to the NHS. They could easily be amended.

Poster campaigns need careful thought in terms of:

- Location (situation, level);
- Messages;
- Objectives; and
- Matching posters to staff awareness;
- Training.

A series of customised charts for the NHS has been developed by the author and is available from him. Successful communications using posters necessitate continually changing and improving the quality messages being broadcast with new posters on a periodic basis.

> The next person
> through this door
> is *your* customer

> Poor quality
> costs money

> Quality starts
> here

> Delight your
> patient!

> Get 'it' right
> first time

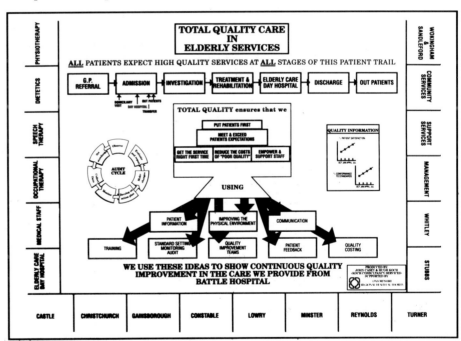

2. Customised booklets

To keep staff up to date with more in depth information that can be achieved by poster (possibly linked to training opportunities) is the use of booklets giving information, description, tools, and techniques and examples of their use.

Total Quality Management International have produced a series of *Handbook, Pocket Book of Tools and Techniques, Project Team Leaders Pocket Book*, which are well worth considering, although again need to be customised to the health care sector. See Figure 8.2.

INTERNATIONAL

Total Quality Management

Pocket Book of
Tools and Techniques

INTERNATIONAL

Total Quality Management

Project Team Leaders
Pocket Book

INTRODUCTION

This pocket book contains our definition of Total Quality Management and explains the basic principles behind TQM.

It also contains guidelines on the use of many of the Tools and Techniques which can be used as part of the Total Quality Improvement Process.

It provides for each technique a summary of:
- What is it?
- When do we use it?
- Why do we use it?
- How do we use it?

and is intended as a handy reference for members of Total Quality Project Teams and others involved in the Total Quality process.

*Figure 8.2.
Customised
booklets cont'd*

3. Suggestion schemes/boxes

Many hospitals have tried this idea with varying success. In a Unit where *total quality* was well accepted staff will use the opportunity to tell *management* about a new idea with the confidence of knowing that the idea will be seriously considered and either implemented, or returned with an explanation as to why it was not felt appropriate. Publicity and recognition are given to these ideas — whether implemented or not.

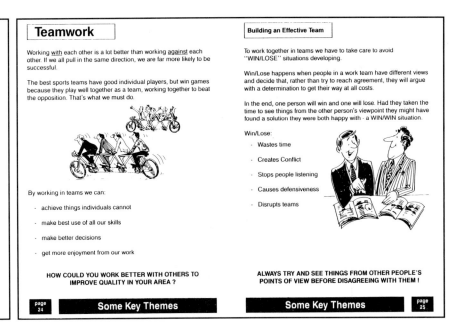

cont'd. Figure 8.2

4. In-house newsletters

To achieve *regular* communication of the *quality improvement* message is often a daunting task. The in-house newsletter is an effective way of communicating to *all* staff the recent success stories in increasing quality of health care. It helps to maintain enthusiasm and momentum, generates new ideas and *cross-fertilises* old ideas.

The innovations and creativity of the Newsletter editor is crucial. An example is shown in Figure 8.3.

Figure 8.3. Newsletter

Medical Records Services ALTNAGELVIN GROUP OF HOSPITALS

'ACTION — QUALITY'

Services for Patients include Medical Records Library and Admissions/Appointments functions, Medical Secretarial services and Ward Clerical activities, all of which are vital to the smooth delivery of high quality care and service here at Altnagelvin.

In order to maintain and help improve these many services, we have developed a "Quality Improvement Group" (Q.I.G.) which includes:

Kathy Funston   Ward Clerk Ward 1
Geraldine Carr   Personal Secretary, Main Block Surgical
Breda Campbell   Appointments Services
John Havord   Medical Records Library
Catherine Gillen Paying Patients and 'Front Line' Services
Marie Dunne   Patient Services Manager

and the support of Hugh Koch, Management Consultant in Quality Management. This Team intends to meet fortnightly and its objectives are as follows:

- to increase staff satisfaction within the services specified.
- to increase staff satisfaction of 'users' of the specified services.
- to increase patient satisfaction with aspects of Medical Records they encounter.
- to help establish and agree service standards and how to measure our performance against these standards.
- to ensure the best use is made of our resources.

- to continuously improve by helping to solve operational problems as they arise.

Progress so far

Following the initial meeting we have agreed the following:
- to identify main issues/problems in each part of Medical Records.
- to identify the effects of these problems, potential solutions to the problems, and obstacles/constraints which might prevent these solutions being successful.
- to plan the specification of standards and their monitoring.
- to ensure all Medical Records staff know about 'Managing Quality Improvement' and feel able to contribute.

How can you help?

We know that 'Quality is part of everyone's job' – most, if not all, staff have already been working to improve services wherever possible.

However it is intended that the Q.I.G. team will help to accelerate this process.

Attached to this progress bulletin is a sheet which is provided for you to jot down any Quality Improvement issues which you would like the Team to address, what effects you feel these issues have on ourselves and on our service provision, and any possible solutions together with any obstacles which you think might be in the way. When you have completed this form pass it on to one of the Team members who will raise you issues at our next meeting.

Regular newsletters like this will be issued to advise you of progress.
Thank you!

Controlled subversion — Quality improvement team (QIT)/circle/action team

A QIT is a cross-functional, multidisciplinary team working on one or more problems which typically affect more than one department. It can either be temporary/time limited — to be disbanded once a problem is resolved — or continuous/permanent — to continually address problems and improve service quality. The establishing and monitoring of QIT's involves several issues:

- Strategic vision — QIT as part of TQM;
- Understanding of quality improvement (QI) process;
- Selection of QIT members;
- Skills in problem solving, QIT — tools and techniques;
- Leadership and meeting management skills;
- Training;
- Documentation and reporting; and
- Overcoming obstacles.

Many of these issues are dealt with in Koch and Sabugueiro (1992) article *Trust in Teams*.

1. Strategic vision

As mentioned at the outset of this chapter, the development of QIT should not be seen as a one-off initiative. It is an integral part of a TQM approach which is established with commitment from senior managers and clarity of objectives, supported by training as required. It has greatest effect when set up as a *Total* project, ie QIT in each main operational service (eg surgery, medicine, outpatient department).

2. Understanding of quality improvement (QI) process

The greater the understanding by QIT members of the QI process the better. However, this takes time and will not occur necessarily until after several, if not many, QIT meetings. However, QIT members need to be aware of:

- General aims of QI
  - Increase staff satisfaction working in Service.
  - Specify and agree standards of service.
  - Measure and increase conformance to standards.
  - Decrease costs of 'poor quality'.
  - Increase 'Internal' and 'External' Customer satisfaction.
  - Increase awareness of staff of Quality.
  - Develop continuous Quality Improvement Process in Quality Improvement Team.
- Main aspects of QI; and
- Main steps to *quality action* via QIT.

See Figures 8.4 to 8.7. An example of how one Social Services Director 'started the ball rolling' to develop *quality action groups* is shown in Figure 8.8.

3. Selection of QIT members

This illustration in Figure 8.9 outlines the groups to consider when looking at selection.

In terms of internal unit staff who will take up, typically eight of the group places (eight is the magic number for a group with variations between five and ten), the following characteristics need to be taken into account:

- Any *major* group of staff needs to be represented, eg medical, nursing;
- Members should be picked for their creativity and positive approach to problem solving;
- Grade should *not* be relevant — the better groups have a mixture of grade/ skill; and
- Volunteers.

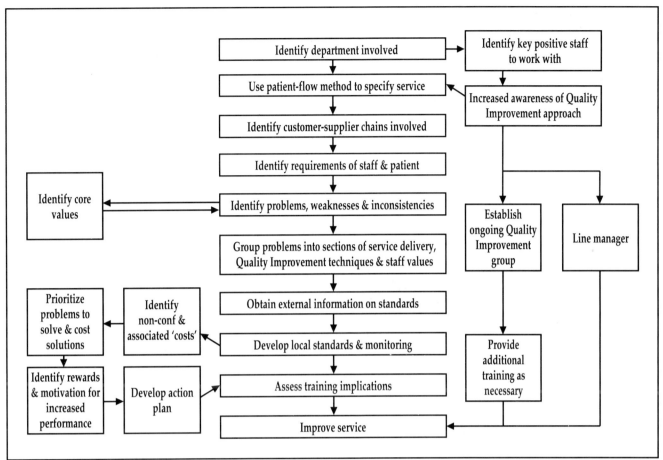

Figure 8.4. Service quality
improvement process

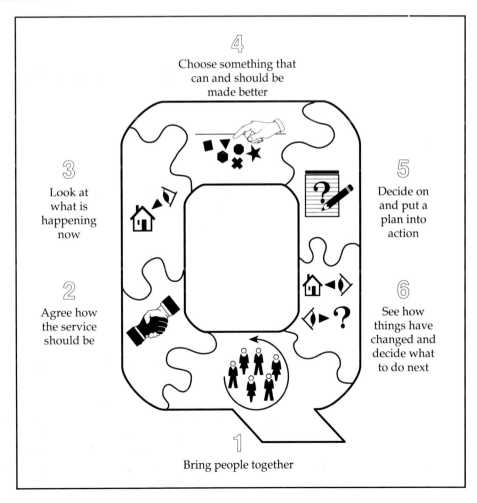

Figure 8.5. Six steps to quality
action

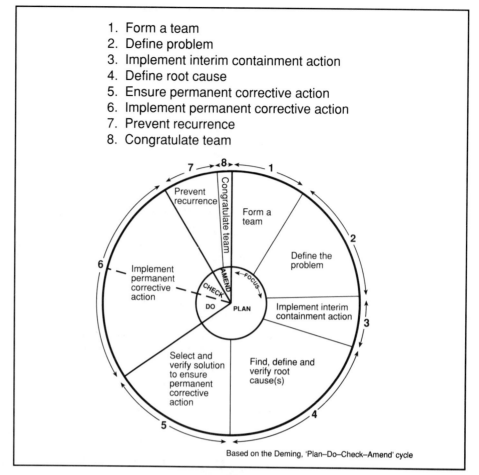

1. Form a team
2. Define problem
3. Implement interim containment action
4. Define root cause
5. Ensure permanent corrective action
6. Implement permanent corrective action
7. Prevent recurrence
8. Congratulate team

Based on the Deming, 'Plan–Do–Check–Amend' cycle

Figure 8.6. The Eight Step Problem Solving Approach

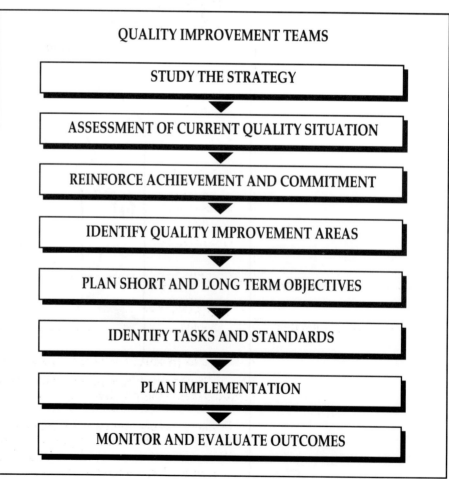

QUALITY IMPROVEMENT TEAMS

STUDY THE STRATEGY

ASSESSMENT OF CURRENT QUALITY SITUATION

REINFORCE ACHIEVEMENT AND COMMITMENT

IDENTIFY QUALITY IMPROVEMENT AREAS

PLAN SHORT AND LONG TERM OBJECTIVES

IDENTIFY TASKS AND STANDARDS

PLAN IMPLEMENTATION

MONITOR AND EVALUATE OUTCOMES

Figure 8.7. Implementing the strategy

MEMO

Date: 25 April
To: Director of Social Services
From: Harry Carr, Training Officer
Re: Quality Action Groups

I would like to confirm my intention to develop Quality
Action groups in the Willows Day Centre and 35 Craddock
Street. This will involve myself and Sue Anderson sharing
the role of coordinator, with the first-line managers
acting as group leaders. This will involve considerable
time and commitment from the four of us, as well as from
the group members. I also expect that the QA groups will
have implications for service management in terms of
proposals for changes in policy and practice, requests for
more resources, etc.

The benefits which we anticipate from running QA groups
include:
- A clear operational definition of the aims and methods
  of the two services concerned.
- A better fit of service to individual need and therefore
  an improved quality of life for service users.

Figure 8.8. Memo

Checklist — who I want in the group, and why

It may be helpful to use this checklist to think about who you want in the group, and why.

	Who	*Why*
Service users		
Advocates		
Staff		
Relatives		
Others		
Group leader		
Co-ordinator		
Total group size		

Figure 8.9. QIT members

4. Skills in problem solving, tools and techniques

Gradually as a result of support, raising awareness, and training, members should develop these skills:

- Problem solving approach: see Figures 8.10 and 8.13;
- Tools and techniques: see Figures 8.11 and 8.12;
- With reference and simple exercises which aid brainstorming and are not complicated, eg weightlifting exercise: see Figure 8.14 and 8.15.

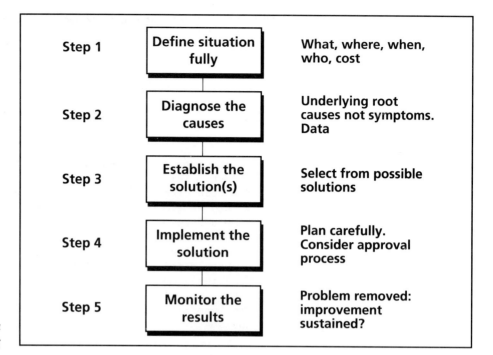

Figure 8.10. Systematic approach to problem solving

SYSTEMATIC PROBLEM SOLVING	DATA COLLECTION
SYSTEMS AND PROCESSES	DESIGNING AN EXPERIMENT
PROCESS FLOW DIAGRAM	DISPLAYING DATA
BRAINSTORMING	PARETO ANALYSIS
CAUSE AND EFFECT ANALYSIS	ASSESSING SOLUTIONS
INFORMATION PLANNING	PLANNING IMPLEMENTATION

Figure 8.11. Quality Improvement tools and techniques

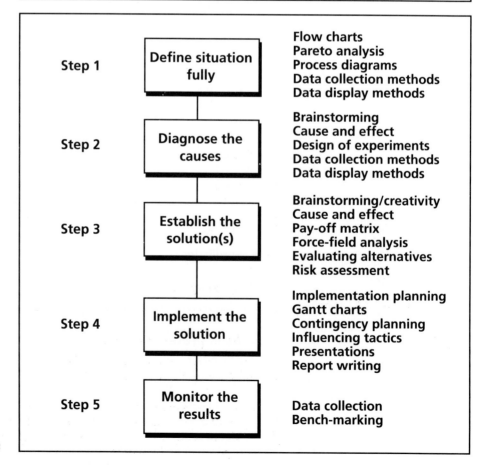

Figure 8.12. Problem solving tools

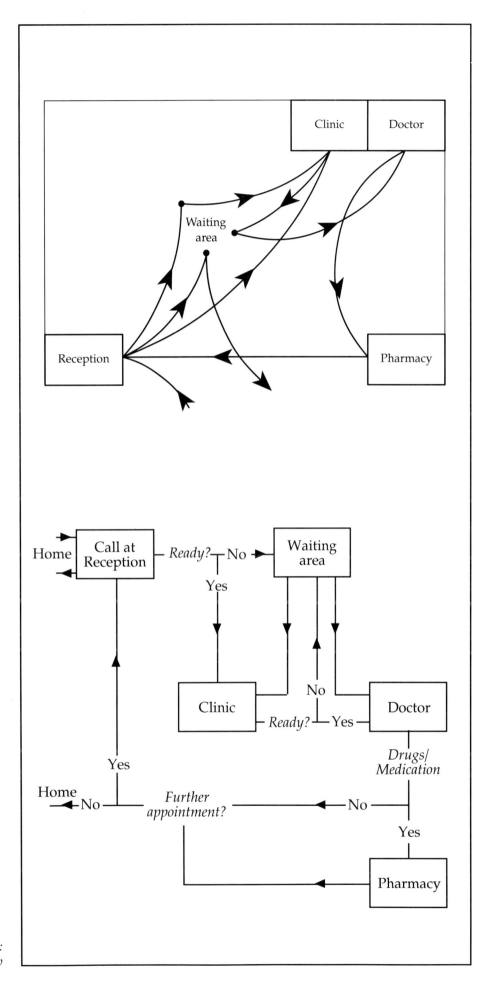

Figure 8.13. Process flow diagram:
work-flow

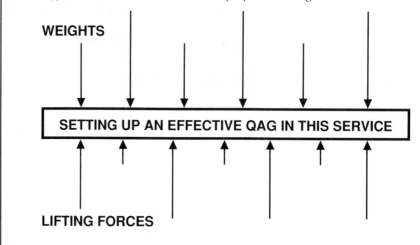

Weightlifting exercise

This exercise will help you get a clearer picture of forces for and against change in your organisation.

In the centre of a sheet of paper write the objective, e.g.: 'setting up an effective QAG in this service'. Think about all the forces against this happening (weights) and write these in above the box with arrows pressing down. You can give the strongest forces the thickest lines. Next think about all the forces that could help (lifting forces) and write these below the box with arrows pressing up.

Once you have got a clear picture of what you are up against, think about ways to **strengthen** the positive forces and **weaken** the negative ones. It may be helpful to do this exercise with other people in the organisation or service.

WEIGHTS

SETTING UP AN EFFECTIVE QAG IN THIS SERVICE

LIFTING FORCES

Figure 8.14. Weightlifting exercise

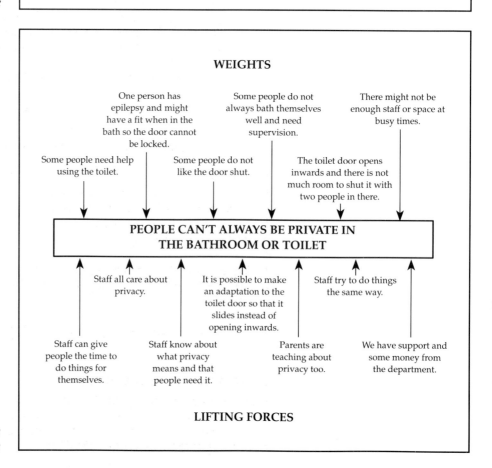

WEIGHTS

One person has epilepsy and might have a fit when in the bath so the door cannot be locked.

Some people do not always bath themselves well and need supervision.

There might not be enough staff or space at busy times.

Some people need help using the toilet.

Some people do not like the door shut.

The toilet door opens inwards and there is not much room to shut it with two people in there.

PEOPLE CAN'T ALWAYS BE PRIVATE IN THE BATHROOM OR TOILET

Staff all care about privacy.

It is possible to make an adaptation to the toilet door so that it slides instead of opening inwards.

Staff try to do things the same way.

Staff can give people the time to do things for themselves.

Staff know about what privacy means and that people need it.

Parents are teaching about privacy too.

We have support and some money from the department.

LIFTING FORCES

Figure 8.15. Weightlifting exercise
— example

5. Leadership and meeting management skills

All members of the QIT, and especially the leader (facilitator or coordinator) require interpersonal skills which enable them to lead and manage QIT meetings. Team Meetings are effective if:

- All members contribute verbally;
- Their contributions are seen as important and involved;
- The discussion stays on track;
- People listen; and
- Progress is regularly summarised.

Teams will be successful if helped by the leader to focus on:

- Effective communication;
- Focused problem solving;
- Good use of time; and
- Wish to be successful and action orientated.

If establishing the first agenda, this example can generate useful discussion:

66 *Suggested agenda*

Introductions

Explaining what Quality Action is and what QA groups do

What do people want — aims of the group

Planning the meetings:
- *who will chair them*
- *who will take minutes or notes about what goes on*
- *how will information be recorded and passed on*
- *ground rules of the group (things the group do and do not want to happen, like smoking, how decisions will be reached and so on)*
- *how often the group will meet, and what time of day suits everyone best*

Run through what has been discussed and decided at the meeting

Remind people of the date of the next meeting. **99**

Subsequent agendas, preferably informal, could include:

- Previous action update;
- Any discussion arising from this action;
- New items to discuss (small number);
- Review of action and next steps; and
- Date of next meeting.

Notes of meetings are important, if not essential, but QIT meetings should not become bureaucratic — they should be fun and action orientated. The best notes involve:

Topic	Issues	Action	Responsibility (Person/Date)

6. Training for QIT members

An important part of any quality strategy is to ensure training and support are available for those involved. An example of a three-day training programme consisting of two consecutive days, six-week gap, followed by a third training day, given to *all* members of *each* QIT is:

WHO SHOULD ATTEND?

The Workshops are organised as part of our Unit's "Towards Total Quality Management" Strategy. It is intended for members of the Quality Improvement Teams (for each Service and Estate and Support Services area). The first will be a two day Workshop and the second one day. Participants must ensure they can attend the whole three days.

OBJECTIVE

The Workshops are intended to develop an understanding of the role of Quality Improvement Teams and introduce participants to Quality Circles' techniques.

1st WORKSHOP — DAY ONE

10.00 A.M.	COFFEE/INTRODUCTION
10.10 A.M.	GETTING TO KNOW EACH OTHER
10.45 A.M.	UNDERSTANDING THE UNIT'S "TOWARDS TOTAL QUALITY MANAGEMENT" STRATEGY
11.15 A.M.	REASONS FOR INTRODUCING QUALITY IMPROVEMENT TEAMS (Q.I.T.)
11.45 A.M.	Q.I.T.s — SKILLS (PART ONE) • WORKING TOGETHER • BRAINSTORMING • DEALING WITH PROBLEMS IN GROUPS • COLLECTING DATA (PART 1)
12.45 P.M.	LUNCH
01.45 P.M.	PROBLEM ANALYSIS AND SOLVING
02.45 P.M.	PRECONDITIONS FOR STARTING A QUALITY CIRCLE (Q.C.)
03.30 P.M.	TEA AND END OF SESSION

1st WORKSHOP — DAY TWO

10.00 A.M.	COFFEE/PRESENTING SOLUTIONS TO MANAGEMENT
11.00 A.M.	STAFF EMPOWERMENT
11.45 A.M.	FORUM
12.45 P.M.	LUNCH
01.45 P.M.	PRACTICAL APPLICATION OF Q.I.T./Q.C. • FIRST IMPRESSIONS • IMPROVING INFORMATION
02.45 P.M.	ACTION PLANNING FOR SECOND WORKSHOP
03.30 P.M.	TEA AND END OF WORKSHOP

2ND WORKSHOP— DAY THREE

10.00 A.M.	COFFEE/FEEDBACK ON Q.I.T./Q.C.EXPERIENCE
11.00 A.M.	PROBLEMS IDENTIFIED IN EACH SERVICE
12.00 P.M.	COLLECTING DATA (PART 2) • FURTHER SKILLS AND TECHNIQUES
12.45 P.M.	LUNCH
01.45 P.M.	Q.I.T.s — (PART 2) • RELATIONSHIPS IN THE TEAM
02.30 P.M.	BENEFITS OF Q.I.T./Q.C.
03.15 P.M.	WHAT ARE THE NEXT STEPS/BENEFITS OF FURTHER TRAINING
03.30 P.M.	TEA
03.45 P.M.	EVALUATION AND END OF WORKSHOP

7. Communication mechanisms

This is an interesting issue. First of all, who establishes QITs? They sometimes develop spontaneously, ie an operational level need met by operational staff. They usually, however, are part of a unitwide, top-led TQM strategy and can appear to be management led. This implies the word *controlled* in controlled *subversion* in that the outcomes of the *subversion* should be somehow communicated/rather than reported back to senior managers. What power they feel they should exercise over these outcomes (actual or planned) is under-emphasised — equally, for the *subversion* to be fully active, managers should *not* exercise control, partial or otherwise!!

8. Overcoming obstacles

Some of the inevitable obstacles which face QITs are:

- *Lack of time for meetings* — this is both a real problem for busy staff and sometimes an unconscious resistance, even in volunteer, enthusiastic staff. Short regular meetings of an hour are better than long meetings with large time gaps in between.

- *Membership and inclusion of staff groups* — it has been noted that QIT membership can reflect ongoing interstaff problems eg lack of medical or support staff input. It is important to use the QIT process to include such excluded groups, if only for particular meetings and particular topics of relevance to them.

- *Us and them language* — a useful diagnostic test of a QIT group's *corporacy* is the frequency with which they use the words *they/them* in discussion. It is typically a reference to senior managers and/or clinicians. It implies a negative prejudice to their group who are described as if they are all identical, unhelpful, and not very likable. It stultifies honest discussion of problems and makes individual one-to-one action or communication less likely.

- *Lack of action* — the opposite to the *bias for action* often mentioned can afflict QITs as well as any other grouping. Interesting projects (like TQM, QITs etc) can become endlessly process-driven — never actually achieving the desired outcomes. A balance between short term superficial outcome and long term indepth outcome must be kept.

- *Poor communication* — destructive views, interruption, and rudeness can afflict the best!! Guard against this.

- *Senior management style* — bearing in mind the reason why QITs are essential, it is hardly surprising that one of the first obstacles which *is bound* to occur is the anxiety and difficulty of Senior Managers in accepting QITs authority on complex/controversial problems that have *baffled* managers in the past.

  One team facilitator who went to her manager with Solution No 1 was immediately met with 'Oh, we tried that/I'm not sure if it would work/Please go back and consider alternatives'. Not an encouraging response!
  Senior Management style must reinforce QIT activity, effort, and *60/40* solutions as part of an ongoing building process to empower the team.

Practical examples of QI Team activity

As a result of experience gained in several units in establishing and maintaining QITs a number of examples of Quality activities are illustrated with brief explanations.

1. Health records quality improvement group

This collection of middle grade staff, some from each of four health record

sections: medical secretary, ward clerk, appointment desk, library plus their
manager, formed a *group* (not team as the initials Q(U)IT were felt to imply
quitting not persevering). They tackled two complex problems — clinical
coding and waiting list management, and their paperwork is shown in Figures
8.16 and 8.17, with their newsletter following their first meeting, shown
previously in Figure 8.3.

Figure 8.16. Health Records QIG

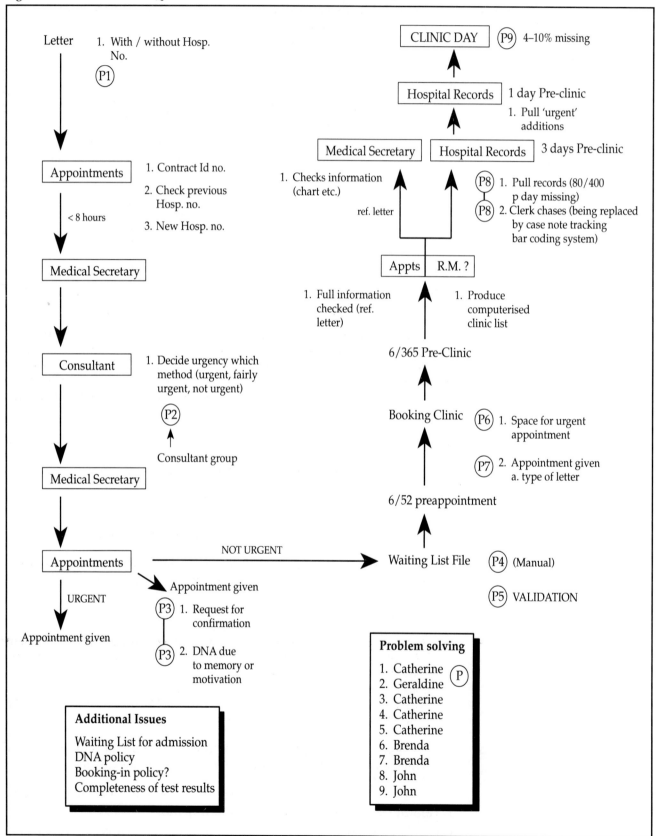

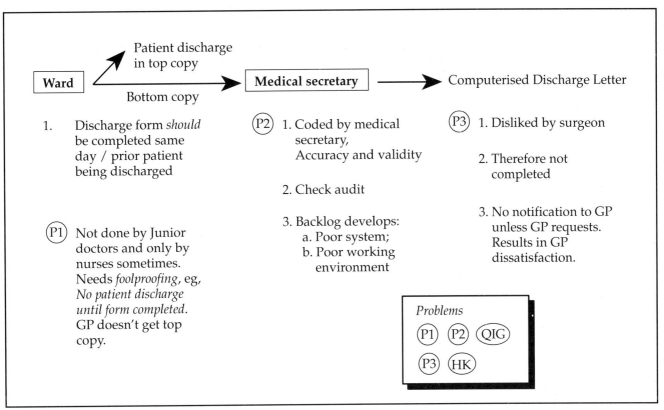

Figure 8.17. Clinical coding

2. Front ramp corridor improvement group

As a result of many complaints from staff in a large Urban DGH about the tidiness (rather than cleanliness) of the main 'arterial' corridor, a time-limited Quality Improvement Group was established and the notes of one of its three meetings is shown below. After three meetings, the 23 problems identified were largely solved and Quality Improvement Group did themselves out of a job! (as a QIG that is!)

FRONT RAMP CORRIDOR (Bottom — Top)

Comments/suggestions for improvement

Number of Entrances — 19   Number of Notice Boards — 14

— Nominated Departments/persons to look after notice boards generally too many. Boards are very tatty – could hessian covered boards improve?

— Ceiling uneven. Paint peeling and cracks. Texture artex might look better.

— Walls – many paint chips especially low down on corners. Looks particularly bad where brown paint at skirting level is chipped. Rubber skirting fitted elsewhere obviously wears better.

— Plastic cover missing from a (BT?) Box containing lots of wiring. Untidy. Dangerous. Also outside neuro theatre.

— Windows many damaged, securing arms and handles bent or broken. Ward door windows have sellotape marks.

— Tyre marks on the floor. Lino has different shades and doesn't match in some places.

— Wire gauze vents in walls torn and badly painted.

— Purple doors – Yuk! Door colours vary. No colour co-ordination.

— Gas cylinders in wooden box outside neuro theatre — health and safety hazard. Needs locking device or storage within the theatre area.

— Fire hose frames very untidy – repaint or build suitable surround.

— Windows dirty next to endoscopy (?no access to clean). Broken window opposite ward 6.

— Notice identifying location of defibrillators currently in dayglo orange paper. Could we have some proper signs?

— Another uncovered wire box near anaesthetics department.

— Rubber doors very scruffy.

— Very old metal doors on some wards, not attractive old fashioned.

— Recess – wooden benches could be improved upon. Ash trays very old and tatty. Is the kit kat machine still in use? Looks very old and unused.

— Near newsagent walls and doors are very dirty.

— Uniform doors and door handles throughout the corridor would improve overall look of corridor.

— Top link corridor – cracked concrete and adhesive marks on glass

— Top recess – is the phone point in use? If not needs removing.

— Drain covers; some not flush with the floor; metal; surrounds dirty; generally untidy.

NOTES OF MEETING OF FRONT RAMP CORRIDOR IMPROVEMENT GROUP

Present: Nurse manager   Hotel services manager
              Support services manager   Management consultant

The purpose of the group is to consider the overall impression created by the corridor in terms of decor, fabric, standard of maintenance, collection point for rubbish bags and to identify ways of making improvements.

The list of staff comments was used as a basis for discussion.

(1) *The corridor being the collection point for rubbish bags.*

Was identified as a key issue to be addressed. A number of options were considered:
— containers outside the ward in the corridor;
— containers outside the ward in the area between each ward;
— greater reconciliation between the time bags are put out for collection and the time of collection;
— frequency of collection;

  — reintroduction of electric trucks in the corridor;
  — retaining cages outside each ward; and
  — mechanical handling.

It was agreed to investigate the option of large containers being placed between 2 or 3 wards. Hotel services manager to identify the number of required and locations. Nurse manager to obtain costs of containers and costs associated with cleaning containers.

(2) *Decor*
Special art group has been commissioned to put forward a proposal for improving the decor of the corridor. This is awaited.
    The current arrangements for redecoration is on a piecemeal basis. There are no monies in this financial year's programme to redecorate the corridor. Total cost for corridor £16,000.

(3) *Flooring*
Flooring is replaced as and when it can be funded and in association with any other work being undertaken in the corridor. Seventy five metres of the corridor floor covering has been replaced. This leaves 225m outstanding. Overall the flooring is not in poor condition.

(4) *Window Replacement*
Nurse manager to arrange for a contractor to assess the need to modify/replace windows in the corridor for safety reasons.

(5) *Excess Wiring*
Nurse Manager to assess and remove/tidy up as appropriate.

(6) *Litter bins/ash trays*
Hotel Services Manager to review provision, identify number required, location and cost .

(7) Windows adjacent to endoscopy which cannot be cleaned to be bricked up, Nurse Manager to action.

(8) Frames around fire hoses to be removed once the decision not to allow electric trucks onto the corridor has been confirmed.

(9) Some of the rubber doors to be replaced within this financial year's works programme.

(10) Defibrillator signs to be replaced with coloured signs which meet British Standards.

(11) Replacement of duct covers is undertaken on an ongoing basis.

(12) Vending machine at top of corridor to be reviewed with WRVS.

As improvements are made to different aspects of the corridor, it is important to make staff aware of these. Hospital Newsletter would be an appropriate means of doing this.

The next meeting of the group will be held on:....

3. Aylesbury Vale Community Health Care NHS Trust QITs

As a result of fully integrating QITs in the Trust's TQM strategy, several QITs were established and their members trained in QIT techniques — at least one team in each area of:

- Physical rehabilitation;
- Palliative care;
- Adult mental health;
- Elderly mental health;
- General community services (including community hospital); and
- Learning disability.

Team progress is shown in Figure 8.18. The hospital pamphlet mentioned in a project by the community hospital is also shown. It was a model then used by all other QITs in compiling their own pamphlets (see Figure 8.19).

Figure 8.18. Team progress

PROGRESS WITH QUALITY IMPROVEMENT TEAMS — JUNE 1992								
	P.C.	**C.C.**	**P.R.**	**L.D.**	**Hosp.**	**Gen. Comm.**	**A.M.H.**	**E.M.H.**
PROJECT	Part of operational meeting. Regular monthly meetings.	Team re-formed. Possible sub-groups. Involve Manor House. Fortnightly meeting. Given Budget (1K).	Regular monthly meetings.	Regular monthly meetings.	Regular monthly meetings.	Regular monthly meetings.	Regular fortnightly meetings.	Regular monthly meetings.
PROCESS	1. Training 'Volunteer Receptionist' programme and accountability to V.S. co-ordinator. 2. Liaison with undertakers. 3. Care Planning assessment documentation review.	1. Quality Cost Assessment of environmental changes. 2. Communication about fencing. 3. Name badges. 4. Leaflet to relatives on Access to Service. 5. Encouraging Q.I. in Regional Capital Works and Estates Service.	1. Catering Survey and Improvements (re-survey in 3 months). 2. Review communication 3. Name badges and photo board review. 4. Reception area. Costing and receptionist post advert.	1. Improved communication on Quality improvement in service. 2. Identify problems with staff. 3. Review of environmental improvements. 4. Badges and photograph board progressing. 5. Co-ordination of annual leave information. 6. Logo development. 7. 'News' board. 8. Ward/Dept. 'Action groups'.	1. O.P. leaflet completed. 2. Casualty leaflet preparation. 3. Ward leaflet preparation. 4. Alteration of notices following '1st Impressions' Review. 5. Patients telephone re-instituted. 6. Security Review.	1. Car parking survey action. 2. Staff room progressing. 3. Reception notice board and information. 4. Q.I.T. Poster. 5. Referral form issue. 6. Wheelchair service access. 7. Service profile 'pack' for staff.	1. Team 4 Satisfaction Survey. 2. Information board in reception (T). 3. 'Bright ideas' competition. 4. Information leaflet.	1. Ward round attendance of patients. 2. Newsletter. 3. Vending machine for staff. 4. Staff rest room. 5. Information Booklet for patients.
CONSUMER INVOLVEMENT	Consider relative involvement.	Reviewing involvement of client and/or Advocacy Group.	Regular input from user.	Regular input.	Consumer involvement	Consumer involvement needs to be addressed.	Under consideration.	Under consideration.

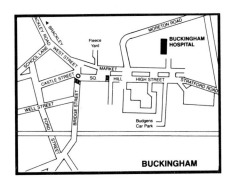

AYLESBURY VALE COMMUNITY HEALTHCARE N.H.S. TRUST

BUCKINGHAM HOSPITAL

High Street, Buckingham MK18 1NU
Telephone: (0280) 813243

X-Ray	0280 823983
Occupational Therapy	0280 822634
Speech Therapy	0280 812862
Dental	0280 813023
Physiotherapy	0280 812342
John Hampden Unit	0280 813062

Reception is open	9am – 5pm
Outpatients	9am – 5pm
Ward Visiting	2pm – 6pm 7pm – 8.30pm
Minor Accident Unit	Open 24 hours

A doctor is on call for minor accidents at all times.

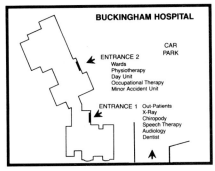

WELCOME TO BUCKINGHAM HOSPITAL

The Hospital provides in-patient services to patients of Buckingham General Practitioners and out-patient services to the local community.

The staff are happy to assist with any queries.

HOSPITAL STAFF

All Hospital staff wear identity badges.

CAR PARKING FACILITIES

Visitors and patients are requested to use the car parks provided.
It is important that spaces provided for ambulance and medical staff are kept clear.

PUBLIC TELEPHONE

A public pay-phone is based at the Physiotherapy entrance.

MONEY AND VALUABLES

The Aylesbury Vale Community Healthcare N.H.S. Trust will not accept responsibility for the loss of or damage to personal property left on Hospital premises.

PUBLIC TRANSPORT

The bus stops are within walking distance of the Hospital.

FIRE AND SAFETY

We ask for the assistance of visitors and patients to ensure that the fire precautions in the Hospital are observed.

SMOKING POLICY

It is not in harmony with the Hospital environment to encourage smoking. However in-patients who desire a cigarette, may use one small room.

LEAGUE OF FRIENDS OF BUCKINGHAM HOSPITAL

Information on joining the League of Friends and donations can be obtained by contacting the Hospital.

SUGGESTIONS/COMMENTS/COMPLAINTS

Should you have suggestions, comments or complaints, please contact the Sister-in-Charge at the Hospital.
Telephone: 0280 813243.

Alternatively the Community Health Council would be pleased to give independent advice and information.
Telephone 0296 83222.

Figures 8.19 and 8.20. Buckingham Hospital leaflet

4. Accident and Emergency QIT

In one unit, the developing TQM strategy and particular interest in QITs in accident and emergency coincided in the development of a QIT in accident and emergency. Several problems were identified initially as shown in Figure 8.21. The results of its second meeting are shown in Figure 8.22.

A & E Quality Improvement Group

Issues/problems identified

1. Developing triage (June 1st);

2. Signposting — Reception, Main entrance etc;

3. Access to PAS in A & E (eg fracture clinic);

4. Focus flow at main A & E entrance;

5. Communication to patients;

6. Communication to public;

7. Gathering and monitoring information:
   (a) Waiting times (seen and assessed),
   (b) Patient satisfaction with service;

8. A & E staff training in *quality management*;

9. Developing written standards and ownership;

10. Training staff in triage evaluation of patients and monitoring flow;

11. Different models of care including *nurse practitioners*;

12. Adequacy/deployment of medical staff;

13. Education of junior medical staff; and

14. Addressing patient feedback, eg car parking.

Figure 8.21. A & E Problems

A & E QUALITY IMPROVEMENT GROUP

PRESENT: Consultant
Senior Sister
Secretary
Medical Records
Plaster Technician
Quality Facilitator
Business Manager

ACTION

1. A very brief overview of the purpose, structure and remit of The Quality Improvement Group was given by Q.F.

2. Membership was further discussed and it as suggested a volunteer is sought from portering and a junior nurse.   SS.

3. SS gave an update on the implementation of triage
   Unit not yet delivered
   Staff not all appointed
   No start date decided   SS.

   Various sheets of documentation distributed.
   Classification of priority documentation to be further discussed outside of group meeting.   SS./Cons.

4. Staff Training —Short update sessions on triage suggested for staff who experienced pilot.
   ? more in depth for new staff   SS

Figure 8.22. Results of second meeting of A & E QIT

cont'd. Figure 8.22   5.   PT had reorganised plaster room and waiting area making the whole area more welcoming and friendly. Extend initiative to main waiting room.

? Local schools to provide artwork.   Cons./QF

6.   Consultant — A & E telephone enquiry service for advice, eg

? Whether A&E visit necessary
? Local help line numbers etc

It would need a dedicated telephone line possibly sponsored   QF.

Meeting closed

7.   Date and time of next meeting.

Two postscripts

Many varied and interesting events occur in any group, not least QITs! Two examples occurred which are both amusing and serious. Those who took part may, if they read this, recognise themselves, but no-one else will!!

(a). Content: Elderly mental health — the sensitive issue of ward round

Every week we have a ward round which starts late because we have to wait for the consultant psychiatrist, Dr Jones to arrive. We have medical, nursing and paramedical staff attending this round. It is the opportunity, the consultant says, for him to call each patient in for five/ten minutes and interview them. It is the only time he sees them.

It is a bit of a sensitive issue which we are gradually getting round to sorting out:

QIT facilitator: Is it appropriate to see patients in ward round like this (*Response: No.*)

Is it professionally appropriate for nurses to reinforce this approach? (*Response: No.*)

Director of Nursing Services: Would you like me to talk to the consultant? (*Response: Yes, please.*)

TIQ facilitator: Hold on — wouldn't you (the Team) like a little more time to sort it out yourselves? (*Response: Yes — give us 2 weeks and we will address the problem.*)

Two weeks later — problem sorted out!!

(b) QIT in acute hospital

Membership: Doctor, Nurse, Nurse Manager, Support Services Manager, Quality Facilitator, Business Manager, External management consultant.

First meeting: All on first name terms except consultant, who was addressed by all clinical staff as Dr X. When this was commented on by Management Consultant (also called by first name!) Nurse Manager and Consultant

	agreed it was appropriate that consultant be called 'Dr'.
Ability of team to be:	Open; Honest; Argue; and Speak their minds was raised and discussed.

Two meetings later all were on first name terms!!

Chapter 9   Responding to the customer

'You should think of your customers as partners, or better still, family'
— *Victor Kiam, President & CEO, Remington Products Inc.*

Introduction

When walking into any major national, successful organisation in the manufacturing or service sector, one is immediately usually met with many varied indications that you — the customer — are important. This is the tone of Virgin airlines, Mercedes Benz Garages, Marks and Spencers. In many parts of the NHS this is also true, and increasingly so. So what are the key features of the health care provider unit which offers good *customer* service (Reynolds S, 1991)

1. **Clear definition of who the 'Customer' is**
    It is difficult to reproduce the service *right first time* unless one is clear to whom, or to which groups, this service has to be provided. The NHS Unit has to deal with the *multiple customer* concept as its customers are:
    *   Patients and potential patients;
    *   Relatives and visitors;
    *   Purchasing authorities;
    *   GPs — fundholders and non-fundholders;
    *   Other agencies; and
    *   Its own staff.

    In the first and last group — the patients — there needs to be a clear understanding of the external/internal customer chain — see Figure 9.1.

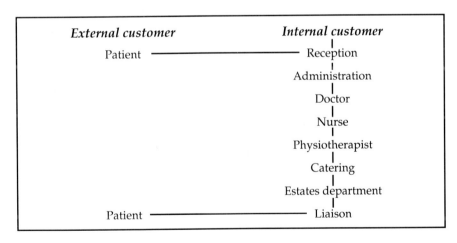

Figure 9.1. External/internal customer chain

2. **Definition of customer services/care policy**
    Hopefully, within the context of a TQM framework, the unit needs to set out its stall and define what its aims and objectives are for meeting, if not exceeding (delighting!) its several customer groups.

3. **Assessing customer expectations and needs**
    Senior staff, managers and clinicians, must have their finger on their customers' *pulses* in terms of consistently wanting to find out what they think of the services provided. On the basis that staff believe they offer a good, high quality service, they should be motivated to assess customer expectations and needs to locate the *'small areas'* where the service falls down. Again, the multiple customers' concept applies.

4. **Contracting and service strategies**
   It is perhaps worth stating the obvious that as standards are set and monitored for the aforementioned issues, these will increasingly appear within the purchasing contract setting.

5. **Customer satisfaction measurement criteria**
   As in any part of the TQM approach, it is important to have a baseline measure plus ongoing quarterly measures of customer satisfaction for each main service — without this, well intentioned but subjective, often self-reinforcing information/feedback will be the order of the day!

Question: To what extent does your unit have a Patient/customer service based on these five features?

To ensure these features satisfy the *Total* part of TQM, it is important to establish good response to *all* external and *all* internal customers as indicated by South Warwickshire's Quality Strategy as in Figure 9.2.

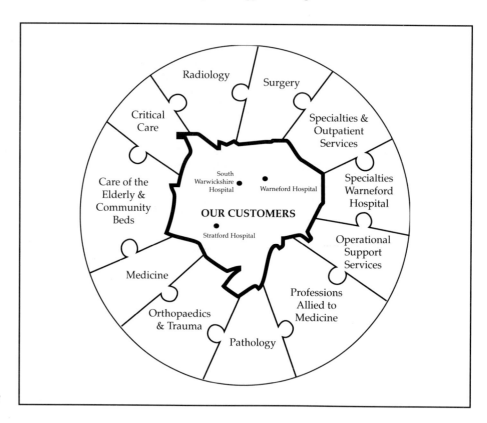

Figure 9.2. Quality strategy

Before continuing with more in-depth investigation of customer responsiveness in the NHS, a small but illuminating depression into other service industries. In the first of a series of Quality Executive Travel Tracking Source studies to monitor travel industry performance, Opinion Research Corporation asked 400 executives from US companies what is most important to them when it comes to Business Travel. The results are reproduced in Table 9.1.

Gaps are identified between what frequent travellers *say* is important and what their perception of actual source delivery *is*. The largest (negative) gaps appear in the airline services and highlight a concern in the travel industry that companies are not giving travellers what they really want. It would be instructive to apply this approach within the NHS using related criteria to identify gaps in what *our patients* reasonably expect.

A progressive model, as in Figure 9.3, for responding to the customer(s) shows a progression from culture/attitudes through *listening to customers* to behavioural action.

Table 9.1

Table 1
Opinion Research Corporation Executive Travel Tracking Service: Airline Industry

	Importance	Performance	Gap
On-time arrival	89%	39%	−50%
Check-in procedures	75%	53%	−22%
Checked baggage delivery	75%	31%	−44%
Pre-assigned seating	75%	65%	−10%
Cares about the customer	75%	40%	−35%
Replacing aging fleet	72%	26%	−46%
Convenient schedules	70%	47%	−23%
Doesn't overbook	68%	33%	−35%
Comfortable seating	67%	34%	−33%
Clean, attractive cabins	60%	49%	−11%
Carry-on room	59%	33%	−26%
Friendly and efficient in-flight service	56%	48%	−8%
Quality frequent flyer programme	35%	23%	−12%
Quality in-flight food service	31%	21%	−10%

Table 2
Opinion Research Corporation Executive Travel Tracking Service: Hotel Industry

	Importance	Performance	Gap
Billing accuracy	91%	83%	−8%
Efficient check-in	80%	55%	−25%
Reliable message and wake-up service	79%	76%	−3%
Cares about the customer	77%	54%	−23%
Competitive room rates	72%	52%	−20%
Reasonable charge for in-room phone service	72%	37%	−35%
Express check-out	68%	63%	−5%
Attractive and generously sized rooms	59%	55%	−4%
Fast breakfast service	54%	48%	−6%
Well lighted and ample work space	48%	51%	3%
Availability of non-smoking rooms	47%	49%	2%
Quality frequent traveller programme	41%	34%	−7%
Multiple dining and lounge facilities	36%	54%	18%
Late evening room service	24%	38%	14%

Table 3
Opinion Research Corporation Executive Travel Tracking Service: Car Hire Industry

	Importance	Performance	Gap
Good mechanical condition	96%	75%	−21%
Reservations in order	88%	77%	−11%
Clean cars	76%	65%	−11%
Express auto return	71%	61%	−10%
Cares about the customer	68%	47%	−21%
Express pick-up	66%	47%	−19%
Short walk to cars	60%	60%	0
Non-smoker cars	30%	11%	−19%
Quality frequent hirer programme	24%	34%	10%
Makes and models	23%	53%	30%

Note: Percentages indicate those who gave a rating of 8, 9, or 10 on a 1 to 10 scale. Results reported on an *industry* basis. Negative gap indicates service delivery is not meeting importance. Positive gap shows delivery exceeds importance or delivers more of a specific item than is required.

Responding to customers					
Raising staff awareness and improving attitudes to *customers*	Increasing staff willingness to elicit customer's views			Response to customers' views	Accountability to customers
	(a) Patient views	(b) Purchaser views	(c) Staff views		

Figure 9.3. Responding to customers

Raising staff awareness and improving attitudes to customers

As the debate as to whether and how to measure customer satisfaction increases, it becomes apparent that for many staff in the NHS the concept of checking their own professionally based judgements as to *what the patient needs* against the views of other *non-professionals* is somehow less than palatable.

Some examples of this attitude becoming apparent are:

1. **Consultant Physician**   when faced with GP feedback on his and colleagues' style of delivery, stated that his view was the prevailing most important one, not the GP and not the patient.

2. **Ward Clerk (Orthopaedics)**   when faced with patient's husband visiting at 10.30 am very politely asked him to return at 6.00 pm as there were three ward rounds that day — who was being put first here!

3. **Psychiatrist**   who parked in short term stay (2 hour) spaces in front of hospital to attend an all day conference. When encouraged (at lunchtime!) to move, she moved into an adjoining space. She won the final argument — who else was parked there? The UGM!

4. **The internal consumer sensitive catering manager**   when regaled by the nurse member of his Quality Circle because of an *apparent* problem being served quickly at lunchtime, put up a sign — 'Would visitors please let staff be served first'!! Poor visitors charged more, now having to move backwards, not forwards, in the queue.

Somehow TQM has to be implemented in a way in which staff are encouraged to look at their own attitudes and commitment to *quality* in general, and their ability to *put customers first* in particular.

Increasing staff willingness to customer views

Patient views

Once one is committed to responding to customers in whatever way resources allow, then the next step is to take every reasonable opportunity to find out what the various customers expect and require and to match this with what they think *they* get and also what *staff* think they provide.

Various studies on patient feedback have been reported — only a small number are summarised here to illustrate the importance of customers' views in informing service providers.

1. Starting on a positive note, but nevertheless one that contradicts *traditional* psychiatric opinion about discharge from large asylums, interim findings from a large project in N E Thames (1992) showed that most mentally ill patients discharged from hospital into community care preferred their new homes and greater degree of autonomy and freedom.

2. Community care service users at a strategy development meeting in London confounded the professional experts by demands for empowerment: ability to speak for themselves; being asked, not told, what they needed; listened to; not *consulted* to death.

3. In a study of psychiatric patient views of which aspects of care they rated most highly (Sharma T, 1992) patients were clearly *not* convinced of the benefits of psychotropic medication or being interested in ward rounds or case conference — their views were at variance with those of the nursing staff. Clearly to improve the Quality of Care we need to look at why patients perceive psychotropic medication as being unhelpful.

4. In the Audit Commission paper (1991) *Patients' views on Day Surgery* patients felt day surgery led to:
    - Faster and better recovery at home;
    - Home sooner (especially important for parents of young children); and
    - Good for NHS resource use.

    Negative views (15%) included:
    - Feeling unwell at home;
    - Not appropriate so soon (2-3 hours) after general anaesthetic;
    - Nervous at home in night; and
    - Onus on partner as carer.

    The last three sections are reserved for *special* patients — three professionals who used the NHS for their own care and made a point of recording their views.

5. Bhopal R (Professor in Epidemiology) (1992)
    Problems: Time to book in (Outpatient Department)
                $1\frac{1}{2}$ hour wait for consultation

6. Ward C (Nurse) (1992)
    Problems: Poor pain relief
                Poor catering
                Night nurse noise
                Medical/nursing crossed lines
                Staff attitudes

7. Ram A (Communication Consultant) (1992)
    Problems: Lack of preparatory information
                Poor discharge preparation
                No bedside light switch
                No television
                Missing call button
                Staff attitude
                Poor team liaison

All these studies reinforce the need to elicit information from customers as to their views, but how should this be done?

In their important work on *customer feedback surveys* (Dixon P and Carr-Hill R, 1989) reviewed methods of patient/customer surveys commonly undertaken by Health Authorities, highlighting good practice. It looked at surveys of inpatient, outpatient, accident and emergency departments, and general population. Readers are referred to this for detailed information. Several different formats (part only) for collecting patient information which show the variation in possible presentation are demonstrated in Figs 9.4 — 9.9.

Arriving at hospital

We would like to know what happened to you before you were admitted to the ward this time.

► 1. What form did your admission to hospital take?

I came in as an emergency patient ☐

I received a letter/phone call asking me to come in ☐

I was transferred from another hospital. ☐

NB IF YOU WERE UNCONSCIOUS ON ARRIVAL AT HOSPITAL, PLEASE GO TO PAGE 8. IF YOU WERE AN EMERGENCY PATIENT PLEASE GO TO QUESTION 8 ON PAGE 4.

► 2. Did you manage to get into hospital the first time you were asked to attend, or were you turned away because there were not enough beds?

I got into hospital the first time ☐

I was turned away for the first time ☐

► 3. How long were you on the waiting list before you were admitted to hospital this time?

Less than 2 weeks ☐

2 to 4 weeks ☐

1 to 3 months ☐

Between 3 and 6 months ☐

Between 6 and 9 months ☐

Between 9 months and 1 year ☐

Over 1 year (please specify) _____

► 4. How much warning did you get of the actual day you were to be admitted to hospital?

No more than a few hours ☐

A day or two ☐

Three days to a week ☐

More than 1 week ☐

Figure 9.4. 'What the patients think' Health Policy Advisory Unit, Sheffield. 'Arriving at Hospital' (Page 3 of comprehensive 43 page Quality Manual, in full analysis provided).

PATIENTS' EXPERIENCES OF SURGERY

First, we would like to ask about what happened before you went into hospital.

1 Did you receive any written or printed information about your treatment *before* you went into hospital?

Please tick one   1 ❏ Yes   2 ❏ No

2 Did anyone explain your treatment to you *before* you went into hospital?

Please tick one   1 ❏ Yes   2 ❏ No

Now we would like to ask you about the time you spent in hospital.

3 What operation did you have?
You may tick more than one

1 ❏ Hernia repair   11 ❏ Custoscopy
2 ❏ Arthroscopy   12 ❏ Laparoscopy
3 ❏ Myringotomy or grommets   13 ❏ Sterilisation (women)
4 ❏ Removal of skin growth   14 ❏ Vasectomy
5 ❏ Anal fissure dilatation/excision   15 ❏ Cataract extraction
6 ❏ Nasal fracture reduction   16 ❏ Breast lump biopsy
7 ❏ Circumcision   17 ❏ Carpal tunnel release
8 ❏ Removal of ganglion   18 ❏ Termination of pregnancy
9 ❏ Orchidopexy for undescended   19 ❏ Dilation & curettage
     testicles   (D&C)
10 ❏ Varicose vein surgery   20 ❏ Cervical cautery/biopsy
                                         21 ❏ Other *(please specify)*

                                         _____

4 How long did you stay in hospital?
Please tick one

1 ❏ For the day or less   2 ❏ For one night or more

Figure 9.5. 'Patients' experience of Day Surgery' Audit Commission May 1991. Meaning Quality: the Patients' view of Day Surgery

Out-Patient Questionnaire

Getting to the Clinic

The...Hospital is keen to tailor services to suit as closely as possible the needs of patients and so it is conducting surveys on different aspects of the services provided.

This survey is about your experience of making an appointment and travelling to the Out-Patient Department.

We would be grateful if you would answer the attached questions by ticking the appropriate box and writing comments where you would like to provide us with further information. Your name is not required and the information you supply will remain anonymous.

Please help us to improve the information we provide you with.

Thank you.

Tick YES or NO

1. Is this your first visit as a patient to the Out-patient Department

YES ☐   NO ☐

2. Were you given an appointment for a time convenient to you?

YES ☐   NO ☐

Comments

_____
_____
_____
_____

3. Were you informed about how you could change the appointment time if you needed to?

YES ☐   NO ☐

Comments

_____
_____
_____
_____

4. Were you given a telephone number to ring should you have a query?

YES ☐   NO ☐

Comments

_____
_____
_____
_____

5. Were you given directions to the hospital and information on car parking, public transport etc., on your first visit to the Out-patient Department?

YES ☐   NO ☐

Comments

_____
_____
_____
_____

Continued...

Figure 9.6. Outpatient: Trent Regional Health Authority. Quality Standards for Outpatient

CONFIDENTIAL

A Pilot Service Satisfaction Questionnaire
Sampling C.M.H.T. 3 Clients

Please tick the appropriate box, unless otherwise instructed.

1) Are you currently seeing a member of the team?

   Yes   ☐   For how many months have you been seeing a member of the team?

   _____

   No   ☐   For how many months did you see a member of the team?

   _____

2) How many weeks did you have to wait for the team to first contact you, after you and your G.P. decided to contact the team?

   _____

- -

   If you have never been to the Centre please go to question number 9.

- -

3) Did you have any problems in finding the Centre?

   Yes   ☐
   No   ☐

4) If you came to the Centre by car did you find parking a problem?

   Yes   ☐
   No   ☐

5) On arriving at the Centre did you find the receptionists and other staff helpful?

   Yes   ☐
   No *   ☐

* If no, could you please explain how they could be more helpful?

_____

_____

_____

_____

Figure 9.7. Service Satisfaction: Quality Care CMHT

QUESTIONS TO SERVICE USERS

1. **ADMISSION TO HOSPITAL/UNIT**

   1.1 When you were admitted how long were you kept waiting before you were taken to the ward?

   Please tick

   Less than half hour ☐

   Between half hour and an hour ☐

   Between and hour and two hours ☐

   Cannot remember ☐

   1.2 Did anyone explain to you approximately how long you would have to wait?

   Yes ☐

   No ☐

   Cannot remember ☐

   1.3 Were refreshments available if you needed them?

   Yes ☐

   No ☐

   Cannot remember ☐

   1.4 Did any staff try to reassure you about what was happening to you?

   Yes ☐

   No ☐

   Comments

   _____

   _____

   _____

   1.5 Where were you interviewed before being admitted?

   In a public place ☐

   In a private place ☐

   Other (Please specify)

   _____

   Cannot remember ☐

Figure 9.8. Questionnaire Quality to Hospital Service Users: Aylesbury Vale

AYLESBURY VALE COMMUNITY HEALTHCARE N.H.S. TRUST

A Question of Healthcare

Here in the Aylesbury Vale Community Healthcare N.H.S. Trust we care about the service you receive. We want to be sure that however and whenever you receive a service from us that it is efficient and friendly and meets your own personal needs.

We would be very grateful if you would take a few moments to complete this questionnaire.

We will use this information to ensure our high standards are maintained and improved.
Thank you very much.

How well did we meet your expectations?
(Please tick as appropriate)

WHEN WE WROTE TO YOU   EXCELLENT · GOOD · OK / FAIR · POOR · VERY POOR

1. Clarity of letter ❑ ❑ ❑ ❑ ❑
2. Courtesy of letter ❑ ❑ ❑ ❑ ❑
3. Necessary information ❑ ❑ ❑ ❑ ❑
4. Feeling of choice ❑ ❑ ❑ ❑ ❑

ON ARRIVAL AT HOSPITAL

5. Ease of car parking ❑ ❑ ❑ ❑ ❑
6. Signposting to reception ❑ ❑ ❑ ❑ ❑
7. Level of courtesy of staff ❑ ❑ ❑ ❑ ❑

OUT-PATIENTS RECEPTION

8. Check-in speed ❑ ❑ ❑ ❑ ❑
9. Level of courtesy ❑ ❑ ❑ ❑ ❑
10. Level of helpfulness ❑ ❑ ❑ ❑ ❑
11. Dealing with difficulties ❑ ❑ ❑ ❑ ❑
12. Facilities a. Magazines ❑ ❑ ❑ ❑ ❑
13.   b. Tea/coffee etc. ❑ ❑ ❑ ❑ ❑
14.   c. Telephone ❑ ❑ ❑ ❑ ❑

ON ADMISSION TO HOSPITAL   EXCELLENT · GOOD · OK / FAIR · POOR · VERY POOR

15. Overall care from
     a. Medical staff ❑ ❑ ❑ ❑ ❑
16.   b. Nursing staff ❑ ❑ ❑ ❑ ❑
17.   c. Other staff ❑ ❑ ❑ ❑ ❑
18. Catering Services ❑ ❑ ❑ ❑ ❑
19. Cleanliness ❑ ❑ ❑ ❑ ❑
20. Facilities (Magazines, telephone, etc) ❑ ❑ ❑ ❑ ❑

Was this your first visit to Aylesbury Vale Community Healthcare N.H.S. Trust

Yes ❑   No ❑

If you needed to, would you be happy to return here in the future?

Yes ❑   No ❑

Are there any of our staff who deserve a special mention?

_____

_____

Additional comments

_____

_____

Thank you for completing this questionnaire. Please hand it to:

Figure 9.9. A Question of Healthcare: Aylesbury Vale

They all have strengths and weaknesses, not least in their blanket applicability to any unit. However, Figures 9.4 and 9.9 are recommended for serious consideration. Figure 9.4 as a comprehensive, externally administered, and analytical approach with full outcome report and therefore ease of operation. The last as an internal easy/quick to administer table to provide an overall scope to monitor on a regular/quarterly basis.

Purchaser Views

District Health Authority purchasers have made their views on quality of provider services clear to providers in the run up to 1992/93 contracts — but variably. Some have been highly prescriptive, others have left much of the quality specification to provider units. Some in the prescriptive camp have gone on to describe how they intend to monitor provider services and obtain customer satisfaction data themselves.

Most provider units and purchasing agencies have been meeting with their GP colleagues (fundholding and non-fundholding) to ascertain their views of local provider services. One such collection of views is shown with the response of the provider unit.

In a recent research project into ongoing open feedback between hospitals and GPs, King and Coventry (1992) asked about the main referral information issues facing them and the problems they foresaw in the immediate future:

66 *COMMENTS ARISING FROM VISITS TO GENERAL PRACTITIONERS*

Introduction
1. *As part of the Unit's philosophy of developing closer links with GPs, visits have been made to the majority of surgeries during the last three or four weeks. The purpose of the visits has been to:*

    (a) *Reinforce the development of a single acute unit*

    (b) *Obtain the views of GPs about the services being provided by The Group of Hospitals, identifying specific problem areas and seeking views about the priority of service developments.*

    (c) *Identify information needs.*

    (d) *Obtain views on GP Fundholding status.*

Summary of Key Concerns
2. *The most frequent comments were as follows.*

    (a) *Whilst there is some feeling of loyalty to the hospitals, it is quite clear that GPs will increasingly refer patients elsewhere in the key specialties referred to in 2(b).*

    (b) *Concern about waiting times between the initial letter of referral and the outpatient consultation date in the following specialties:*
        Specialty A
        Specialty B
        Specialty C

    (c) *Concern about inpatient waiting times in the same specialties.*

    (d) *Difficulties associated with emergency medical admissions (including the elderly). Comments relate to the process of obtaining information about bed availability and actual availability.*

    (e) *Discharge letters are frequently illegible and contain insufficient information, including clinical diagnosis*

(f) *Lateness of discharge summaries and, in some cases, no discharge letter.*

3. *Whilst it would be impracticable to provide a complete picture in this brief report, other comments included:*

(a) *Waiting time in the Accident and Emergency Department and senior medical cover outside 9.00 a.m. to 5.00 p.m.*

(b) *Physiotherapy waiting times — greater open access to services.*

(c) *Open access ECG service.*

(d) *Long waiting time for treatment Problem A.*

(e) *Long waiting time for Specialty 7 outpatient consultations.*

(f) *Waiting time for Specialty Y outpatient consultations.*

(g) *Reduce number of follow-up outpatient attendance and reinforce the point that patients who DNA waste valuable resources.*

(h) *Waiting time for access to the X Service.*

(i) *Opportunity for direct access to a surgical fitting service.*

(j) *GPs to be advised by telephone of births.*

(k) *GPs not always advised of death of a patient.*

(l) *Development of specimen service as part of the courier service.*

(m) *Development of computer links between GPs and the Unit.*

Future Action

4. *Some issues can be dealt with quickly by directorates, whilst others are on the agenda in discussions with purchasers, particularly waiting times in Specialties 1,2,3.*

5. *In addition to the action that can be taken in the short term, the quality strategy and Business Planning process, will offer the opportunities to develop service strategies to overcome the more serious deficiencies in service provision.*

6. *It is essential to reduce waiting times, particularly for the first outpatient consultation. Assuming equality of care between Providers, waiting time becomes the critical factor which determines referral patterns.* **99**

This highlights the UKwide need to speed up hospital to GP communication. More important than this prescription is the method used in this study to bring these staff together to share their different perspective of the services provided.

Staff views

As the third group of customers, staff themselves have very important and valid perceptions of what the services provided by their colleagues in a hospital or community service are like and how they could be improved. Developing *Total Quality* relationships between services and the staff users of that service is based on:

- Regular dialogue;
- Education and awareness about service provided and required;
- Open shared monitoring of performance; and
- *Win-win* dialogues over *quality improvement.*

The central value of *putting the customer first* is as important in the internal customer chain as with the external patient-hospital chain. Four examples of *internal customer feedback* questionnaires are shown in Figures 9.10 to 9.13.

The one in Figure 9.13 developed by the author with colleagues in the Aylesbury Vale Community Health Care NHS Trust is a generic questionnaire which can be used by any department to canvass opinion from its other *user* departments. It can be scored easily.

To all Wards & Departments

TOWARDS TOTAL QUALITY (TTQ)

Dear Colleague,

It has been suggested that the quality of our service to you our "customers" could be improved.

To help us in the pursuit of a better service, we would be grateful if you would answer the following questions.

1) Have you experienced any problems with our service?   Yes ☐   No ☐

   If yes please let us know in writing.

2) Is our service to you?   Excellent ☐   Very Good ☐   Good ☐   Poor ☐

   If poor could you tell us why.

3) Are our staff efficient and helpful?   Yes ☐   No ☐

   If no please give examples.

4) Are your works requisitions responded to within a reasonable time?   Yes ☐   No ☐

   If no please give examples

Please return this questionnaire to the Works Dept. Thanking you in anticipation of your cooperation in this survey.

Yours faithfully,

Senior Engineer,   **Senior Building Officer,**
Works Dept.   **Works Dept.**

Figure 9.10. Estate service to all other staff

SUPPLIES DEPARTMENT – CUSTOMER SERVICE QUESTIONNAIRE

Please state your Name _____

Title _____ Unit _____

Hospital _____ Department _____

Your newly established Supplies Department is responsible for providing you with a total supplies service. Please indicate your views on the service you receive by marking on the dotted line with a cross where appropriate. Questions 1 to 21 relate to your Supplies Department. Questions 22 to 28 relate to stores.

1. Do you find that the Supplies Department answers your telephone enquiries promptly:

   Always   Sometimes   After some delay   Very slowly

   ....

2. When you telephone Supplies, do you find them:

   Very helpful   Helpful   Unhelpful

   ....

3. Do you find the service provided over the telephone:

   Very good   Good   Average   Poor

   ....

4. Do they phone you back when they promise they will:

   Always   Sometimes   Hardly ever

   ....

Non-Stock requirements (ie items *not* obtained from Stores)

5. When you send your requisitions to Supplies, do you find they are dealt with:

   Very quickly   Quickly   Slowly   Very Slowly

   ....

6. When Supplies come back to you with a query over the phone about your non-stock requisitions are they:

   Very helpful   Helpful   Unhelpful

   ....

7. If your request has to go out to Quotation/Tender, are you aware of the necessary delay?   YES / NO

8. Do you find such delays are   Reasonable   _____

                                        Too Long   _____

9. When orders are placed, one copy is meant for the originator of the requisition, do you get a copy:

   Always   Occasionally   Never

   ....

10. When you require an urgent order placed, are your requests dealt with:

    Quickly   Slowly   Very Slowly

    ....

11. How often do you contact Supplies?

    Regularly   Infrequently   Never

    ....

12. How is the majority of your contact made?

    Telephone   Correspondence   Visit to Supplies

    ....

13. Is your contact concerned with

    a) order queries _____

    b) stores queries _____

    c) need for product information _____

14. Is the response from Supplies:

    Very good   Good   Fair   Poor

    ....

Figure 9.11. District Supplies Department to all other departments cont'd

15. Have you ever been visited by a member of the Supplies staff
    YES / NO

16. Do you feel a visit from Supplies staff would be helpful to you?
    YES / NO / DON'T KNOW

17. How often do you feel a visit would be helpful?

_____

18. Do you feel that advice obtained from Supplies has
    contributed to financial savings   YES / NO

19. Would you welcome the opportunity to hear about the role of
    Supplies?   YES / NO

20. How would you rate the overall supplies service provided to
    you by the Supplies Department:

    Very good   Good   Fair   Poor

21. Indicate in priority order (1,2,3) what you look for in the goods
    Supplies obtains for you:

    Price   Quality   Service
    ____   ____   ____

Please detail any additional or expanded comments on the service
provided by your Supplies Department and state what
improvements you would like to see.

_____
_____
_____
_____
_____

Items received from stores

22. When staff contact you with queries on your requisitions, do
    you find them:

    Very helpful   Helpful   Unhelpful

23. When you need an item added or amended on your
    requisitions, do you find staff:

    Very helpful   Helpful   Unhelpful

24. When you have an urgent request for items from stores, do
    you find staff:

    Quick to respond   Moderately quick   Slow

25. When you have an urgent request, do you find delivery is as
    agreed:

    Always   Most times   Occasionally

26. Do stores deliver your goods on the agreed day:

    Every time   Most times   Not often   Hardly ever

27. On a scale of 1–10 (1 represents 'not important') to you is:
    a) reliability of delivery on the right day _____
    b) frequency of delivery _____
    c) time taken from requisitioning to delivery _____
    d) stock availability (no stock outs) _____
    e) emergency deliveries _____

28. What is your overall opinion of the stores service :

    Very good   Good   Average   Poor   Very poor

Please detail any additional or expanded comments on the
service you receive from stores and state any improvements you
would like to see.

_____
_____
_____

Many thanks for your help. Please pull out and return the
completed form to : District Services Manager

cont'd. Figure 9.11

HEALTH RECORDS DEPT.
"HEALTHY RECORDS SERVICES"?

The Health Records Department in Altnagelvin Hospital is anxious to ensure that it is meeting the needs of **all** it's customer including it's internal customers i.e. medical, nursing and para-medical staff.

In order to monitor how well we are doing, we would be grateful if you would take a few moments to complete this questionnaire and return it to the Patient Services Manager, within 10 working days. We will use the feedback we obtain to maintain and improve our standards.

Thank You!

HEALTHY RECORDS SERVICES?

How well do we meet your needs and expectations? Please tick and comment below. Comments will be particularly helpful where you feel our service is less than good.

How did we rate?

Are you – Medical ❑
Nursing ❑
Paramedical ❑

Column headings: NOT APPLICABLE / DON'T KNOW · EXCELLENT · GOOD · FAIR · POOR · VERY POOR · **Comments?**

1 Outpatient Services:
a Efficiency of GP referral process ❑ ❑ ❑ ❑ ❑ ❑ _____
b Organisation of appointments ❑ ❑ ❑ ❑ ❑ ❑ _____
c Efficiency of throughput of patients ❑ ❑ ❑ ❑ ❑ ❑ _____
d Availability of complete case notes and x-rays ❑ ❑ ❑ ❑ ❑ ❑ _____
e Response to changes ❑ ❑ ❑ ❑ ❑ ❑ _____
f Quality of PAS letters ❑ ❑ ❑ ❑ ❑ ❑ _____

2. Inpatient Services:
a Efficiency of booked admission process ❑ ❑ ❑ ❑ ❑ ❑ _____
b Efficiency of emergency admission process ❑ ❑ ❑ ❑ ❑ ❑ _____
c Efficiency of "short notice" admission process ❑ ❑ ❑ ❑ ❑ ❑ _____
d Availability of complete case notes and x-rays ❑ ❑ ❑ ❑ ❑ ❑ _____
e Ward clerk service ❑ ❑ ❑ ❑ ❑ ❑ _____

3 Secretarial Services:
a Quality of work produced ❑ ❑ ❑ ❑ ❑ ❑ _____
b Response to 'one off' demands ❑ ❑ ❑ ❑ ❑ ❑ _____
c Efficiency of discharge letter process ❑ ❑ ❑ ❑ ❑ ❑ _____
d Efficiency of clinical coding process ❑ ❑ ❑ ❑ ❑ ❑ _____

4. Consumer Issues:
a Courtesy and politeness to you ❑ ❑ ❑ ❑ ❑ ❑ _____
b Appearance/presentation of staff ❑ ❑ ❑ ❑ ❑ ❑ _____

Thank you for completing this questionnaire.

Figure 9.12. Health records service

AYLESBURY VALE COMMUNITY HEALTHCARE N.H.S. TRUST

A QUESTION OF HEALTHCARE SERVICE

What do our colleagues think of the......... service?

APRIL 1992

Part of managing the quality of our service involves periodically and regularly finding out what our colleagues think of our service provided to them.

Please take a few moments to complete this questionnaire. We will use this information to ensure our high standards are maintained and improved.

Thank you very much.

(signed Head of Dept.)

_____ Department

(Please return to: (HOD))

How well do we meet your needs and expectations?
(Please tick and comment as appropriate)

	Excellent	Good	OK/Fair	Poor	Very poor	Additional Comments
1.	❏	❏	❏	❏	❏	_____
2.	❏	❏	❏	❏	❏	_____
3.	❏	❏	❏	❏	❏	_____
4.	❏	❏	❏	❏	❏	_____
5.	❏	❏	❏	❏	❏	_____
6.	❏	❏	❏	❏	❏	_____
7.	❏	❏	❏	❏	❏	_____
8	❏	❏	❏	❏	❏	_____
9.	❏	❏	❏	❏	❏	_____
10.	❏	❏	❏	❏	❏	_____
11.	❏	❏	❏	❏	❏	_____
12.	❏	❏	❏	❏	❏	_____
13.	❏	❏	❏	❏	❏	_____
14.	❏	❏	❏	❏	❏	_____
15.	❏	❏	❏	❏	❏	_____

ARE YOU

Medical ❏   Nursing ❏   P.A.M. ❏ Non-clinical ❏

Figure 9.13. A question of healthcare services

Response to customer views

By this stage in the process *responding to the customer*, the staff have *customer-first* service attitudes. They are willing to elicit customer views. Then what.....?

Sometimes, consciously or unconsciously, staff adopt the Jean-Paul Sartre model of surveys typified by the statement — 'I asked, therefore I am (customer-sensitive)'. It reminds me of a patient in a therapy group I ran in Cardiff in a previous life (1984) as a psychotherapist — the patient entered the group room early and asked me if I minded if he smoked — faced with the usual dilemma, I adopted a *personal reaction* approach and said 'As you asked, I would prefer it if you *didn't*'.....and he lit up!! Slightly bemused, I waited a little while and asked him 'Why did you ask?'; 'Oh,' he said 'it's polite to ask.'!!

Some staff act a little like him in that they know they should ask patients what they think of the service, but once the information has been requested and even collected, the process stops short there.

The key question to ask of any service is:

• What have you *changed* in your service over the past 3 months as a result of customer information?

Well....?

Examples of paperwork that could predict or reflect action now or imminently are shown in Figures 9.14 to 9.20 and are self-explanatory:

Customer satisfaction surveys and action					
Hospital	Area	Survey Completed	Findings Available	Action in Hospital	Action in Unit

Figure 9.14. Customer satisfaction surveys and action

WHAT STEPS DOES THE PRIORITY CARE SERVICES UNIT NEED TO TAKE IN ORDER TO OBTAIN A GREATER NUMBER OF REFERRALS IN THE FUTURE?
(Please tick)

	NOT IMPORTANT	QUITE UNIMPORTANT	NEITHER IMPORTANT NOR UNIMPORTANT	QUITE IMPORTANT	VERY IMPORTANT
Much shorter waiting time	1	–	3	16	18
Improve speed that letters are sent	–	–	4	17	16
Improve quality of information in letters	2	–	4	24	8
More personalised service	2	–	5	18	11
Improve mechanism for arranging appointments	1	–	13	20	5
Encourage greater links between consultants/senior professionals & GPs	–	1	6	16	19
Hotel services should be improved	1	2	13	14	5
Improve physical accessibility for patients	2	2	14	17	1
Improve quality of care	1	1	6	13	14
Improve information given to patients receiving long-term care	1	–	3	21	12
Improve aftercare arrangements	1	–	6	17	12
Improve arrangements for urgent appointments	1	–	6	12	17

Figure 9.15. Increasing referral numbers

DIRECTORATE OF PATIENT SERVICES
Notification of Catering Problems

Ward/Dept: _____

Date Time of Occurrence: _____

Nature of Problem: _____

_____

_____

Name of Catering Manager notified:

Action Taken: _____

_____

Signed: _____

Grade: _____

Please return to: Miss I. D., Senior Nurse Manager, 1st Floor, Altnagevin Area
Hospital.

Figure 9.16. Notification of catering problems

**QUALITY ASSURANCE REPORT FOR MEETING OF UNIT
MANAGEMENT BOARD**

1.   **On-going Environmental Issues**

1.1 **Manning of Cardiac Arrest Phone**

Quality Assurance Officer involved in the duties of the DGH telephone
staff, to ensure that they can have a continuous answering service of the
Cardiac Arrest phone, even when there is only one operator on duty.

A survey was done over a weekend and the results showed that the phone
was unmanned for a total of 59 minutes, with a call put out 2 minutes after
the telephonist had returned from a visit to the toilet. A proposal was put
forward by Mr. M. to re-vamp the room adjacent to the switchboard as a
toilet/washbasin area with a facility to still be able to hear, answer and
activate the Cardiac Arrest bleep.

1.2 **Complaint by Mr. and Mrs. K. on lack of a single-unit designated
disabled toilet** for use by male/female persons in O.P.D.

Q.A.O. involved in a suggested scheme put forward by Mr S. and Mr A.to
alter the separate male and female toilets opposite Pharmacy. This would
then become a designated disabled toilet for use by male or female persons,
with improved access, wide door, low wash basin, adequate rails and
signposting.

1.3 **Complaint by Mrs. H that she fainted due to the high temperature in
Clinic A, Out-patients**

Q.A.O. involved in complaint; scheme already suggested. Mr. F to install a
new system of ventilation and ductwork (replacing the existing one). This
would increase the ventilation rate and each clinic would then have control
of its own system. Total cost of this work would be £69,000 plus £5,000 per
annum running costs.

**POINTS 1, 2 AND 3 FOR DISCUSSION AND DECISION DURING
U.M.B. MEETING**

Figure 9.17. Quality assurance report

IN-PATIENT SURVEY - WARD 11

ITEMS RAISED — ACTION PLAN

1. *Entrances* to Hospital difficult for disabled.
   Signposting to Ward — Environmental audit
   Car parking difficult — Report to U.G.M.
2. *Visiting Times*
   Longer in evenings requested — Local negotiation with Sister.
   Two only to bed
   Provision for children
3. *The Ward*
   Needs redecoration, upgrading) — In conjunction with Mrs. P identify planning
   Provision for bed radios and headphones) — arrangements
   Day room for non-smoking)
     and smoking patients)
   Long waits on admission & day before operation — Feasibility of pre-admission clinics Mrs P/Miss J.
   No shower)
   One bath for ward)
   Not enough toilets) — To be addressed in upgrading ward programme: Mrs. P.
   No hairwashing facility)
   Need for shaverpoint)
   Need for mirror)
   Need for better lighting in wash areas)
   Separate wash facilities from toilets
4. Communication between staff variable) — Local professional issues.
   Attitude between staff variable) — Customer care training package.
   Noise levels)

Figure 9.18. In-patient survey — Ward II

CATERING SURVEY - MARCH 1990

ITEMS RAISED	ACTION PLAN	Responsibility
1. Overcooked vegetables	Review cooking techniques.	AB
2. More healthy eating foods, e.g. prunes	Promote healthy eating on menu cards.	MA
3. Temperature of food variable	Monitor temperature of food.	CD
4. High percentage wastage of food on plate	Menu choices appropriate for patients' needs.	HS
5. Cutlery not always clean	Monitor closely and spot checks.	MA

Figure 9.19. Catering survey — March 1990

EYE O.P.D. - CUSTOMER SURVEY 1989

ISSUES RAISED — ACTION PLAN

1. More seating and chairs comfortable
   1. Seating reorganised to give maximum amount in small area.
   2. Have bought high backed chairs which are easier for elderly patients.
   3. Anticipate more room when E.N.T. O.P.D. moves. Discuss with Mrs. P.
2. Need for play area
   1. Reception desk moving, and that area going to be utilised as a play area.
   2. Sister currently buying more toys for department.
3. Decoration
   1. Need for redecoration, and plants.
   2. To discuss with Mrs. P. upgrading department.
4. Reliance on staff to phone for taxis
   1. Need for dedicated taxi telephone line. In hand.

Figure 9.20. Eye O.P.D. — customer survey 1989

Complaints

What do we learn from Complaints? Complaints can usually be collated and analysed into categories of:

Matters relating to conduct   Medical Staff
                                    Nursing Staff
                                    Other Staff
Communication   Medical Staff
                                    Nursing Staff
                                    Other Staff

Waiting times
Hotel services
Other

An extract from the *Report of the Health Services Commission* indicates the specific types of major complaint (albeit small in number) that reach the Commissioner's level:

CONTENTS

	Case Reference Number	Title	Page Numbers Epitomes	Full Text
England	W.545/89-90	Deficiencies in midwifery care during a patient's labour 1		11
	W.677/89-90	Treatment and care in an accident and emergency (A and E) department 2		20
	W.21/90-91	Lack of attention to an elderly A and E patient 2		31
	W.231/90-91	Deficiencies in discharge, homecare and aftercare arrangements for a juvenile patient 3		38
	W.380/90-91	Delay in treating an injury sustained in hospital 4		48
	W.438/90-91	Refusal to release the full text of the report of an independent professional review 5		54
	W.452/90-91	Correspondence about a complaint kept with patient's medical records 5		62
	W.459/90-91	Advice to ante-natal patient 6		66
	W.508/90-91	Actions of ambulance crew and response to complaint 6		73
	W.590/90-91	Response to emergency ambulance request 7		82
	W.676/90-91	Remedial treatment at a dental hospital 8		89
	W.839/90-91	Charge under the Road Traffic Act 1988 8		93
Scotland	SW.47/90-91	Arrangements for discharge to nursing home 9		96
	SW.70/90-91	Deficiencies in supervision and communication in a labour ward 9		102

Figure 9.21. Report of the Health Services Commission

In quoting one *remedy* for one of the above complaints:

❝ Remedy   *The DHA apologised for the shortcomings I identified and agreed to remind medical staff of the importance of accurately dating and timing entries in clinical records. They agreed to satisfy themselves that staff involved in dealing with complaints fully understood what to do and their roles in the complaints procedure.* ❞

It begs the question that when a complaint has been addressed, hopefully to the satisfaction of the complainant, the remedy for this *particular* complainant affects the *whole* system (as appropriate) so that this particular problem under normal circumstances can *never* reoccur. The *Get it right first time (and if a failure occurs, prevent it happening again, ever)* model must be applied when a service receives feedback either through surveys or complaints.

One specific area that patients frequently comment on, either via elicited feedback, or through verbal/written formal complaints is the *shop window* of the hospital — reception desks, outpatients, catering and A & E departments etc. A patient's first impression as they come into a hospital is very important — the physical and social environment is important to someone who is anxious and unsure (as most of us are in our *patient* status. The warmer the welcome, the better. As a result of feedback received, many hospitals are aiming to give patients a more positive first contact with their hospital. This warmer welcome should consist of:

• Providing directions;
• Providing preparatory information;
• Accompanying people to their destination if lost;
• Putting patients at their ease; and
• Showing welcoming behaviour.

Two references for this work are Smith S (1991) and Nelson A & Gordon M (1986).
Training packages of relevance are:

1. *Person to Person* Mersey Region; and
2. *Face to Face* Chartwell Bratt Bromley.

Two areas before moving on:

1. Avant Hotels Group — a privately owned company in North Humberside — have developed the following front desk procedure for guest arrival/ check-in procedure:

❝1. *Each guest must be acknowledged immediately upon arrival at Front Desk and served on a first come first served basis.*

2. *All registration transactions must include:*
   (a) A welcoming smile.
   (b) Eye-to-eye contact.
   (c) Response to guest arrival, eg. 'Good morning', 'Good afternoon'.
   (d) The use of the guest's name at least once.
   (e) Confirmation of room type and length of stay.
   (f) Confirmation of method of payment and offer of express checkout, if applicable.
   (g) Handing over the key and key-card with rate clearly shown, and directions to room.
   (h) No room number should be mentioned for security reasons.
   (i) Offer to assistance with luggage.
   (j) An appropriate conversation close, eg. 'I hope you will enjoy your stay'.

3. *Guest registration should be an unbroken sequence. Should an unavoidable interruption occur, an apology must be offered to the guest.*

4. *Every effort must be made to accommodate individual guests immediately. A guest with a confirmed reservation should not be required to wait if his/ her arrival is after checkout time. If this is the case then the guest must:*
   (a) Be given an apology and, if feasible, be offered coffee, tea or a drink.
   (b) Be informed of the time when his/her room will be ready.
   (c) Be offered storage facility for luggage.
   (d) Never be sent to a room which is not ready for letting. **❞**

A different kettle of fish to the typical DGH outpatient department on a Monday morning. Or is it?

2. Many service jobs in the NHS contain large sections of prolonged contact with customers, even if the task is simple, the pressure of giving prolonged good customer care is immense and stressful. The role of the manager of front line staff is crucial to support, appraise and encourage staff.

Accountability to customers

An extension to *putting customers first* is to behave in a way that illustrates a service's accountability to its customers who ultimately *pay your wages*.

Two main ways in which a provider unit service displays this is via:

1. Explicit standards and specifications which it is shown to meet, if not exceed; and
2. Explicit charters embodying the main standards or values of the service.

Both these mean that patients (and staff) are constantly aware of what patients should, under normal circumstances, expect, and, by implication, this means that the service *expects* and *wants* to hear from patients who feel they *did* not receive the standard of service laid down in the standards and charter.

Two examples of charters, one NHS and one from Comet Electrical Suppliers Customer Services Department, as in Figures 9.22 and 9.23, are shown to compare and contrast:

NORTHWICK PARK HOSPITAL
PATIENT'S CHARTER

CARE — CLINICAL EXCELLENCE — COURTESY

Northwick Park Hospital Patients can expect:-

*   To receive all hospital care that is necessary for the proper diagnosis and treatment of your illness or injury

*   To receive respect, privacy and dignity at all times

*   To be informed about all aspects of your illness if you so choose

*   To be involved in the planning of your care whenever possible

*   To be cared for with consideration for your family and close friends

*   To receive an advocacy service if you are unable to effectively express your own needs

*   To be discharged from hospital at a time and on a day determined by your health care needs

*   To have continuing care specific to your needs arranged for you

*   To have any complaint investigated thoroughly and a response made within a reasonable time

Signed _____

CHIEF EXECUTIVE
On behalf of staff at N.P.H.

Figure 9.22. Patient's Charter at Northwick Park Hospital

Comet
Customer Pledge

Our aim is to help you make the right choice and ensure your remain satisfied with your purchase

Product Information
Each product area has its own Information Display explaining key features, and demonstrations are available wherever possible.

Price Promise
If you buy any product from Comet, then within 14 days find the same offer on sale locally at a lower price, we'll willingly refund the difference, plus 10% of that difference.

Extended Warranties
All parts and labour are included and you don't have the inconvenience of paying the engineer for repairs and then claiming your money back.

Delivery Service
For a small charge, delivery can be arranged morning or afternoon. Most stores can also arrange delivery in the evening. When we deliver, we'll also remove your old (disconnected) appliance if you wish.

14-Day Exchange
If the product doesn't suit, simply return it within 14 days — as new with the original packaging — and we'll exchange it for another product of equivalent value or, if you prefer, give you your money back.

After Sales Service
We want you to enjoy continuous use of any product, and as we have the biggest dedicated service operation in the country, staffed with our own fully-trained engineers, you can be confident of specialist attention should the need arise. If the product can't be repaired in the first 12 months, we will replace it.

Telephone Enquiries
You will find the telephone number and the name of the store manager on your receipt in case you have any problems or further queries about your purchase.

Total Customer Satisfaction
Our aim is total customer satisfaction. If we fail to achieve this please let us know by writing to:
Peter McTague
Customer Services Director, Comet Group PLC
George Street, Hull HU1 3AU

Figure 9.23. Comet customer pledge

Chapter 10   Sustaining commitment for TQM

With the increasing awareness of quality management systems by those delivering health care, and the expectation from District *purchasers* that *provider* hospitals and community services will build quality management into their service specifications, most units have begun to plan for *total quality*. Of these, some services are 18-24 months down the road towards total quality.

Like all public sector services in the UK, the NHS is attempting to drive quality of care and service higher and higher through its developing customer orientation. However, these services implementing total quality have encountered a key issue in the long term process, which, depending on how it is dealt with, predicts success or failure in realising the benefits of TQM.

This issue is the ability, having embarked on TQM, to sustain the commitment of all staff to quality improvement processes in health care delivery.

Provider units vary considerably in the comprehensiveness of their strategies for quality improvement, depending as they largely do on the quality approaches of quality assurance, professional standards setting and developing awareness of the clinical audit. Some units, including many of the Department of Health's funded demonstration projects, have forged conceptual links with TQM models applied outside health care.

The initial vision of total quality in health care depends on an awareness and commitment to the cultural values inherent in successful and sustainable TQM, as illustrated again in Figure 10.1.

Most managers and clinicians (doctors, nurses and other therapists) will acknowledge the essential nature of these values. However, they vary in their behavioural/practical application and consistency of application. The initial audit of staff attitudes and subsequent explicit *operationalising* of these values and how they relate in a practical way to everyday patient care are crucial to this issue.

The more controversial of these values is the one which links quality improvement to reducing quality costs of health care. The *tension* between perceived need for *additional* funding to improve quality (in addition to quantity/throughput of care) and possible *reducing* of costs, resulting from quality improvements, needs clear understanding and sensitive management due to the considerable pressures and public expectations on direct patient carers.

The vision also depends on a clear and comprehensive model of TQM and its implementation, which can be applied in a health care setting and seen as relevant by clinical and non-clinical staff alike. Key components of such a model have been outlined previously.

Provider units, currently implementing TQM in either hospital or community settings, could compare their own models with this to establish their comprehensiveness.

This implementation plan has been explored throughout this text illustrating the several steps to TQM shown in Figure 10.1. These steps are not quite as ordered on this *staircase* with some steps being, in fact, the same level, ie occurring simultaneously.

It has been my experience working with provider units throughout the United Kingdom and abroad that it is not so difficult to get a positive initial response from a service to *establishing* TQM. The most important part is how they *keep* the process of TQM *going* once established.

Ten key components have been identified in health care provider units which, if addressed, can help sustain staff commitment and maintain the initial momentum established by introducing the TQM approach:

- Maintaining senior management and clinician commitment;
- Practising *total* communication;

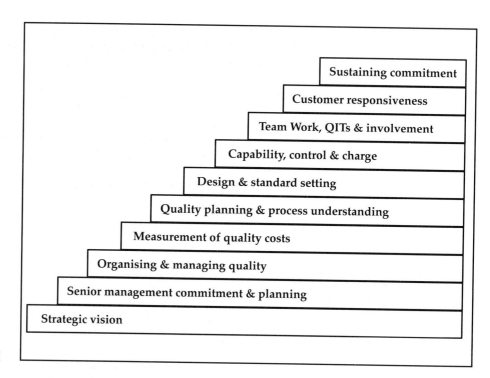

Figure 10.1

- Measurement and audit;
- Emphasising tangible results;
- Integration of clinical activity monitoring with quality monitoring and applying both to purchasing strategy;
- Introducing concept and practice of benchmarking;
- Continual review of structure for quality;
- Training and education;
- Identifying and overcoming barriers and obstacles; and
- Continual transformation of the unit's culture towards vision of TQM.

Maintaining senior management and clinician commitment

For TQM in health care to be effective and *drive quality on* it must be both *top-led* and *bottom-fed*. Chief Executives and members of his/her executive board (both general managers and consultants/clinical directors) must lead from the top, by example, attitude, and actions. They must be individual in the strategic operational aspects of quality and give full support to others who are focusing their efforts on particular services, clinical and non-clinical.

The lack of top management commitment has been cited by 97 of the 100 firms in the United Kingdom surveyed recently by ODI (1991) as one of the most significant barriers to implementing a *quality programme*. The NHS and its provider units can learn from this and many other similar studies, some cited earlier in this text, and ensure that senior management and clinicians obtain high quality training and advice to help ensure their ongoing commitment to both words and actions.

The challenge for both of these groups is to continually:

- Identify and define successful health care delivery in terms of *adding value* through meeting patients' and other customer quality requirements;
- Reviewing and reformulating a clear and mutually shared vision of quality and model the commitment to achieving that vision;
- Motivate, reward, and develop key staff in a commitment to quality;
- Develop the systems and technology to support *quality improvement and management*.

One practical step to ensure staff in a provider unit understand the senior management commitment to *quality* is to emulate David O'Neill in Trafford

(O'Neill, 1992) who describes his *plan of attack* in which he regularly appears in front of large groups of staff and discusses commitment to their TQM programme citing four important reasons:

- *To allay staff concerns — as has already been mentioned many had been interviewed and were wondering what was going on.*
- *To create a high profile for the programme.*
- *To demonstrate to the cynics that this was not a 'flash in the pan' or a 'flavour of the month', but something which would be here for good.*
- *To further demonstrate my commitment by standing before staff and telling them of our plans.*

Practising *total* communication

The key meaning of the word *Total* in TQM has to be the involvement of staff in the action — not just some staff, eg the committed, enthusiasts, but *all* staff. Some of the less likely staff have tremendous contributions to make, albeit sometimes unlikely ones, to the Total Quality Management approach, for example:

- **Argumentative Doctors** can share their intimate experiences of dis-eased patients and GPs and use the ability to make their lot a better one — the desired outcome of any *management initiative.*

- **Resistant Nurses** are the ones who bear the brunt of over-stretched wards and can use their everyday (and night) experience to equate quantity, quality and cost of health care in a meaningful way.

- **Unenthusiastic Managers** can turn round their 'I've seen it all before' attitudes and tie over-visionary interpretations of TQM down to more realistic and practical application to the very busy world of operational management.

- **Unmotivated support staff** can remind senior managers and clinicians that years of poor recognition and disempowerment (let alone less wages than Croesus would work for) by senior colleagues has an effect on anyone's motivation.

The importance of effective communication is shared over and over again in *How to develop Total Quality Management* type publications — yet in everyday management it is amazing how total communication is not achieved and even not attempted because:

- *We'd never get to all the staff*
- *They don't all come to the meetings*
- *They wouldn't all be interested*

Well informed staff become interested, motivated and the standard bearers (literally) of Quality Management. It is important to take the trouble to ensure any part of TQM reaches *all* staff to whom this message is appropriately targeted. At the end of the day, check staff against a list to ensure *you* get through to *all* of *them*.

Measurement and audit

Hospitals and community providers of health care are large complex organisations. It is very difficult to have a comprehensive overview of the Quality of all the functions involved. The unit must corporately develop its

QUALITY MONITORS IN PLACE

A.   Finance
Monthly operating statements for
   CEO and Finance Committee
Daily/weekly/monthly
   reconciliation of accounts
Annual and bi-annual audit
   including management letter
Payroll accuracy (x 2 weeks)
Audit of master file system

B.   Personnel
Recruitment audit – speed,
   appropriateness
Benefit enrolment
Audit of hospital-wide
   performance appraisal program
Employment Standards Act audit
Analysis of union grievances

C.   Medical Records
Monthly count of incomplete
   charts
Complaints of charts not
   available
Audits on transcription/chart
   deficiencies/coding and
   abstracting techniques
External audit – HMRI

D.   Admitting
Concurrent audit of admitting
   procedure (random sample)
Audit of accuracy of A/D/T lists
Assessment of discharge/transfer
   system

E. 1. Occupational Health and Safety
Audit of Workers' Compensation
   Board Claims
Safety inspections, weekly/
   monthly
Ministry of Labour inspections
Investigation of employee
   incidents and lost-time
   accidents

  2. Infection Control
Investigation of reported
   infections
Analysis of hospital-acquired and
   community-acquired infections
Audit of aseptic procedures
Sterilizer monitoring

F.   Staff education
Program evaluations/list of
   program attendance
Competency-based evaluation/
   program effectiveness—based
   on incidents
Recertification of delegated acts

G.   Psychology
Chart audit
Audit of psychological
   assessment reports
Workload analysis: direct vs.
   indirect care hours

H.   Engineering
Record of breakdowns
Quality of air (winter)
Boiler efficiency (percentage)
Heating system efficiency
   (percentage)
Testing of emergency power
Chemical treatment of water
   system

I.   Maintenance
Preventative maintenance
   program
Monitoring maintenance
   requisition system
Weekly inspections
Ontario Hydro random
   inspections of new work
External inspections

J.   Materials Management
Reconciliation of purchase
   requisitions to receipts (weekly)
Client satisfaction survey
Weekly inventory control (stock
   level check)
Audit of follow-up requests
Audit of quota system

K.   Housekeeping
Weekly inspection
Monitoring pest control contract

L.   Dietetics and Food Services
Nutritional audits (retro, chart)
Menu audit
Tray audit
Tray returns (therapeutic diets)
Patient satisfaction
   questionnaires/interviews
Accuracy of food production
   scheduling
Sanitation inspections, daily
Public Health inspection of
   kitchen
New food evaluation
Temperature checks
Trayline assessments

M.   Social Work
Case book audits (retro. chart
   audit)
Peer review audit
Patient satisfaction survey

N.   Chaplaincy
Review of on-call activity
Review of numbers (1) at
   worship; (2) in counselling
Reports of education programs
   for external students/pastors

O.   Physiotherapy
Patient outcomes: comparison of
   status on admission and
   discharge
Health status rating forms
Chart audit (retro.)

(1) documentation; (2) patient
   care
Patient questionnaires

P.   Occupational Therapy
COTA accreditation for OT
   student placement

Q.   Fire Preparedness
Monthly fire drill/standby drills
Monthly monitoring of fire
   equipment and alarm systems
Biennial external inspection: fire
   marshal's office

R.   Radiology
MOH radiation protection branch
   inspections
Reject/repeat rates
Accuracy and timeliness of
   report/audit of dictation
Audit of patient waiting time
Spot check on film library
Outages/breakdowns
Dose measurement
Check on automatic processor
Monthly statistics

S.   Laboratories
LPTP (Laboratory Proficiency
   Testing Program)
Incidents— reported internally
   and by external department
Turnaround times
Lab orders
Quality control data
Preventative maintenance control
MD and patient surveys

T.   Pharmacy
Errors in dispensing
Delays in dispensing
Weekly inspection—in pharmacy
   and/or units—and restocking
Narcotic controls
Drug utilization review

U.   Nursing
Concurrent nursing audit
Nursing practice standards
Analysis of incidents, quarterly
Nursing workload management
   system: consistency and
   appropriateness
Mini-audits:
   Documentation of response to
      PRN medications
   Documentation of patient
      teaching and response
   Nursing histories (completion)
   Nursing care plans (currency)

Figure 10.2. Quality monitors in place

measurement and audit function so that quality monitors are in place *throughout* the Unit. Wilson (1987) succinctly describes this approach throughout one particular hospital in Figure 10.2 which reflects the considerable measurement and audit taking place. Most NHS hospitals have suitably comprehensive programmes but they are not as coordinated and explicit as this programme indicates they could be.

Emphasising tangible results

Benefits of effective health care delivery via the adoption of a TQM approach are:

- *Greater Consistency of Care/Service.*
- *Increasing standards of care.*
- *Reduced* errors.
- *Greater confidence of staff.*
- *Better communication of what is expected and available.*
- *Better understanding of patients and staff views.*

- Increased patient satisfaction:
  — Greater overall satisfaction values
  — Improved customer relations
  — More effective care and service
  — Greater access and convenience
  — Greater involvement in own care

- Greater organisational effectiveness:
  — Existence and consistency of standards
  — Raising standards
  — Rising consistency of conformance to standards
  — Integrated resource management (Quantity, quality and cost)
  — Increased market share (when possible)
  — Cultural change (incorporation of Quality into documentation, policies, induction and training)
  — Involvement of *all* staff groups and decrease barriers

- Increased staff satisfaction
  — Reduced staff turnover
  — Reduced sickness/absence levels
  — Improved staff training and conditions
  — Greater job clarity and satisfaction
  — More time to use specialist skills
  — Greater recognition from others
  — Improved staff communication
  — Increased team coherence

- Reduced quality costs and increased value for money
  — Reduction in failure costs
  — More appropriate inspection and monitoring
  — Higher prevention costs
  — Improved budgetary control

Although only one of several important variables, customer satisfaction is the key to successful TQM. When a provider unit can display *improving customer satisfaction* ratings from each directorate, locality or service, it is likely that TQM is in place. (See Figure 10.3).

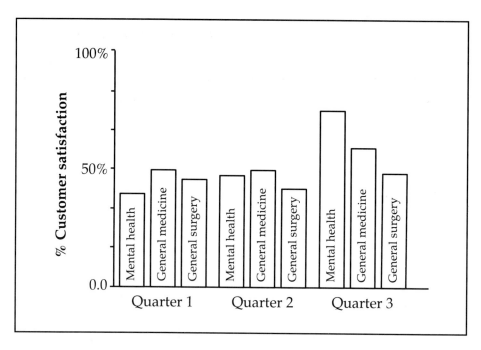

Figure 10.3. Customer satisfaction

The most effective way to evaluate a TQM programme is to compare the performance of a Total Quality Hospital or Community Service with other services in terms of the variables identified above. The TQM service should be significantly better than average on these measurements. These types of benefits should be achievable, not in periods *over two years*, but within six months of the start of the programme. Quality improvement is measurable. Concentrate on a few key patient-focused measures and *benchmark* your service against other similar services, especially *the competition*. One of the most common characteristics of a successful total quality programme is an emphasis on tangible results. Cultural change is crucial and long term. While transforming the culture, it is essential to drive for early results to reinforce the cultural change, attitudes, and core values of QI.

Integration of clinical activity monitoring with quality monitoring

At a strategic level it has already been mentioned that a TQM policy must be integrated fully with the unit's overall business planning approach. It makes no sense to separate them. Similarly, at operational level, where doctors, nurses and managers meet to discuss the ongoing function of services for patients at ward, specialty, or directorate level, it is important to integrate the variables of:

* Clinical Activity, throughput, facility (beds, day places, outpatients);
* Cost of this activity; and
* Quality possible for these resources.

Key issues in achieving this interpretation are:

* Availability of simple, reliable and valid information on activity cost and quality
* Information on over/underachievement of monthly/quarterly activity and/or cost/quality targets
* Agreed and owned action to remedy missed targets
* Interpreted approach to waiting times, *two-year waiters* and waiting list initiatives
* Awareness and discussion of effects of changing the equilibrium between Quantity, Quality and Cost. Eg Increased quantity after decreased quality.

Some examples of simple and highly practical data which apply to these issues alone are shown in Figure 10.4.

Figure 10.4

																Cumm.	Cumm.	

CONTRACT ANALYSIS APRIL/MAY 1992

INPATIENTS: ALL CONTRACTS

SPECIALTY	1992/93 Contract Level	April	May	June	July	Aug.	Sept.	Oct.	Nov.	Dec.	Jan.	Feb.	March	Cumm. Total	Cumm. Target	Variance
Surgery	6,410	497	471											958	1,068	−100
ENT	1,485	91	110											201	248	−47
Orthopaedics	3,108	238	233											471	518	−47
Urology	1,964	163	161											324	327	−3
Ophthalmology	1,196	83	84											167	199	−32
Oral Surgery	320	50	47											97	53	44
Paediatrics	2,359	196	208											404	393	11
A&E	1,932	135	136											271	322	−51
Dermatology	176	25	21											46	29	17
General Medicine	7,707	618	606											1,224	1,285	−61
Haematology	481	36	46											82	80	2
Pain Relief	214	28	22											50	36	14
Rheumatology	942	33	74											107	157	−50
Plastic Surgery	2,550	191	197											388	425	−37
Well Babies	0	399	463											862		
Gynaecology	2,382	236	222											458	397	61
Obstetrics	6,100	533	597											1,130	1,017	113
Geriatrics	2,975	224	208											432	496	−64
GP Obs	890	74	86											160	148	12
GRAND TOTAL	43,191	3,451	3,529											6,980	7,199	−219

1. Inpatient Activity
Note: Annual contract activity divided into monthly *targets* with over/under achievement shown (variance)

OUTPATIENT WAITING TIMES FOR NON URGENT APPOINTMENTS
Position as at 31st July 1992

Specialty	Consultant	Waiting Time (Weeks) Previous Month	Waiting Time (Weeks)	Date of Next Non Urgent Appointment
Medicine	Dr. Adam	6	8	20.7.92
Medicine	Dr. Bede	6	10	10.7.92
Medicine	Dr. Cone	5	4	16.6.92
Medicine	Dr. Dealy	4	6	9.7.92
Medicine	Dr. Elstead	8	11	14.8.92
Medicine	Dr. Finer	4	4	26.6.92
Gastroenterology	Dr. Hone	6	6	8.7.92
Gastroenterology	Dr. Irwin	4	6	9.7.92
Diabetes	Dr. Jones	5	7	16.7.92
Geriatrics	Dr. Kenwood	4	3	17.6.92
Geriatrics	Dr. Lander	4	4	23.6.92
Surgery	Mr. Miller	(25)	(24)	10.11.92
Surgery	Mr. Norway	(17)	(17)	21.9.92
Surgery	Mr. Orton	(16)	(16)	14.9.92
Surgery	Mr. Petra	11	8	21.7.92
Paediatrics	Mr. Quartz	4	3	19.6.92
Paediatrics	Dr. Rosser	4	4	22.6.92
Paediatrics	Dr. Shean	4	3	15.6.92
Orthopaedics	Mr. Toller	(46)	(48)	28.4.93
Orthopaedics	Mr. Underwood	(91)	(101)	2.5.94
ENT	Mr. Viner	(22)	(18)	29.9.92
ENT	Mr. Winwood	(16)	(16)	18.9.92
ENT	Mr. Allen	(14)	(16)	14.9.92
ENT	Mr. Beacon	(17)	(20)	30.9.92
Oral Surgery	Mr. Coleridge	6	5	1.7.92
Oral Surgery	Mr. Dean	(21)	(22)	30.10.92

2. Waiting Times for non-urgent Appointments (Access)
Note: Allows identification of key long waiting lists (circled) for further discussions and action (where appropriate)

cont'd. Figure 10.4

WAITING LIST ANALYSIS								
Inpatients as at 31st July 1992								
Speciality	No. With Date	No. Without Date	TOTAL	0-2	3-5	6-8	9-11	12-23	24+
General Surgery	86	850	936	367	285	173	81	30	-
ENT	118	185	303	81	50	29	20	123	2
Orthopaedics	55	628	683	248	128	108	88	111	-
Urology	122	322	444	300	100	32	6	6	-
Plastic Surgery	153	340	493	173	166	107	28	19	-
Oral Surgery	32	291	323	115	79	39	45	45	-
Ophthalmology	172	811	983	265	137	150	111	262	58
Pain Relief	-	90	90	46	20	17	6	2	-
General Medicine	5	72	77	47	18	9	-	3	-
Dermatology	14	-	14	14	-	-	-	-	-
Rheumatology	-	93	93	74	19	-	-	-	-
Gynaecology	5	245	250	97	36	32	27	58	-
UNIT TOTAL	762	3,837	4,599	1,781	1,018	679	406	657	58

3. Waiting List analysis for Admission (Access)
Note: Allows the identification of 24+ month-waiters for immediate action and 12-23 month waiters for projection of growth in 24+ month waiters over next 12 months

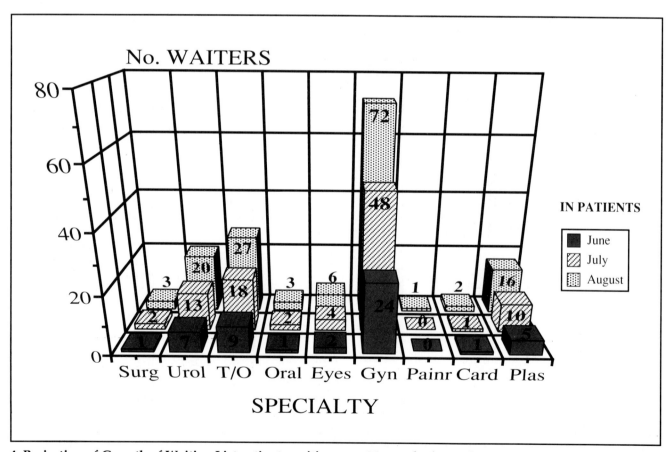

4. Projection of Growth of Waiting List patients waiting over 24 months (access)
Projecting forward from current 20-23 month waiters, to level of 24+ waiters over next 2-3 months.

It is crucial to identify the several tensions which exist between:

- Activity increases (or selective activity increases) cost and/or quality;
- Selective action on 24+ months waiter can affect cost prediction and workload later in the year;
- Selective Action on 24+ month waiters can affect ability to deal with urgent cases; and
- Increase in outpatient activity can affect quality of individual outpatient appointments.

Continual review of structure for quality

Very few organisations establish and feel confident that their structure for monitoring total quality is right. On at least an annual basis they review different aspects of their structure as their ideas develop, business pressures change, and customer requirements and demands alter.

Key structural issues include:

- Capability of management structure to support TQM eg relevance/success of clinical directorate model or locality management model, or hospital/ community model of health care;
- Adequacy of composition and activity of Senior Quality Improvement Steering Group;
- Success or otherwise of Human Resource Organisation to help managers empower, support and develop staff;
- Appropriateness of resource management strategy in helping clinicians have the appropriate resource use information;
- Integration of profession medical machinery with overall way of managing the unit;
- Structure of quality systems;
- Internal quality system;
- Accreditation; and
- *BS 5750* certification

These structural issues need frequent review to ensure they meet the needs for coordination within the service.

Training and education

Poor quality or good quality health care delivery is a reflection on our ability to train and educate staff in QI. Education and training affects service delivery and hence patient satisfaction.

Education and training have different meanings but are both essential. Figure 10.5 indicates the different roles they play. Training for Total Quality health care delivery is not just an activity for staff *close to the patient*. Senior management and clinicians must be among the first to be trained in:

- *an understanding of the change process and how to manage it*
- *leadership skills, such as self-management, how to empower people and team-building*
- *developing skills to improve organisational effectiveness, such as process analysis and improvement, and customer/supplier skills*
- *developing skills of problem-solving, running improvement teams and using the tools and techniques of total quality*
- *communication skills to enable them to share their vision of the future and to be able to deal more effectively with their customers and suppliers.*
- *coaching skills to enable them to develop people.*

Seath (1992)

Education	Training
• Customers' requirements (Patients and Purchaser) • Current performance in meeting requirements • Vision and values of Health Care Quality • Determinants of Health Care service quality	• Managing the TQM change process • Leadership skills (Consultants and Managers) • Process improvement skills • Customer/Focus skills • Problem-solving skills and QIT skills • Communication skills • Teamworking skills
Desired Outcome = **Awareness**	Desired Outcome = **Improvement Action**

Figure 10.5. Different roles for education and training (Modified from Seath (1992)).

All other staff will have training needs which are similar to those for managers and can be met through workshops, coaching by senior managers, HOD, consultants, supervisors, and facilitators and concentrate on the determination of *service quality*.

❝ ❑ *Reliability:*   *Consistency of performance and dependability*
   ❑ *Responsiveness:* *Willingness of employees to provide service*
   ❑ *Competence:*   *Skills and knowledge to perform the service*
   ❑ *Access:*   *Approachability and ease of conduct*
   ❑ *Courtesy:*   *Politeness, respect and consideration of contact staff*
   ❑ *Community:*   *Keeping customers informed*
   ❑ *Credibility:*   *Trustworthiness, believability and honesty*
   ❑ *Security:*   *Freedom from risk, danger or doubt (physical and financial)*
   ❑ *Understanding and knowing the customer:*
                    Making the effort to understand the customer's needs
   ❑ *Tangibles:*   *Physical evidence of the service (facilities, appearance of staff, tools and equipment)* ❞

Source: Parasuraman, Zeithamel and Berry, 1985

In developing the unit *training for quality* strategy, key dimensions to bear in mind are shown in Figure 10.6.

The broad timeframe for education and training of staff needs to be sensibly scheduled. An example is shown in Figure 10.7. Training style is crucial to the success of any programme and some elements of successful training style are shown in Figure 10.8.

Detailed information on training packages/approaches and content can be found in Koch (1991). In addition the reader is referred to training packages on Total Quality Management in Health care:

• *Total Quality Management in Public Sector Service* (Koch 1991)
• *Exceeding Expectations — Total Quality Management in Mental Health Services* (Koch 1991)
• *Implementing Total Quality Management* (Koch 1992 in preparation)

A final note on training and the customer — apart from ensuring all training materials are of a very high quality (including no errors in OHPs — a quality

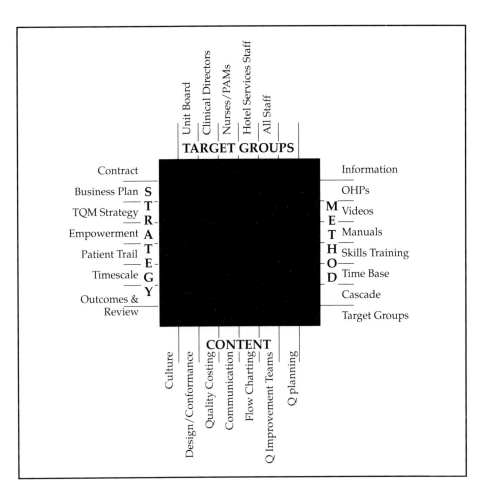

Figure 10.6. Training for quality
— developing a strategy

activity \ month	1	2	3	4	5	6	7	8	9	10	11	12
Initial Service Management TQM Awareness Seminars	▬	▬										
Train TQM Manager & QIT Facilitators			▬	▬								
TQM Education Cascade Programme												
Hospital A					▬	▬	▬	▬	▬	▬	▬	▬
Hospital B					▬	▬	▬	▬	▬	▬		
Hospital C						▬	▬	▬				
Extend Consultant Seminars on Key Tools & Techniques					▬			▬			▬	
Quality Systems Training					▬							
QIT Training Seminars						▬		▬			▬	
Phased Roll-out – TQM												
Hospital A								➔	▬	▬	▬	
Hospital B								➔	▬	▬	▬	
Hospital C									➔	▬	▬	▬

Figure 10.7. Broad timeframe — education

TRAINING STYLE						
	Trainer					
	1	**2**	**3**	**4**	**5**	**6**
Appearance						
Movement						
Non-verbal Behaviour						
Humour						
Confidence						
Specificity of Brief						

Use of
    a)   **OHP**
    b)   **Written Information**
    c)   **Video**
    d) **WhiteBoard/Flip Chart**						

Reinforcing Audience & **Audience Assets**						
Encourage Participation						
Use of Service Examples						
Use of positive, action-oriented **language**						

Figure 10.8. Training style

issue close to my heart!), use the training experience to model customer responsiveness — find out by verbal means and evaluation questionnaires what the 'trainees' thought of the training. An example of a questionnaire is given in Figure 10.9 which was developed for a Total Quality Management seminar for Hong Kong professionals in 1992.

Identify and overcome barriers and obstacles

In a study of barriers to TQM implementation in United Kingdom firms. A. Wilkinson and B. Witcher (1991) identified the main barriers:

1.   Short-termism;
2.   Organisation and segmentation; and
3.   Reluctant managers.

R. Boardman and Weyndling (1992) considered total quality implementation barriers under the headings of:

• People
• Processes

These notions and others encountered in NHS work are now explored.

The framework on page 10.10 identifies many of the key dimensions of Total Quality Management implementation, with obstacles or barriers being found at the lower end of each vertical dimension. These will be taken together and key obstacles identified.

Evaluation Questionnaire
Seminars on Quality Management in Health Care

Dates: 14 - 17 February 1992   ❑   To be returned to: Training & Development Unit
        18 & 19 February 1992   ❑   Hospital Authority
        20 & 21 February 1992   ❑   28/F Hennessy Centre
                                                     500 Hennessy Road
                                                     Causeway Bay
                                                     Hong Kong

Please tick as appropriate

1. Did the programme meet the training objectives as stated?

   ❑ Completely   ❑ Very well   ❑ Fairly well   ❑ Not very well

   Comments: _____

   _____

2. Did the programme meet your training needs?

   ❑ Completely   ❑ Very well   ❑ Fairly well   ❑ Not very well

   Comments: _____

   _____

3. Were the subjects relevant to your job needs?

   ❑ Very relevant   ❑ Relevant   ❑ Relevant in part only   ❑ Not relevant

   Comments: _____

   _____

4. Was the level of the subject treatment about right?

   ❑ Too advanced   ❑ About right   ❑ Too shallow

   Comments: _____

   _____

5. How satisfied were you with the length and pace of the programme?

   ❑ Very satisfied   ❑ Satisfied   ❑ Moderately satisfied   ❑ Not at all satisfied

   Comments: _____

   _____

6. Did you find the group discussions useful?

   ❑ Very useful   ❑ Useful   ❑ Fairly useful   ❑ Not useful

   Comments: _____

   _____

7. Was there enough time for questions?

   ❑ Too much   ❑ About right   ❑ Too little

   Comments: _____

   _____

Figure 10.9 cont'd

8. How satisfied were you with:–	Very satisfied	Satisfied	Moderately satisfied	Not at all satisfied	Comments
(a) trainers' presentation?	❏	❏	❏	❏	_____
(b) the trainers' training materials?	❏	❏	❏	❏	_____
(c) the planning and organisation of the programme?	❏	❏	❏	❏	_____
(d) the A-V materials, if any?	❏	❏	❏	❏	_____
(e) the venue?	❏	❏	❏	❏	_____

9. Please give your assessment of the content:–	Very good	Good	satisfactory	Poor	Comments
Session 1: Quality in Health Care in Private & Public Sector	❏	❏	❏	❏	_____
Session 2: Definition of Quality	❏	❏	❏	❏	_____
Session 3: Current Quality Improvement Initiatives	❏	❏	❏	❏	_____
Session 4: Quality Assurance, Quality Management & Clinical Audit	❏	❏	❏	❏	_____
Session 5: Overview of TQM Culture & Values	❏	❏	❏	❏	_____
Session 6: Overview of TQM Techniques	❏	❏	❏	❏	_____
Session 7: Devising a Quality Management Strategy	❏	❏	❏	❏	_____
Session 8: Possible Obstacles to Implementation	❏	❏	❏	❏	_____
Session 9: Implementation Plan	❏	❏	❏	❏	_____
Session 10: Quality Planning	❏	❏	❏	❏	_____
Session 11: Quality Improvement Teams	❏	❏	❏	❏	_____
Session 12: Action Plan	❏	❏	❏	❏	_____

10. Please give suggestions to improve the programme for future participants.

Comments: _____

_____

11. Please suggest topics for future management programme.

Comments: _____

_____

12. Other Comments: _____

_____

cont'd Figure 10.9

Figure 10.10. TQM elements

	Commitment to quality by senior manager	Quality management systems organisation and structure	Health care business performance	Staff development training	Relationships with patients	Staff attitude to quality management	Communications	Staff technical awareness of quality	Quality management system	Quality performance indicators	Improvement teams
1	Fully committed and actively involved in all areas of service	Well established and widely understood TQM systems	Activity completed within budget at expected quality	Programme fully developed and ongoing	Active partnerships taking place with patients involved with care and feedback	Totally committed and openly enthusiastic	Well established system, fully implemented	Full practical understanding	Fully documented and implemented	Performance indicators as standard management tool integrated with contracts	Several teams with patient involvement
2	Part time involvement with quality improvement activities	Objectives defined, and implemented in a constructive fashion throughout service	Budget control established separate from activity & quality control		All management involved in developing relationships with patients	Voluntarily cooperative	Established system, partially implemented	Application of theory	Partially documented and implemented	Regular measurement	Improvements identified and implemented
3	Quality manager the driving force	Problem identified and remains unsolved	Budget problems identified	Programme fully developed but partially implemented	Patient expectations reviewed and agreed	Cooperate when ordered	Function exists but lacks direction	Partial understanding		Structure for measurement is complete	Teams identified and trained in TQM tools & techniques
4	Senior managers give spasmodic support & encouragement to quality initiatives & short termism	Objectives defined but partially implemented	Budget established	Programme under development budget allocated	Recognition of concerns of patients	Indifferent	Policy exists but system is disorganised		Informal QMS in place	First regular measurement	Improvement project identified
5	Managers are sceptical of benefits of TQM	Organisational segmentation fragmented & ill-defined partially documented	Activity and quality data available	Importance of programme recognised but not initiated	Patient-centered activities well intended but prone to atrophy	Privately hostile	Importance recognised but no coordinated policy exists			First performance indicators identified	Improvement programme established and budget allocated
6	No interest from managers	Non-existent quality objectives	No budget control, no activity or quality control	Not recognised as important	Suspicious and defensive of patient views	Openly hostile	No recognition of need	Unaware	Non-existent	None	None

1. Commitment to quality

Barriers

(a) Senior Management and Consultants's personal commitment

(b) Unclear quality manager role

(c) Short termism — no long term vision

Solutions

(a) Senior staff seminars

(b) Gentle confrontation of individual behaviour

(a) Clear responsibilities

(b) Explicit accountability to chief executive

(a) Allow short term tangible results to fit with long term strategy

2. Quality management system and structure

Barriers

(a) Incomplete, incoherent 'system' for coordinating different thrusts of TQM

(b) Quality steering group with unclear direction

Solutions

(a) Application of customised TQM structure with/without elements of *BS 5750* type structure

(b) Clear terms of reference accountable through chairman to chief executive officer

3. Health care business performance

Barriers

(a) Lack of availability and integration of activity, quality and cost information

Solutions

(a) Resource management/TQM integration

(b) Availability of simple, regular activity, cost and quality of information by specialty

4. Staff development and training

Barriers

(a) Lack of investment in training and staff development

(b) Poorly implemented IPR

Solutions

(a) Funded *training for quality* programme given high priority in business plan

(b) Strategy for offering *all* staff some form of appraisal

(c) Management training for appraisal skills

5. Relationship with patients

Barriers

(a) Patients seem, in part, as obstacles to efficient running of service!

(b) Lack of involvement with patients in their own care/in giving feedback

Solutions

(a) Train managers and clinicians in customer responsiveness

(b) Establish customer feedback strategy:
— corporate
— in all areas
— quarterly feedback of simple numerical score for patient satisfaction

6. Staff attitudes to quality planning

Barriers

(a) Resistant, reluctant staff

Solutions

(a) Senior management and consultant modelling of TQM related attitudes and behaviour

(b) Reinforcement and recognition of staff necessary

(c) Clear expectation of performance of staff in quality areas

7. Communication

Barriers

(a) Inadequate and incomplete communication

(b) Selective communication

Solutions

(a) Establish clear communication strategy

(b) Team briefing

(c) Total staff involvement

(d) Regular open forum meetings

(e) Tolerance of *open* expression of disagreement in conducting meeting

8. Staff technical awareness of quality

Barriers

(a) Partial understanding

Solutions

(a) Education and training

(b) Everyday practical application of TQM ideas and principles

9. Quality management system

Barriers

(a) Undirected activity in standard setting, audit, customer feedback

Solutions

(a) Develop structure for fully documented (and implemented) manual for TQM to reflect activity and provide coordination

10. Quality Performance Indicators

Barriers

(a) No clear indication of good/bad quality

(b) Lack of measurement of performance

Solutions

(a) Identify and measure five key quality performance indicators

(b) Ongoing discussion of performance, data and revision of quality performance indicators

11. Improvement Teams

Barriers

(a) Senior management support for QIT actions

(b) Insufficient skills development of Quality Improvement Team members

Solutions

(a) Support and encouragement from managers to *let the strings go*

(b) Training for QITs

Implementing TQM in a Health care provider unit is about identifying normal obstacles and barriers which in some ways exist in *any* organisation and helping that part of the unit feel less anxious about *using* these barriers to better quality management. These barriers are inevitable and have to be dealt with sympathetically. They disappear if consistently and gently challenged.

Conclusion

The European Foundation for Quality Management in designing the European Quality Award early in 1990 places great value on achieved results and improved performance in:

❝ The European Quality Award criteria and weightings.

Customer satisfaction — the perceptions of external customers, direct and indirect, of the company and its products and services. **(20%)**

People — the management of the company's people and the people's feelings about the company. **(18%)**

Business results — the company's achievement in relation to its planned business performance. **(15%)**

Processes — the management of all the value-adding activities within the company. **(14%)**

Leadership — the behaviour of all managers in transforming the company towards total quality. **(10%)**

Resources — the management, utilisation, and preservation of:
• Financial resources.
• Information resources.
• Technological resources. **(9%)**

Policy and strategy — the company's vision, values and direction, and the ways in which it achieves them. **(8%)**

Impact on society — the perceptions of the community at large of the company. Views on the company's approach to quality of life, to the environment and to the need for preservation of global resources are included. **(6%) ❞**

Ref: EFQM (1991) TQM October, p. 266

The weightings show the relative importance of each of these eight variables.
Health care provider units can establish their own quality and quality management in terms of these variables — many already have.
The critical success factors for Total Quality Management which need to be understood are many and varied. I have tried through this text to identify and describe them in practical terms.
I would like to end by reinforcing some of the fundamental factors that are perhaps less easy to define, yet are crucial to doctors, nurses, therapy staff, managers and support service staff in hospitals and community services who are already implementing their own particular versions of *quality management*:

• There must be a shared belief that TQM (or whatever *'doing the job right'* is called!) is the right and appropriate thing to do;

- There must be sustained patience because TQM change takes time and the service must allow for this;
- Small, and large, successes must be engineered, communicated, and applauded.
- There must be a desire to make a service the best possible one within resources available.

Finally, although anything worthwhile tends to be hard work, it can and should be fun — management is fun — it maintains an interest in providing health care at the highest possible quality.

References

Atkinson P 1990
Creating cultural changes
TQM **Feb** 13-15

Audit Commission 1992
Community care review
HMSO

Audit Commission 1992
Homeward Bound
HMSO London

Avant Hotels 1991
Beyond stars & crowns.
Managing service quality **Jan** 97-100

Berwick DM Enthoven A & Bunker J P
1992
Quality management in the NHS: the
doctor's role
BMJ **25** 1/92

Bhogal R 1992
Health Services Journal **30** 1/92 p19

Blades M 1992
TQM **Apr**

Boardman R & Weyndling C 1992
Measurement of business success.
TQM Conference
177-183. IFS Bedford

Brooks T 1992
TQM in NHS
Health Services Journal **Apr** 17-19

Kuston W & Rowbotham R (1986)
Levels of work
Brunel University

Carr-Hill R 1989
The NHS & its customers
Centre for Health Economics York

Carr-Hill R Dalley G 1990
Questions of quality
Health Services Journal **Aug** 2

Carson J 1991
Role Modelling
Managing Service Quality **Jan** 72-81

Chase R L 1991
Targetting the message
TQM **Oct** 259

Chase R 1991
The road to recovery
Managing Service Quality **Jan** 101-103

Clifford P 1990
FACE IQMS unpublished document

Dale B 1991
Starting the road to success.
TQM **Apr** 125-128

Dale B 1992, *TQM*

Dash P 1992
Quality doctors
*International Journal of Health Care and
Quality Assurance* **5**,2,25-26.

Davies P 1992
Easy as ABC
TQM **Apr** 69-70

De Kievit D & Finlow-Bates 1992
Keeping tales
Managing Service Quality **Jan** 91-94

Department of Health 1992
The patient's charter
HMSO

Eccles S 1992
A better pill
Health Services Journal **Apr 16**, 22-23

EFQM 1991
TQM **Oct** 265-6

Ferguson I 1991
Goal for the Future
Managing Service Quality **May** 233-335

Fitzgerald L 1991
This Year's Model
Health Services Journal **Nov 11**

Goldstone L A 1987
*Quality counts in nursing: the monitor
experience*
Newcastle-upon-Tyne Polytechnic
Production Ltd

Handy C 1988
Understanding organisations
Penguin

Hewitson P 1991
Collaborative care planning
*International Journal of Health Care and
Quality Assurance* **5**12,12-16

Hinks M D 1973
Spotlight on shop window staff
King's Fund

Hopkinson E 1991
BS 5750: quality standards
ambulance services part I
*International Journal of Health Care and
Quality Assurance* **4**,6,22-29

Hopkinson E 1992
BS 5750 Part II Ambulance Services
5,2,27-36

Howard D (1991)
A limited understanding
TQM **Apr** 91-94

Iles V 1992
The importance of talking shop
May 7

Koch H C H 1991
TQM in Health Care
Longman

Koch H C H 1992
Sustaining commitment
Managing Service Quality **Mar** 157-160

Koch H C H 1991
Public sector services
Managing Service Quality **Sept** 10

Koch H C H 1991
*Exceeding expectations. TQM in Mental
Health Services*
Pavilion Publishing

Koch H C H 1991
TQM in Public Sector
Pavilion Publishing

Koch H C H 1992
Implementing TQM
Pavilion Publishing
in preparation

Koch H C H & Chapman E J 1991
Planning for high quality care
*International Journal of Health Care
and Quality Assurance* **4**,6,10-1

Koch H C H & Higgs A 1991
What does quality health care
cost
*International Journal of Health Care
and Quality Assurance* **4**,4,4-7

Koch H C H & Sabugueiro J 1992
Trust in teams
Managing Service Quality **Jul** 279-281

Lacey P 1991
Discovering hidden truths
TQM **Apr** 107-110

Lowenhaupt M 1991
Win/win opportunity
Managing Service Quality **Nov** 56-57

Maxwell R 1984
Quality assessment in health
BMJ **13** 31-34

Marsh J 1991
Different Approaches
Managing Service Quality **Nov** 49-54

Mathew D 1990
Management team effectiveness
GMTS Scheme London

McDonald I 1991
Coming up to standard
*International Journal of Health Care
Quality Assurance* **4**,4,17-20

McCarthy J & Hicks A 1991
*International Journal of Health Care
Quality Assurance*

McColl L 1992
letter in *Times*, 4th April

Millner L, Ash A & Ritchie P 1991
Leading quality in action
Nora Fry Research Centre

National Audit Office 1991
Review of NHS outpatient services
HMSO

N E Thames 1992
Health Services Journal **Apr 2** 39

Nelson A Gordon M 1986
Promoting a public image
N E Essex H A Colchester

NHSME 1991
Day surgery: Making it happen
UFM Unit
HMSO

NHSME 1991
Demonstrably different
DoH

Oakland J 1989
TQM Heineman

ODI 1990
Quality in NHS **Jul**

ODI 1991
Quality: the next steps

O'Neill D 1992
Plan of attack
Managing Service Quality **Mar** 163-165

Ovretreit J 1991
Quality health
services
Brunel University

Ovretreit J 1991
Costing quality
Health services management **Aug** 184-5

P A Consulting 1989
Total Quality Initiative
Trafford General Hospital

Para-Swaman A Zeithamel & Berry
1985
Journal of Marketing 33-36

Peters T & Waterman R H
In search of excellence
Harper & Row, New York

Pfeiffer N 1992
Strings Attached
Health Services Journal **Apr**

Pollitt C Harrison S Hunter D J
Marnock G 1991
Quality & general management 83-88
*International Journal of Health Care
Quality Assurance* 3,6,33-36

Ram A 1992
Communication breakdown
Health Services Journal **Mar 12** 24.

Rea A 1992
Gang mentality
Health Services Journal **Mar 26** 31-34

Reynolds S 1991
Applying common sense
Managing Service Quality **Nov** 23-25

Roy A 1991
Getting the message across
TQM **Oct** 275-275

Rooney M 1991
Applying common sense
Managing Service Quality **Nov** 23-25

Spiby J & Griffiths S 1991
Tightrope Management
Health Services Journal **Dec 12**

Seath I 1992
Training-a-waste of effort?
Managing Service Quality **May** 185-187

Seddon J 1991
Middle managers' new role
Managing Service Quality **Jan** 71-72

Seddon J & Jackson S 1990
TQM & cultural change
TQM **Aug** 213-216

Sharma T 1992
Health Services Journal **Nov 10** 21

Shaw C Hurst M & Stone S 1988
Towards good practice in small
hospitals
NAHA

Smith J 1991
Total quality development in Mid-
Staffs
*International Journal of Health Care
Quality Assurance* 4,4,9-11

Smith S 1991
Welcoming patients to your hospital
Royal Berkshire Hospital
*International Journal of Health Care
Quality Assurance*

Sashkin M 1989
*Structured activities for management.
Training in communications*
OD + Development Inc
Health Services Journal

Stewart J D & Ramelli D 1992
Firing on all cylinders
*International Journal of Health Care
Quality Assurance* **Jan** 85-89

Timmers J G & Van Der Wiele T 1991
A Question of Quality
TQM 3 **Apr** 2 87-90

Trent RHA 1990
Quality standards for outpatient services.

Tucker J 1992
Costing GP hospitals
Health Services Journal **Jan 1** 24-25

Ullah P 1991
Psychology of TQM
Managing Service Quality **Jan** 79-81

Van Cylenburg P 1990
Why TQM?
Managing Service Quality **Nov** 31-34

Ward C 1992
From the other side
Health Services Journal **Jun** 4 26

Webster C 1992
Bevan on the NHS
Oxford University

West Midlands RHA (1991)
Collaborative care planning

Western Health & Social Services
Board 1992
*Mental health unit quality development
programme*
N Ireland

Wilkinson A Witcher B
Fitness for use
Management decisions **29** 8 46-51

Wilson C, 1987
Hospital-wide quality assurance
Saunders, Ontario, Canada

Wythe R 1990
Agenda for change
TQM **Aug** 209-212

NHS Clients

Aylesbury Vale Community
Health Care
NHS Trust

Altnagelvin Hospital
Londonderry

Dudley Acute Unit

Northwick Park Hospital
Harrow

Trafford Hospital
Manchester

South Warwickshire
Acute & Maternity Services

West Glamorgan
District Services Unit

Acknowledgements

Chapter 1: Figures 1.2, 1,3 and 1.4, Timmers & Van der Wiele (1991); List of Characteristics of Continuous Business Improvement, Figures 1.5 and 1.6, Dale; Figures 1.7 and 1.8 KPMG (1988); Figure 1.14, Liverpool HA.

Chapter 2: Figures 2.1 and 2.2, *Managing Service Quality*, **Jan** 1992 87, 158; Figure 2.3, John Sabugueiro, Director of Quality, Manor House Hospital, Aylesbury; Figure 2.4, John Butler, W. Glamorgan HA; Figure 2.5, BIS Nynex Company; Figure 2.6, Atkinson (1990), TQM Journal; Figure 2.7, De Kievit & Finlow-Bates, *Managing Service Quality*, **Jan** 1992; Figure 2.8, Roy (1991); Figure 2.9, David O'Neill, UGM Trafford (& PA Consulting); Figure 2.12, Marsh (1992), *Managing Service Quality*.

Chapter 3: Figure 3.4, Brunel University; Figures 3.5 and 3.6, John Sabugueiro, Aylesbury HA; Figure 3.7, Paul Brennan.

Chapter 4: Figure 4.1, QA Manager, Merton & Sutton HA; Figure 4.2, Trafford HA; Figure 4.5, Aylesbury Vale Priority Care Services; Figure 4.6, South Western Regional Health Authority; Figure 4.8, Hinks M D, Kings Fund; List of The Outpatient Process, Bruce Liddle, Trent Regional HA; List of NHS Outpatient Services, National Audit Office; Figures 4.9 and 4.10, Clifford (1991); Probes 1 and 2, Audit Commission (1992); List of Contents, forms for Surgery & Anaesthesia, Maternity, General Medicine, Care of the Elderly, Shaw 1988; Figure 4.11, Kings Fund; List of Contents, Figures 4.12 and 4.13, NHSME VFM Study (1991); Figure 4.15, Goldstone *et al*; Figures 4.18 to 4.27, adapted from Koch H & Higgs A, What does health care cost?, *International Journal of Health Care*

Quality Assurance; Figure 4.29, Bruce Liddle, Trent RHA; Figure 4.30, Aylesbury Vale HA.

Chapter 5: Figures 5.2, 5.3 and 5.4, Jane Chapman; Figures 5.7 to 5.10, Aylesbury Vale HA; Figure 5.18, Lauerhaupt International, *Journal of Health Care Quality Assurance*; Figure 5.19, Ward K (1991) Project Approach to Quality Management, *International Journal of Health Care Quality Assurance*; Figure 5.21, Coventry Community Care Unit.

Chapter 6: Figure 6.6, Smith (1991); Figure 6.8, South Western Regional Health Authority Medical Records Standards; Figure 6.17, Koch H, Chapman J, *Health Services Journal*; Figure 6.18, DoH; Figure 6.19, *International Journal of Health Care Quality Assurance*, Nottingham (1991); Figure 6.20, Clinical Psychology Forum **May**, 1992; Figure 6.21, Trent RHA.

Chapter 7: Figures 7.8 and 7.9, Merton and Sutton Acute Unit; Figure 7.10, Jaguar; Figures 7.12 and 7.13, RCN Standards of Care Project (1991); Figure 7.14, Trent RHA; Figures 7.15 and 7.16, Eccles (1992); Figures 7.17 to 7.19, Coventry Clinical Audit Programme.

Chapter 8: Figure 8.2, Total Quality Management International; Figure 8.3, Altnagelvin Group of Hospitals; Figure 8.5, Pavilion Publishing; Figure 8.6, Avon Industries, Polymer Ltd; Figures 8.7 to 8.9, Pavilion Publishing; Figures 8.10 to 8.13, Worthing HA; Figures 8.14 and 8.15, Pavilion Publishing; Figures 8.16 to 8.19, Aylesbury Vale HA; Figures 8.21 and 8.22, Russells Hall Hospital, Dudley.

Chapter 9: Figure 9.2, South Warwickshire HA; Table 9.1, Opinion

Research Corporation; Figure 9.4, Health Policy Advisory Unit, Sheffield; Figure 9.5, Audit Commission May 1991; Figure 9.6, Trent RHA, Figures 9.7 to 9.9, Aylesbury Vale HA; List of Comments arising from visits to general practitioners, King and Coventry (1992); Figure 9.10, Aylesbury Vale HA; Figure 9.11, Dudley HA; Figure 9.12, Altnagelvin Group of Hospitals; Figure 9.13, Aylesbury Vale Community Healthcare NHS Trust; Figures 9.16 and 9.17, Altnagelvin Group of Hospitals; Figures 9.18 to 9.20, Cheltenham HA; Figure 9.21, Health Services Commission; Figure 9.22, Northwick Park Hospital; Figure 9.23, Comet.

Chapter 10: Figure 10.2, Wilson; Figure 10.5, Seath (1992).

Despite our best endeavours, we have been unable to trace the authors for Figures 4.14, 4.28, 5.20, 7.2, 7.3, 7.4, 9.15, 10.3, 10.4.